HUMANISTIC TEACHING FOR EXCEPTIONAL CHILDREN

An Introduction to Special Education

Edited by

WILLIAM C. MORSE

SYRACUSE UNIVERSITY PRESS
1979

371.9
H88
1195-49
out.1981

Library of Congress Cataloging in Publication Data
Main entry under title:

Humanistic teaching for exceptional children.

Bibliography: p.
1. Exceptional children—Education—Addresses,
essays, lectures. I. Morse, William Charles.
LC3965.H85   371.9   79-20332
ISBN 0-8156-2199-X
ISBN 0-8156-2215-5 pbk.

Manufactured in the United States of America

THIS BOOK IS DEDICATED to a long-time friend and professional colleague, Dr. Carl Fenichel. He was preparing Chapter 3 when he died. We hope that his chapter is a memorial to this most unusual special education leader. A very long time ago he had already arrived at the humanistic concepts of special education expressed in this book. He cared about children, not categories or cases. He cared about families and parents, not patients but people.

Carl founded the League School which espoused psychoeducation —an educational focus combined with a deep psychological understanding. With the help of parents he raised the money for the magnificent new building in Brooklyn which stands as a physical recognition of his greatness, for there his work goes on. He taught at Columbia University, consulted many places, and led in the discovery that those impossible cases of seriously disturbed children had potential for growth. He never gave up. He was a model. His presence is with so many of us. He stood for seeing the essential human being in the special child.

PREFACE

There are certain ironies in contemporary special education. We are entering the new era of federally legislated, mandated special education which provides the greatest opportunity for special children, but we operate with conflicting processes. Our goal is to help children with special needs, but we do this almost exclusively only when they fit a given category. The categories are holding companies for the money. We are fixated on their "schooling" when that is only a part of their education for life. We have meetings about children with reams of data which often take the place of knowing the actual child. We get so tied up in regulations and certification of a youngster that we dehumanize the services we have which are at best short of what is needed. We expect teachers with marginal training to accept major responsibilities for children they may not understand.

But it does not have to be thus. The purpose of this book is, first of all, to put the special children at the center of it all. What is a special child's life like in spite of as well as because of the handicaps? At every stage from infant to young adult, special education is about a person. This article of faith permeates the volume: Once we understand the children as human beings, we will empathize with their condition, listen to them, and be better able to be useful helpers. We learn they are special, but this does not mean they are all that different from children we have known, or even all that different from the child or adolescent that was us. Through this understanding we develop the concern that moves us to find ways of helping as we would do for any child.

Who needs to benefit from such an experience? All who teach and work with exceptional children. Old-timers who are experiencing the well-known "burn out" syndrome need sensitivities reawakened. The new professionals who often get more sterile information and gimmicks need a balance of the core which makes a teacher—the sense of the human beings that are special children. And the mainstream teachers who have been outsiders, but are no longer—while they are not without the potential for helping, they are often uneasy because they forget they are experts in helping children. If we concentrate only on the stereotyped categorical differences, it is easy to forget these are children the like of which regular teachers have known and helped. They will find children who are essentially more like than different from the so called normal ones.

And parents are no longer in the dark; many keep up with the literature, serve on boards, and are the new semi-professional lay personnel in special education. Parent leaders need to know their children and other special children better. These chapters will help them see the total picture.

There are of course many others who are involved in special education nowadays—administrators, ancillary personnel, aides, and those in collaborative disciplines. For them, too, this approach through the lives of special children will both clarify the role of special education and integrate it with other parts of a total program which they help provide.

Ann Arbor, Michigan   WCM
Summer 1979

CONTENTS

TABLES

FIGURES

HUMANISTIC TEACHING
FOR EXCEPTIONAL CHILDREN

WILLIAM C. MORSE

William C. Morse has spent his professional career working with socially and emotionally disturbed children. For many years he was director of the therapy camp for disturbed children operated by the University of Michigan as a service and training agency. Under his direction a strong therapeutic program was devised around the central themes of camping activities, educational assistance, and group work. Graduate students from education, social work, and psychology learned by doing in a twenty-four-hour-a-day intensive experience with children combined with seminars and supervision.

Morse is Professor of Education and Psychology at the University of Michigan. He was responsible for undergraduate special education for emotionally disturbed children as well as doctoral training in this area. At present he is Chairman of the Combined Program in Education and Psychology and a regular consultant to public school and institutional programs for disturbed children and youth.

1

The Societal Role of Special Education

WILLIAM C. MORSE

THE GOAL OF SPECIAL EDUCATION can be stated in simple terms: to make the educational opportunity for pupils who are handicapped equal to that for those who are not. States have passed mandatory special education laws, in some instances covering from birth to twenty-five years of age. Federal law now mandates free and appropriate public special education in regular public school classes whenever possible, or in special classes and special institutions when necessary. In 1975 Public Law 94–142, (Education for All Handicapped Children Act) was passed and must be adhered to in order for state and local agencies to receive federal funds. The provisions include free public education with an individual educational plan (IEP) for each pupil in hopes that the child will reach his or her maximum potential. Careful evaluation is required. Parents must be consulted and approve the plan. Progress toward explicit goals in the plan must be reviewed periodically. Priority is put on unserved and inadequately served pupils. Because of the added costs to accomplish this mandate for the estimated seven to eight million children, states will be given augmented financial aid.

The new plan appears to be simple and direct until one begins to examine the complications of executing the legislation. Ideological, financial, administrative, and methodological issues take over. In the resolution of such forces, the individual experiences of the millions of children and their families often get lost. Hence the focus of this book, humanistic teaching. As any teacher knows, the real nature of special education will not be found in the legislative code numbers of statements of purpose. It will be found only through examining the lives of children.

This book is about the lives of special children. Around these lives,

3

the nature of the given handicap is explained and various remedial procedures are described. Since the severity of a given limitation often defines where and what help is needed, these matters are also included. Attention is given to what can be done in a regular classroom and what additional services may be needed. When there are differences of professional opinion about treatment, these are explained. But we are just as interested in the lives of these children beyond formal schooling. The educational experience in itself should be meaningful to the child and have relevance for his or her contemporary life, but this is only half the story. Schooling is more than a holding operation where the child grows up. It should be conducted to maximize the quality of the long span of life as well. It is said that many students live in spite of their schooling rather than because of it. With the handicapped the opposite is more likely: the quality of their entire life experience will be determined to a significant degree by the astuteness of their educational program. For certain special persons, the quality of the training will determine the potential for employment or even be critical in the decision as to whether life will be in an institution, a protected care setting, or independent. It is myopic to think of special education apart from education for life.

Present attention in education is focused on mainstreaming every handicapped child, which is to say provide the optimal education in the regular school setting. What the real goal should be is "life streaming" or the plan which will maximize the ability to lead as normal a life as special education can provide. Because of our primary concern for the eventual outcome of schooling, the examples in this book describe or project the adult life of exceptional individuals and clarify what role education did or could play in a most favorable outcome. It is not uncommon for the formal educational establishment to consider schooling an end in itself, especially if a youngster makes it into the mainstream. This error is compounded by another error: schools accept the mandate to provide for all the needs of the special youngster when those needs can only be provided through total community services. For example, the resources of mental health, medical services, and welfare and family protective services along with vocational rehabilitation are required to make life plans in given instances. These services are all independent and require discussion and cooperation. The responsibility for the handicapped is a community responsibility. The nature of "education," as differentiated from, say, "mental health," is not clear. The integration of the required services usually depends upon interpersonal relationships beyond formal agreements. As a teacher reads the cases in this book, the multifaceted responsibility for a program for the handicapped will become evident. The school has a vital and often catalytic role to play, but it cannot expect to go it alone.

Kirk (1962) has provided a concise definition of the special education pupil as one "who deviates from the average or normal child in mental, physical or social characteristics to such an extent that he requires a modification of school practices, or special educational services, in order to develop his maximum capacity." This definition brings out two interesting matters. The less any regular school program accommodates to individual differences, the greater the percentage of special children. Also, the goal to develop the child to the child's maximum capacity generates considerable planning and evaluation and accountability.

The number of significantly deviant children is hard to determine. One reason is the matter of definition, as Wedell (1975) has pointed out. If by exceptional we mean non-normal, is this to mean deviation from the statistical average? We could use a psychometric, medical, or educational yardstick. In practice we apply mixtures of all three. Not only do overall figures for the total special population differ considerably but percentages given by the experts for each category also vary greatly. Somewhere around 14 percent of the total school population can conservatively be considered an overall estimate of the special education responsibility. It is obvious the topic of this book is a significant portion of the educational task, especially since each such child should have a greater investment than the regular pupil.

The intent of this book is to put the person back into special education. For teachers who deal with many pupils and much variation, it is a continual task to respond to every person with the empathic concern which our profession requires. While the case approach helps to foster this empathic concern, we can also be aware of certain other aspects which sometimes are lost as we concentrate on the differences from typical growth found in the various handicapped areas. The ramifications of special education are anything but simple, as discussion of six fundamental issues in the field of special education will show.

1. There is no "class" of handicapped set apart from others. We do not have handicapped pupils: we have pupils who have handicaps. We all have the same basic motivations and feelings. As Fromm (1973) says, we all share the desire to understand and relate to our world as best we can. We generate patterns of love, anxiety, hope, and despair. For example, until recently the fact that retarded adolescents had the sexual drives common to others was largely ignored. This responding to only one aspect of a person and ignoring the total is dehumanizing. Our first task, then, is to focus on what we all have in common, not on the differences alone. To put the handicap before the person is a distortion. Extending the range of

variation leaves no place for separate categorization. The emphasis should be on what we have in common, not how different we are. There is a test each reader can apply to this issue. Consider several handicapped persons you know well. Then consider what portion of their lives are typical and what portion special.

2. A corollary to the first issue is the fact that most of us are "special" to some degree or another, or at some time or another. The net result of human variation in both endowment and experience is the unique mosaic that comes to be each individual self. Being a candidate for special consideration is not a condition foreign to typical experience—at least for most of us. At one time or another in our development both in and out of school, we required or at least needed more and different attention than was average. If we were fortunate, we got intensified individual help—special education in the generic sense if you will—to manage a hurdle as we grew up. This concept of individualization is the keystone of all educational processes, much talked about and occasionally practiced. Because our schools are organized on a supposedly homogeneous age group basis, it is sometimes thought that every member of the class is going through the same experience and learning the same things. Nothing could be further from the truth. Special education is providing for individual differences, a process every teacher knows about from day one in the classroom.

If we look at the life span of so-called normal persons, it is evident that at some period in their history they could well be categorized as "special." Visual problems, hearing problems, emotional difficulties—who will not be classified sometime? Lowder (1975) found that "only 17% of the physically handicapped population were born impaired in some way. The other 83% acquired their disability through disease, traumatic injury, war, or advanced age." Thus, our second major theme: being handicapped is not a condition set apart from general human experience. It is not a matter of "we" normals and "they," the handicapped. All are of one family. The test for the reader relative to this issue is to review several well-known persons who have lived to retirement age and list characteristics which could be considered in a "special" category. Or better still, as we review our own life history, have there been times when we were temporarily in some special category?

3. The third issue is the cultural core which defines the nature of special education. It is logical to ask that, if being handicapped is not really that different from experiences many of us have to some degree, then why all the additional societal programs such as special education? There are basic reasons why certain types and degrees of deviations re-

quire special assistance. These reasons depend upon a prior philosophical position that all citizens, young and old, have the right to maximum life experience. We are dedicated to this proposition of equality, and it is now the law of the land. Our regular institutions do not, and for some handicapping conditions cannot, provide equal opportunities for the total range of human variation. While the current emphasis is rightly to expand the regular school accommodation to wider variation, there are barriers, prejudices, and restrictions to rights in employment and certainly in education. Our society does not in fact accept everyone on a par. While there are the very few instances where the general public is actually endangered (by a rare mental patient, for example, or certain delinquents), the more significant side is the need of handicapped persons for more protection, care, and services.

What is needed is not segregation to warehouse those who are different because of popular fears or distaste, not separation because it costs less in a rich nation such as ours, but that degree of separation which is required to provide the best life for the individuals. Schools and agencies are bound first of all to the concept of least extrusion from the normal, and they are obligated to accommodate. Special classes are legitimate only when the intensity of need and the nature of providing specialized services requires such separation. Regular employment should be open to all qualified handicapped people. Only when limitations are severe are sheltered workshops proper. Then they become a protective right. Such decisions require good will, new approaches, and pressure on agencies to reduce the segregated special programs to the minimum required.

4. Much of the segregation of the handicapped is a consequence of social attitude and has nothing to do with features of the handicapping condition itself. Probably none of us is free from prejudice of various sorts in this connection. If we hope to humanize special education, we must recognize in ourselves and in society at large the significance of the irrational fear of children and adults who are different.

We can sense the generic nature of negative social attitudes as a producer of handicap. The damage to self-esteem fostered by social rejection and ostracism is a major factor in special education. We tend to behave as we believe others expect us to, the self-fulfilling prophesy. The only individual difference admired by our society is the superior end of the distribution, and even here there is often envy and rejection.

To be a member of any subgroup which is the object of prejudice is an obvious handicap. Attitudes toward minority groups and racial stereotyping are prime examples. Bandura (1974) has outlined how "normal" people manage to generate and justify these devastating emotional attitudes which dehumanize the target persons. When special programs were developed in an effort to counteract and redress the impact of prejudice toward blacks, other minorities such as Chicanos and Native Americans saw the same need. All were and are special. We must remember that we are dealing not only with societal prejudice and attitudes, but also with denial of equal opportunity all the way from educational encouragement to economic opportunity. In truth, there is no end to special education and social provision until we maximize opportunity for every individual. This is the cause which special education represents in society.

A discussion of this complex problem can be found in *Deviance and Respectability* (Douglas 1970) where the moral implications are revealed. We also know that many equate being handicapped with being sick. All of the special education categories suffer from this, some much more than others. There are superstitions and fears which cause many people to reject, shun, and even deride those who look different, act different, or even seem to think in a different way. Some of the historians of special education have pointed out how attitudes toward those who differ have changed at different times and in various cultures. At one time the deviant might be worshipped as a special prophet and seer while at other times be considered a visible manifestation of Satan. Attitudes of fear, disgust, pity, and curiosity were and still are common. It is interesting how we consider ourselves beyond such primitiveness, yet remnants remain in the field of special education and in many of us individually. We still see parents of special children both blaming and denying themselves. The historical rejection of those who were different also has a contemporary counterpart. For a long time rejection was reflected in the style of care which assured the public that they should not have to see or be reminded of imperfections. Many times the responsibility was left in the hands of voluntary religious groups. In fact, the care of special children was for a long time (and still continues) in the minds of many, as a huge home-missionary effort. It was not that these children had a birthright similar to all children but that virtue was accumulated by doing good work helping these unfortunates.

Later, as the responsibility became a recognized obligation of the state, the provision of segregated schools and classes solved two problems at once: one no longer needed to see them and yet one need not feel guilty since the children were being "helped." What is not seen does not exist, and thus the cause of rejection is served. It is encouraging to see that general public attitudes, at least toward the retarded, are improving. There is less rejection and fear, though 49 percent of the population still believes retarded people cannot support themselves, and 14 percent still see reason to fear them. Social stereotypes are still assigned for various special conditions. Special teachers have problems with school attitudes toward their pupils: self-images of the retarded have been shown to be related to the teacher's image of the academic ability of the retarded (Richmond and Dalton 1973).

One of the questions of young special education professionals is how can we go on treating handicapped people as we do and call it helping. This shock usually comes after a first visit to a school or institution where the atmosphere is punitive and restrictive. An overly simple remedy is just to close down all institutions, whatever their nature, and bring every inmate "home" to local institutions or services, which may be well and good in many instances. But it is already evident how the same individuals, still needing special assistance, can be exploited at a local "home" just as well as they can be at state level.

As the reader comes to know each case in this book, the test of understanding is to imagine what it would be like were we the one to have the given handicap. One way to get closer to the actual human experience is by simulation of the conditions. A day of "stuttering" may be a more powerful teaching tool than the pages of print in order to appreciate the condition. Or try ear plugs to minimize sound communication. Fear of loss of sight is simulated by a blindfold. Of course, none of these simulations are the real thing, but they can help us turn the study of handicaps inside out.

5. A fifth and major issue of special education goes to the heart of the matter: it lies at the interface of the person and society and results from the high risk of certain special conditions. We are speaking of risk in the society as it is, not as it might be, or as some would wish it to be. If society operated with a different set of premises, the conditions which would predicate high risk or potential failure would differ too. There have been societies which were less competitive, and less restrictive in what was considered satisfactory for a person to do. But ours is a society, as George Orwell so cleverly described in *Animal Farm,* where all are equal but some are more equal than others. Even in our competitive society and even with inequalities of ability, many exceptional children could participate reasonably well if they were given the rehabilitation and education they need.

The manner in which our society operates causes those who are limited in some way to have a particularly hard time. As we have seen, the individual may have the limitation or it may be a projection of societal prejudice, but it handicaps all the same. Not only the school but most all institutions operate on a competitive basis which puts those with handicaps at a significant disadvantage. Special education is the compensatory support to equalize opportunity as much as possible. We must then ask, what are the factors which predict major misalignment at the person-society interface? Certain predisposing conditions produce risk for certain individuals. It is worthy of note that these conditions are not all included in the eight categories of special children, though the added factors are only too obvious when one thinks of conditions which blight success in this society. Whether special education formally includes these conditions or not, the teacher who thinks generically of those who need special help will recognize the pupils of social bondage.

All else being equal, which is unlikely, the single most pervasive handicap in our society is to be born poor, though the definition of poverty is not simple. Poverty is a relative condition in a society which is materialistic and affluent. You may have enough to survive, but relative to others you may have far too little. While the rags to riches theme has been nourished in our society, the far more common sequence is rags to rags, or as is sometimes said, "Poverty breeds poverty." The shock most middle class, privileged teachers get when they first see the raw life of poverty can be the most traumatic experience they have had. Poverty is known to affect a child's motivations, aspirations, beliefs, and hopes, to say nothing of health.

There are so many negative conditions associated with poverty and low socioeconomic status that these are the number one hazard for normal growth of children in our country. A poverty-stricken mother's inadequate diet results in a baby born with diminished potential. The child's development becomes atrophied and there are related health problems. The necessary stimulation for normal growth is seldom present. The compensatory efforts provided by Head Start and other special programs for the deprived fall far short of meeting the physical and social needs facing a youngster from urban or rural poverty areas.

Not only is there the impact of limitation in overall resources on these children, but the school also punishes poor and minority groups through a higher incidence of school exclusion and higher proportions of negative classification tags like "retarded" and "delinquent."

When we recognize the combined effects of double handicap—economic and racial prejudice—it is clear how the disproportionate percentage of minority children were designated "special." Many are in fact multiply handicapped and deserve their birthright of assistance. Since both the nature and reputation of special education was so negative, giving them such "help" turned out to be adding insult to injury. Like sending a delinquent to the typical training school to be reformed, putting these double-jeopardy pupils into special classes further reduced the chances of equalizing their opportunity. They were categorized, put away, and usually forgotten. This is not to deny that a certain number of teachers and programs were effective, but the overall effect of special education was a failure. It was too limited in scope and substance. The reaction has been to reject the programs, sometimes through the courts as we shall see.

It is a sad commentary that educational programming for those under the greatest handicap of all in our society developed first outside of both regular and special education. Direct governmental grants made it important to "count the poor" in a district to get the maximum money. The issue here is that every teacher must recognize the stultifying result of poverty whether or not the field of special education has formal programs. Combined with other handicaps as a coproducer of hazard, this condition adds greatly to the burden of these children. As particular children are presented in the various chapters, the reader will be alerted to the impact of the socioeconomic handicap as well. Since we have been speaking in average terms, we must remember too that many poor families have resources which overcome such stress. As advocates for children, teachers cannot forget that poverty could be prevented by social planning. It is a matter of values.

Perhaps deprivation has been a maverick area in special education because of the multifactor nature of the causes. The evidence of the handicapping condition is only too clear, but the character of anything beyond a band-aid remediation effort would require strategies not common to special education. For this condition, prevention should replace remediation as in the case of certain special anomalies which medical programs have eliminated (see Chapter 7 on vision, for example). To accomplish similar prevention for poverty and prejudice implies a change in the total culture and the values which determine the resources made available to families and their children. In this regard education has played the establishment role of attempting to repair damage rather than eliminate the problem. What has been tried in schools falls short of what must be done. Of course the answers are difficult to find and even harder to get into practice. This aspect of unrecognized special education remains a huge challenge. Poverty alone is a huge handicap. It is also a societal time bomb. The explosiveness of the ghettos has been proven over and again. Combined with other special education problems, handicapping is not just doubled; it is squared. It is of concern in all the chapter areas in this book.

A second major handicap is a limitation in one's overall mental capacity which reduces the ability to cope with a complex society. Mental capacity includes the ability to learn rapidly, remember well, think, solve problems effectively, and deal with changes in a creative fashion. Life-coping ability is obviously far broader than the cognitive processing which traditional IQ scales measure. It is obvious that intellectual functioning is a particularly vital factor in coping with our very verbal and conceptual society. Alone it is not enough for success, but without it the odds against mastery increase. Limitation in ability to use symbols is indeed sign for risk in our society. It is even more important for being successful in school. In fact, it has been said that for the mildly retarded, the greatest life problem is school survival. Once out in the real world the chances are better.

The formula for school success, even in academic subjects, includes such factors as motivation, relevant past experiences, and the way the material is taught, and no one denies the major role played by intellectual ability. However, even a correlation of +.70 between IQ and reading would indicate only 49 percent of the variance is accountable to intellectual ability. On the other hand, no other factor on the average accounts for such a high proportion of the relationship. It is not without reason that we should admonish youngsters to be born in a high SES family and to be born bright, too, if we wish to reduce risk. Children who are limited in cognitive potential will need special education help if they are to achieve a reasonable role in life. Traditionally, programs for the retarded have been the stronghold of special education and the category long recognized. It is interesting to note that Binet's intelligence test was designed to indicate children who would not benefit from the schooling of his time. Because the ability to deal with life problems is comprised of more than intellectual capacity, we find many people who manage life in a far more adequate way than their formal test scores would suggest. But once stigmatized as retarded this becomes built into personal and social perceptions and adds to the original difficulty. For the severely intellectually limited, the environmental expectations must be tremendously reduced, education radically changed, and the protected surrogate environment attuned to the relative coping capacity. Some will need virtually complete care. Raymond H. Elliott's Chapter 2 on retardation covers this special education category, but the condition may accompany all other disability areas as well.

Because our society makes it difficult for any pronounced deviation, *both* ends of the IQ distribution are candidates for special help, though for different reasons. It is a sad commentary on how things are arranged to recognize that having more or special abilities can become a handicap. The particular problems of the gifted are presented in Treffinger's Chapter 5. While the intellectually retarded have been universally accepted as a responsibility of special education, the very bright and talented are not always included. After all, why should *they,* of all children, need more support? It is interesting to speculate how different our own lives would be if we could add, say, 30 IQ points and throw in a high level of some special talent for good measure. And where might we be with 30 IQ points less? The regular school process is not designed to accommodate to this atypicality any better than it is to the retarded, though one might speculate a natural affinity between the bright and talented and formal education.

Although known for some time, more recently receiving a flood of attention is another handicap which is more specific in nature unless compounded in combination with other difficulties. There are the children who are in the normal range of intellectual capacity but who have more or less specific limitations in perceptual or conceptual ability, symbolic organization, or putting together the right combinations of concepts. This may be found in combination with other special education conditions or alone. Reading is a most common malfunction, but arithmetic and spelling disabilities are also prevalent. One can readily imagine the life of an adolescent with an IQ of 115 but with a severe reading problem who functions with reading ability arrested at the second grade level. School would be a continual threat. Filling out a job application or getting a driver's license becomes a virtual impossibility. Ours is a society which requires the ability to decode symbols in order even to find one's way. In some aspects the condition of the learning disabled is the most difficult for both them and others to appreciate and leads to personal and social consequences as well as skill deficiencies. While school success depends even more on appropriate cognitive processing than does the culture at large, there is no escape even in the out-of-school culture. Special help must be given to those who are at risk because of limited ability to function in this important area. Even the so-called nonacademic subjects require aligning concepts correctly and often incorporate formal reading as well. Chapter 4 on learning disabilities makes it clear that problems are life long, and that schools have much to do to properly accommodate to this disability. He discusses the "they will grow out of it phantasy" which has prevented the needed attention to this problem at all school levels, especially the early school years.

Another broad limitation which is reflected in several special education categories is communication. The child who has any limitation in communication is obviously high risk in our society. We are a nation of communicators. We talk, look, listen, feel, and taste as well as read. There is also the cyclic feedback to the person from the responses of other people as well as the direct experience with environmental objects. We receive communication from gesture, word, tone, and touch. A severe punishment is to "excommunicate." One can experiment with the devastating impact of communication anomalies in a two-hour class where all members are blindfolded, spend an afternoon with tight earplugs, try even one day of enforced silence, or take a trip to a foreign country where one's native language is not understood. The experience is traumatizing.

There are many variations in communication problems, ranging from sight and hearing losses to the problem in symbolization discussed above. The emotionally disturbed youngster often also has communication problems. Feelings can also distort the conduct of social communication.

Typically, special education has focused on the child who has restrictions in communication because hearing, vision, or speech losses cut him off from full participation in the human experience. It is often difficult or impossible for such a child to reach out because of the severe limitations in getting certain messages through the ears and eyes. To those not expert it seems impossible to see how a blind-deaf child even with normal cognitive capacity could assimilate information from the environment. Anything which seriously inhibits the ability to utilize and respond to the environment obviously creates a state of higher risk for a child and is therefore a special education responsibility. Expressive difficulties found in speech atypicalities are evident as soon as the child tries to speak. When this happens, others may not understand, and more than that, the child may face ridicule as a result of communication limitation.

In the subenvironment of the school there are cases where significant visual or hearing problems have gone undetected. A child can sit in a class and not hear half of what a teacher says, even if the child is given lessons on listening skills. The school establishment extorts a high price for any communication inadequacies. Children with speech problems may not be asked to respond, and the teacher loses contact with the state of their learning. The chapters which are largely built around communication difficulties include Sophie French's on hearing, Geraldine Scholl's on vision, and Lawrence J. Turton's on speech.

Physical anomalies are a source of curiosity and frequent rejection. If there are physical handicaps which limit movement, bringing with them restricted environmental contact and a more limited prognosis for development. We have all seen the vast change in a baby's world when he or she learns to crawl, but this is nothing compared to what happens when the child can walk and run freely. This society is designed for those who can move themselves about and control their physical bodies. The mass worship of the physically adroit in games and dance points out the plight of those who suffer motility handicaps. Only recently have even special education training programs provided ramps for wheelchairs. All conditions which limit motility reduce the chances of a normal developmental experience. If you cannot control the appendages of your body, you have further difficulties. Writing requires fine motor control. Gym day is bleak for those who are somewhat awkward let alone significantly handicapped. Not until the annual Special Olympics could the handicapped be considered "competitors." Sometimes it is hard for the hyperkinetic to even stay in line—which can be a federal offense in certain elementary schools. In many jobs dexterity has taken over where intellectual ability leaves off. Special education has recognized the need to provide programs for those with limiting physical stigmata and motor problems of various types since these represent a serious limitation to normal success in our society. William M. Cruickshank and Lawrence Lewandowski have gone into considerable detail regarding the many facets of this complicated condition in Chapters 9 and 10.

Another critical societal and school expectation is for conformity or at given times, overconformity to certain established social conventions, values, and styles of behavior. To be deviant, whatever the cause, makes one high risk. While we pride ourselves on our degree of political freedom compared to dictatorships, deviance is as abrasive in many situations in society. There are two distinct sources of pressure for conformity. One source is the fear people have of those who are different. The quota of anxiety and hostility generated by the presence of members of the counter culture and those with variant life styles is amazing. Punishment is meted out to those with poor fit to the ideological norms. The other source of pressure against deviance results from the social problems produced by certain forms of social and emotional variance. There are individuals with destructive potential, though the number is small. Where the behavior is really threatening to others or the self, the cause of special education is rehabilitation and not merely custody. In fact, mere custody is not legal; help must be provided. In this society social maladjustment portends risk for the child's future. But the responsibility does not end with externalized problems.

The mental health movement has added consideration for the internal emotional state of children. Here the aim is the reduction of undue anxiety or depression and the enhancement of self-esteem. We know that high internal stress predicts difficulty and constitutes a state of risk. While some disturbed children live with their intrapersonal pain in such a way as to inflict no or minimum infringement on the rights of others, this is frequently not the pattern. Special education is equally concerned for internal welfare even when there is no infringement on others. Most children who have emotional deviance also have great difficulty wending a satisfactory way in the home, school, or community. The ability to make good use of environment is distorted, and the general level of tolerance of social institutions is easily exhausted. This results in a system involving both the person and the environmental conditions in a state of dissonance and pain. These children cannot hope to get along without the mediation of specialized help and remedial work. These are matters discussed by Harold Coopchik in Chapter 3. With autistic and schizophrenic children, unless there is special support and programming, even good home, school, or community environment is to little avail. While their future even then may be limited when compared to the normal child, there is a vast range in the possible competency the severely disturbed child may acquire. Through special education and therapy the intent is to maximize their functioning and to elevate the lives they will live. Caring for themselves and living in a semiprotected environment is a far cry from custodial and sometimes punitive institutional existence on the back wards for a lifetime.

In summary, aside from the need for considerable latitude for different patterns of behavior or life style, there is the fact of serious maladjustment brought on by biological and experiential histories: such maladjustment is the companion of personal and social misery. Maladjustment carries the virus for accelerating one's defeat. The problems which the child causes others result in rejection and hostility. Since there is usually at least a quota of the maladjusted behavior which results from environmental pressure (especially in the school) special education is concerned about ways to minimize such stress and to replace stress with support in the child's milieu both at home and in the community as well as the school. The situation is further compounded by the fact that some patterns of maladjustive behavior are transitory and developmental, while others are predictive of life-long stress and defeat. Whatever the implications, we generally assume that the fostering of adequate and personal adjustment is a major responsibility of societal agencies, especially the school, and thus of special education.

Finally, one of the highest risk groups of children, and one which cannot be ignored, are the so-called delinquents. While there are many children who may commit delinquent acts, the nucleus of the true delinquent is a value deviation. The youngster operates on life premises not acceptable to society as a whole. There is usually the absence of guilt when the rights of others are violated. Some live by rules of relatively amoral subsociety code, others by their own expedient codes. Like the deprived they are usually side-stepped by formal special education or mixed with the emotionally and socially handicapped until they become too difficult to manage. Then they are remanded to legal agencies. It is again a sad fact that they represent a most significant personal and social problem and yet are the step children of special education. Often it is by chance whether a youngster becomes a "legal" or "mental" case, each with a quite different destiny. The prognosis for serious delinquents is dire and programs fall short. The delinquents' values will rarely include any priority for formal schooling. Many affiliate with groups of like attitude, defying adults. The ordinary educational program exacerbates the condition; it takes an intensive education program and therapeutic design to reverse the prognosis (Glasser 1965). Since delinquent behavior is not tolerated, though it is seldom really dealt with, society does demand that something be done. It is likely to be done *to* the delinquent rather than *for* him. While tragic things have been done to all children in the name of helping, a continuing sad chapter is what is done in the name of treatment to delinquents. It is obvious, if these very high risk youth are to have a chance, special education must intervene. Chapter 3 deals with social and emotional variance.

Issue five which we have just discussed outlines a generic rationale for special education: simply stated it is to equalize the opportunity for children with various handicaps which constitute risks for normal success in a society which has certain characteristics. Each category is generated by particular societal sanctions and conditions, and it would also be simpler if all special children appeared with only a single risk area. Occasionally a child does have only one risk area such as retardation without socioeconomic handicaps or any learning disability or emotional difficulties. But the truth is, most special children have more than one handicap, even several. Each limitation interacts with the others to heighten the disadvantage: thus the risk for the multiply handicapped is much higher. To be severely intellectually retarded with a significant hearing loss and a spastic condition is more than any human being should have to face. There are those with just such complications and more. Even to diagnose the elements which contribute to the total condition taxes the best clinical services. In the past, the tendency was to categorize the youngster on the basis of the most prominent or presenting disability. Sometimes the categorization was intended to make a child eligible for a particular service which, though not the appropriate one, was the only available. We have moved away from exclusive emphasis on vertical categories (emotionally disturbed from minor to most serious but all in the emotional continuum and likewise with retardation and other disabilities) toward horizontal assessment (mild to serious in degree regardless of the specific area). The theory is that mild retardation and mild disturbance are more alike to educate than are mild and seriously disturbed; hence the new groupings. Such issues as these will find their place in the discussion of various aspects of the children who are the foci of the chapters. The recognition of the interactive, multiple conditions of the seriously handicapped has become a subspecialty. Not all professionals have the stamina needed to help the severely multiply handicapped. The need for early intervention has gained prominence, which leads to a new emphasis on preschool special education.

One test of equalizing opportunity is for the reader to try to apply for a job carrying a paper to show the agent explaining some condition of special education, say retardation, or limited vision. Another device is to list one's biological and environmental assets and limitations and then to think how life might have been altered with changes in the list.

6. The last issue to keep in mind while reading the chapters is the process by which special services are provided. What are possible alternative administrative formats? How early in life should help be provided? What is the school's role and the parents' role? For a long time the major characteristic of special education was separation from regular education. At times the reduction in class size was all that was different. With the advent of special methodologies (and the concurrent requirement of special certification), the divorce from regular education became final. The teacher of normal children was not considered adequately prepared to assist the special child.

Now the mandate is for no change from the normal setting unless necessary to serve the child's needs. The rules have reversed from how to get the handicapped out of the regular class to how to keep them in the regular class.

This is the wrong way to go about offering service. By definition, the handicapped require more teacher investment and more sophisticated teacher skills than are required for the normal youngster. Once the diagnostic study has been made, planning can begin around the needs revealed. A good quality program must be designed within any style of delivery. There are excellent institutional programs for particular children. While *mainstream* is today's catchword, if what is done amounts to inadequate service, this is no help. There are expert differences of opinion as to what is the best technique; such debates will be discussed in the chapters. It is obvious that some handicapped pupils do not differ greatly from the range found in the typical classroom and may be accommodated with reasonably little added. There are even instances, such as with certain disturbed children, where the total intervention program may be out of school, with the family. The sequence of helping starts with the regular teacher and traditional classroom resources; then special training can be given the regular teacher; next is the supplementary service of a resource teacher; from this we may move to various amounts of time in a special class; day schools and all-day programs (especially when many disciplines are required) provide more intensive care, with parent involvement; finally, there is the institutional placement. In each step, excellent or poor service can be provided.

It is worthwhile to look in some detail at the problem of program evaluation. Studies have indicated that segregated classes did no better for the retarded placed in them than for a "matched" group in regular classes. But even here, the efforts to evaluate have often been equivocal. If we ask where the retarded child feels better about his or her academic promise—self-concept of ability—it turns out to be the segregated class. This is to be expected since this is where the child's competitive position is less in jeopardy. In a class comprised of Terman's geniuses, any of us might well feel inferior. One of the issues of concern should be the *nature* of the special provision: is it a quality program, run of the mill, or primitive? Most of the classes for emotionally disturbed were found to be very little different in nature from regular classes except in size and concentration of problem behavior. Few programs provided what was really needed by the children placed there. Also, the studies usually deal with the mythical "average" child and do not differentiate between those who were helped and those not helped in a given program. It would be interesting to study the proper classes with the proper provisions for the pupils selected.

There are many issues regarding the special class as the delivery mode for special education services. The availability of special classes made it too easy for the mainstream to rid itself of certain children. Assessment methods were heavily loaded against certain children, such as the deprived (Mercer 1973). The prejudice of the educational establishment against minority children who did not fit well into rigid systems added to the diagnostic distortions. There were children put away for their school life with what amounted to a criminal procedure of decision-making. Parents were usually kept in the dark. And to top it all, the so-called programs where the children and adolescents were placed were wanting in substance. Re-evaluations of status were rare.

There is still another item on the agenda. As long as regular schools could easily rid themselves of responsibility for children who did not fit in their context, they could continue to operate in an inflexible manner.

Rather than adapting the school to the needs of the child, the child should fit the school or be served elsewhere as a special education student.

The problem of coping with school is illustrated in *Children Out of School in America,* which found that nearly 2 million children of school age are not enrolled, an average of 4.8 percent, but a survey indicated there are far more. Suspensions, counseling out, and push outs account for additional rejection of many children: the study reveals that *153,000* are suspended for a total of 3,200 school years. About double the equivalent percentage of minority students are suspended—all of this when the school is supposed to be serving as a compensatory agency in society for maligned and high-risk children and youth.

However one puts it, the demands made in mainstreaming are severe. A lucid discussion of the substance of the concept is provided by Kaufman (1975): "Mainstreaming refers to the temporal, instructional and social integration of eligible exceptional children with normal peers, based upon an ongoing individually determined educational planning and programming process and requires clarification of responsibility, among regular and special education, administrative, instructional and supportive personnel." We can see that there is nothing simple or easy about the plan. If this plea for research is followed, it is likely that the efficacy issue will be shifted from the special class to the regular class rather than to the question, Are real needs actually being met?

The main question is, How much total milieu control is needed to bring about the change needed to make intervention successful? In the mainstream, we know that social acceptance is as critical as teacher acceptance. There will be discussion of these matters in all of the chapters. Study the proposals for the psychological implications for the pupil, not administrative cost or philosophical criterion. The impacts on the special child, the peers, and the teacher must all be weighed. Kendall (1971) has made it clear that ideological decisions overlook a great many other factors. Nor should cost become the judge, though the struggle for adequate resources continues to grow.

As you read the various chapters, it will become evident that there is a spectrum of ways to deliver special educational services. While many of these are not new administrative designs, the changing special educational theories have encouraged a far more balanced set of opportunities than was true in the past.

For each of the examples presented in the chapters, the reader should explore various designs: How much can be done by astute management in the mainstream? When and why are various degrees of separation indicated as the preferred mode of help? Each chapter will attend to the type of help which can be given, where it can be given, and how. The chapters include discussions of the way one decides this based upon serving the child rather than a philosophy dissociated from psychological reality.

No implication of importance should be drawn from the order of presentation. The first chapter has to do with retardation, followed by disturbance and learning disability. These three have come to comprise the common functional triumvirate in training and programming. Delinquency is included with disturbance. The next area is of quite another nature, the gifted. The communication problem areas of speech, sight, hearing, and motility follow in that order. Of course, as has been pointed out, each illustration of a "category" covers more than one, since a single pure problem condition seldom occurs.

The authors of the chapters have three qualities in common: they are experienced experts in the fields they are presenting, with a command of the research and techniques. From this they have selected the most critical knowledge. The authors are also professionals who have direct knowledge of many children from which they have selected the example. But the breadth of their contacts permits them to explore the parameters of their area. Finally they are known for their humanistic concern. The challenge is to introduce each field through lives of children, to make factual information relevant by the relationship to real youngsters, and to test the actual processes of special education by following the situations to adulthood.

RAYMOND N. ELLIOTT, Jr.

To Raymond N. Elliott, Jr., categories or theoretical generalizations about special children have never been of primary importance. Rather, he has worked to better the lives of individual special children. He was an advocate before the advocacy movement started. Colleagues value his astuteness at sizing up situations, as well as his forthrightness which he combines with fairness.

His contact with special education has included extensive teaching of retarded and disturbed children, university teaching, and consultancy to various public school and special education programs.

For several years he directed the University of Michigan Fresh Air Camp for exceptional children, which included training advanced personnel and a wide spectrum of assistance for various types of special children. He developed innovative ways to make a recreational-therapeutic camp available for special children who would never otherwise have such an experience. At present Professor Elliott is the Area Head of Special Education, College of Education, University of Alabama.

The case of Marty represents the misdiagnosis which can all too easily happen to minority children who come from poor economic circumstances. There are many children like Cely who are normal at home, retarded at school. We see next John, who can be maintained in a regular class. The final brief set of children illustrates serious retardation and what was done for them.

2

Mental Retardation

RAYMOND N. ELLIOTT, Jr.

IN THIS CHAPTER THE READER is introduced to seven individuals who have shared the human experience of being classified as mentally retarded. The partial case histories are strategically placed to highlight textual information as definitions, causes, assessment, characteristics, and educational programs for educable, trainable, and severely mentally retarded individuals are reviewed.

DEFINING MENTAL RETARDATION

The common denominator of most definitions of mental retardation is a characterization of an individual's inability to make adequate adjustments to life situations because of limited intellectual capacity. Disagreements concerning identification and diagnostic procedures, differing etiological variables, and the varying influences of environment are the reasons often cited for dissatisfaction with many of the existing definitions. The definition formulated for the American Association on Mental Deficiency is widely accepted. As originally formulated, the definition was as follows: "Mental retardation refers to subaverage general intellectual functioning which originates during the developmental period and is associated with impairment in adaptive behavior" (Heber 1961) Grossman (1973) revised the Heber definition to read: "Mental retardation refers to significantly subaverage general intellectual functioning existing concurrently with deficits in adaptive behavior, and manifested during the developmental period."

23

There are several differences between the Heber and Grossman definitions. In the Heber definition, subaverage refers to greater than one standard deviation below the mean on an individually administered test of intelligence. Grossman used the term "significantly subaverage" to mean two or more standard deviations below the mean. Heber defined the developmental period as approximately sixteen years; Grossman used a higher age limit of eighteen years.

The focus on impairment or deficits in adaptive behavior is a key element of the AAMD definition. In an expansion of Heber's statement, Grossman defined adaptive behavior as, "effectiveness of degree with which the individual meets the standards of personal independence and social responsibility expected of his age cultural group." Grossman further specified that adaptive behavior may be reflected in the following areas: During infancy and childhood in sensorimotor skills development, communication skills, self-help skills, and socialization. During childhood and early adolescence behavior was reflected in application of basic academic skills in daily life activities, application of appropriate reasoning and judgment in mastery of the environment, and social skills. During late adolescence and adult life the area was vocational and social responsibilities and performances. The following levels of severity of mental retardation were identified with corresponding IQ ranges: mild retardation, 52–67; moderate retardation, 36–51; severe retardation, 20–35; profound retardation, 20 and below.

Problems of definition are most important for children whose intellectual handicaps are relatively mild. These children's abilities to adjust will vary almost as much as that of normal children. Robinson and Robinson (1965) observed that "Some of these children learn to read well; others do not. One child is particularly adept with his hands; another has particular facility in cooking and baking. The need for clarification in our thinking about intellectual handicaps is thus acute."

A CASE OF MISTAKEN IDENTIFICATION

Mislabeling, misdiagnosis, incorrect class placement, and disproportionate representation of ethnic and poor minorities in special education classes are issues directly related to contemporary definitions of mental retardation. Marty's case summary highlights a number of these issues.

Marty is a ten-year-old black male of divorced parents. He lives with his mother and three sisters (ages thirteen, nine, and seven) in a low-middle income neighborhood. Marty was performing below grade level in all academic areas, but he presented no behavior problems in school until the marital problems at home ended in separation. At that time, Marty's behavior was sufficiently disturbing and his academic achievement at such a low level that the teacher referred him for psychological evaluation.

In the referral, Marty's teacher described him as being a "retarded, socially maladjusted sex pervert." She reported that he sucked his fingers and spent most of the school day making obscene finger signals at the other children. The teacher was concerned about the lack of academic achievement, did not know how to cope with his behavior, and was seeking to have him placed in a special education class. She stated that his academic progress was impeded and that his reading had become a serious problem.

The psychological report indicated that Marty was a sensitive child with a fair self-concept, slightly below average in intelligence, and retarded in most academic areas, especially reading. After reporting achievement grade equivalents, IQ, and mental age scores, the report indicated that the child was probably suffering from some emotional difficulty that, in all likelihood, resulted from his parents' recent separation. It was suggested that temporary placement in a special education classroom for the educable mentally retarded might be helpful, and psychiatric counseling for both child and parent was advised.

Such a psychological evaluation report added little to what was already known about the child. The psychologist verified the referring teacher's observations without suggesting alternative remedial solutions. Psychological study that eventuates in a verification process appears to have limited usefulness for instructional purposes. However, the report pleased the referring teacher, since it allowed the removal of the child from her class. Marty was placed in a special education class "temporarily."

The recommendations for psychiatric counseling could not be implemented. Marty and his mother were refused service at the local mental health clinic because Marty's father was a resident of another state and unavailable to participate in therapy sessions. The family did not have sufficient means to employ private psychiatric help. In his recommendations, the psychologist managed to ignore the reality of the family circumstances. A recommendation not related to environmental constraints is a poor prescription.

The receiving special education teacher was left to her own resources to find remedial alternatives for Marty's academic retardation and controls for his behavioral difficulties. As an initial step, the special education teacher summarized information available from both school records and the psychological report. Marty was given independent work to do. In addition, instruction was planned for activities in which Marty would most probably be successful.

As the teacher worked individually with Marty, or as he participated in group activities, the teacher kept anecdotal records of incidents which might require further investigation. On the basis of Marty's past education performance and the results of the informal surveys administered by the special education teacher, educational plans were developed for Marty and shared with him and his mother:

Arithmetic

Marty would work in his fourth grade text independently, with the exception that story problems were to be read to him. A duplicate text was given to his mother, and plans for the next several weeks were scheduled for Marty to work at home on specific pages of arithmetic. As an assignment was finished, Marty was to return the work to school. The goal of such instruction was to maintain his skills at grade level so that he could be reintegrated with regular fourth grade arithmetic classes as soon as possible.

Reading

Marty was to receive intensive instruction in word study skills; such skills included both phonetic and structural analysis. The reading material selected for instruction was published by the Economy Company, which introduces vowel sounds and consonant sounds at the first grade level. A student tutor was selected to help Marty drill on relating sounds with letters and visual word recognition. Independent activities were planned for Marty to practice sound-letter associations using the Language Master. In addition, Marty participated with a reading group in the class who were reading at second grade level. Individual instruction with the teacher included helping Marty quickly master auditory association skills. The mother had agreed to spend a few minutes daily practicing word recognition cards with Marty. The teacher would provide new cards of unknown words as a set was mastered and returned to school. Such word cards were made using words selected from a graded word list and were non-phonetic.

Language

Marty was included in a group practicing language usage using oral group techniques. This practice involved choral reading of simple sentences with verb forms missing. Most of Marty's usage errors had been in using incorrect past tense forms of common verbs.

Spelling instruction was both an individual and group activity. Marty was started in a spelling workbook which emphasized phonetic family word groups.

An in-class tutor worked with Marty, dictating words that Marty was to write on the board. These spelling words were from his spelling workbook, but the goal of instruction was the correct writing of certain letters with which Marty had a great deal of difficulty.

Science and Social Studies Concepts

An effort was made by the special education teacher to parallel the science and social studies curriculum currently being taught in the fourth grade classrooms. Since such texts were often too difficult for Marty to read, the teacher adapted the textual information to his level of academic skills. Class discussions were encouraged, especially using terms unique to these content areas. A partial goal of this activity was to provide Marty with essentially the same content he might have learned had he been enrolled in fourth grade.

Behavior

The misbehaviors reported by Marty's former teacher disappeared when they failed to obtain attention in his present class. The increased interpersonal contact within the classroom (the in-class tutoring and individual attention from the teacher) provided Marty with status and recognition. A great deal of praise was used to help him understand and appreciate his abilities. Corrections were made tactfully and with no emotional overtones ("This is not right," rather than "You've Made a Mistake"). In a private conversation with the mother, Marty's reactions to his father's absence were discussed. Marty's mother realized that Marty would need extra support and understanding, as well as constant reassurance of his value to her. It was felt that his reactions were of a temporary nature. The teacher suggested that a male relative or neighbor might be enlisted to provide Marty with some companionship for the next few months.

The teacher assured Marty's mother that Marty would be re-integrated into regular classes on a part-time basis as soon as possible, with the eventual goal being complete re-integration. During his placement in the special classroom, educational goals included the maintenance of skills he had, a similar curriculum to that of fourth grade classes, and intensive instruction in reading.

At the request of the special education teacher, Marty had been administered an audiometric screening test by the speech correctionist. A minor hearing loss was noted. This was also discussed with the mother. Although the loss was very slight, such a condition should be watched in case the loss became more pronounced. At present, the loss was not severe enough to require any corrective measures. It was this minimum loss which had accounted for Marty's visual attention and which may have interferred with his learning phonetic skills in a regular classroom.

Several contemporary issues are illustrated in Marty's case overview. The special education class to which he was assigned had an enrollment that was 50 percent black. The overall percentage of black students in Marty's school was 6 percent. Marty's mother was puzzled at having her child labeled mentally retarded, because outside of the school setting his behavior was very normal. She had always been very successful in having him correctly complete the school assignments his teacher sent home and believed that the work was "too easy" for him. Unfortunately, it is very clear that the reason for the mental retardation classification and placement was more an administrative convenience for the teacher than a constructive program for Marty. Fortunately, the special education teacher was able to effect positive remedial plans so that Marty could be returned to the regular classroom. The special education teacher performed no miracles with Marty. While some specialized assistance might have been required, a similar type of program plan could have been effectively implemented by the regular classroom teacher.

PREVALENCE: NO TRUE FIGURES

From the review of definitions it is clear that estimates of the number of mentally retarded individuals are valid only for a particular time and place. The figures most often cited are about 3 percent of the entire population or 2 percent of the school-age population. These figures include individuals from the mildly retarded through profound. From 80 to 90 percent of these individuals are in the mildly retarded groups. It is estimated that there are approximately six million retarded individuals in the United States. Less than one hundred thousand are moderate to severely retarded, and over five million are identified in the mild retardation category.

U.S. Office of Education figures for 1971–72 report 2.3 percent of the school-age population as mentally retarded and requiring special education services, with 2 percent of the group identified as educable retarded and 0.3 percent as moderately retarded. Using a 1974 Census Bureau report, Sontag (1977) reported a 2.3 percent figure or 1,507,000 retarded persons from birth to age 19.

Heber (1970) reviewed twenty-eight prevalence surveys and found a median of 1 percent. Payne and Mercer (1975) summarized the findings of surveys of prevalence of mentally retarded individuals in the following manner: (1) there is a higher incidence of mental retardation during the school-age years with lower incidence at the preschool years and adulthood; (2) there is a higher incidence of mental retardation among males; (3) there is a higher incidence of mental retardation among ethnic and racial minority groups; and (4) there is a higher incidence of mental retardation among low socioeconomic groups.

IDENTIFICATION AND TESTING

Testing Intelligence

When testing the intelligence of a child it is important to be constantly aware of the difference between the meaning of several concepts. Instruments and procedures are not currently available to directly measure a person's innate capacity to learn. Furthermore, it is impossible to measure all of a person's knowledge. Even a severely retarded person has acquired a relatively large amount of factual knowledge of many different kinds. It is virtually impossible to exhaust this store of knowledge for the purpose of measuring it. What must be done, therefore, is to select many different samples of knowledge and behavior and infer from the results the person's intellectual level. When this is done, certain things must necessarily be taken for granted. The things which are taken for granted constitute the basic assumptions underlying intelligence testing:

1. Intelligence is "normally" distributed.
2. All children for whom the test is applicable have had essentially equal opportunities to learn.

3. A normal child of a given age will have learned a normal amount, while a superior child of the same age will have learned a greater amount, and a retarded child of the same age will have learned a lesser amount.

Consider these assumptions in order: (1) *Intelligence is "normally" distributed.* Any characteristic which is governed by chance factors alone is distributed normally over the entire population. To illustrate, if it were possible to measure the height of all the women in this country, the vast majority of them (68%) would be found to measure very close to 5 feet, 6 inches, which is the average height of American women. Some would be taller and some would be shorter than this. The actual measure, if drawn in the form of a graph, would be found to conform to a Gaussian curve or "the curve of normal chance distribution."

Intelligence is conceived to be one of the characteristics which are normally distributed. Since no control can be exerted over the level of intelligence an individual possesses, it is assumed that only chance factors determine this, and, therefore, "normal" distribution prevails.

Assumption (2) *All children for whom the test is applicable have had essentially equal opportunities to learn.* This does not mean that all children are assumed to have had the *same* opportunities. For this reason, some poor, black, and ethnic minority children cannot be tested accurately with existing instruments. For the most part, many of these children are from different cultures from the majority and therefore do not conform to the basic assumption of "equal opportunity to learn."

Assumption (3) *A normal child of a given age will have learned a normal amount; a superior child of the same age will have learned a greater amount; and a retarded child of the same age will have learned a lesser amount.* If the reader realizes that intelligence varies individually in both qualitative and quantitative aspects, and accepts Assumption (2)—the quality of opportunity—it will be much easier to understand why this assumption is reasonable.

Assumptions (1) and (2) enter into intelligence testing in yet another way. Intelligence tests are constructed by giving many hundreds of children of each age level many tasks to perform. On the basis of assumptions (1) and (3), the performance exhibited by the most children at each age is designated the "normal" or average performance for that age level. The better than average and poorer than average performances are then scaled out to conform to the normal curve of chance distribution.

The performances of the members of the original group tested (the standardization group) are given numerical scores in terms of years and months of intellectual development, or "mental ages." When children are tested they are given exactly the same tasks to perform as was the standardization group. Each child's performance on these tasks is compared with the performances of the original group of children and the child's score is expressed in terms of his or her "mental age." The mental age thus derived was used to compute "intelligence quotients" in the following manner: the mental age of each child was divided by his chronological age and the quotient multiplied by one hundred in order to remove the decimal. It is apparent therefore that an "IQ" is a *mathematically derived score,* not something that exists within the individual such as intelligence, wisdom, or knowledge.

Consider what an IQ really means. First, it is not a direct measure of an individual's intelligence. It is simply a mathematically derived score indicating how an individual compares with a *group of individuals* in the performance of certain tasks. For an IQ to be meaningful it must be interpreted by a trained person. Many factors are involved in such an interpretation. Some of the most obvious are:

1. Did the examiner succeed in obtaining the child's cooperation in the test situation? If not, the score derived from the test results does not represent a fair sample of the child's ability.

2. Can the child be considered to have essentially the same opportunities to learn as the standardization group? If not, the test is not applicable to the child because he does not conform to basic assumption (2); that is, that *every* child for whom the test is applicable has had essentially equal opportunity to learn.

3. Suppose that all the basic assumptions are met. What kinds of tasks did the child perform successfully and what kinds were failed? It is possible for two children to obtain exactly the same score but to exhibit widely divergent abilities. An IQ of 50 for a passive Down's syndrome child does not represent the same thing that an IQ of 50 represents for a hyperactive child who suffers from organic brain injury.

Many other factors enter into the interpretation of an IQ. The three discussed should serve to illustrate the danger involved in assuming that an IQ is meaningful in and of itself. It has just one purpose when it is interpreted, it serves to classify a person on the basis of his predicted ability to learn (see Table 2.1).

SEVERAL PROBLEMS IN DIAGNOSIS

Cely, age 5½, is an excellent example of a case where a child's school performance manifested "retarded" behavior, but her home and community

32 HUMANISTIC TEACHING

TABLE 2.1

Levels of Mental Retardation and Associated IQ Scores

Educational Term	Degree of Mental Retardation	Standard- Binet IQ	Wechsler IQ
Educable	Mild	67–52	70–55
Trainable	Moderate	51–36	54–40
Trainable	Severe	36–20	39–25
Severe/Profound	Profound	19–below	24–below

behavior was that of a self-sufficent, normal child. Cely's parents moved from Mexico to a large metropolitan area in the Midwest when she was two years of age, leaving her with her grandmother. The parents promised to return for Cely as soon as possible. Three years later the grandmother became seriously ill and the parents were forced to return to Mexico for Cely.

Cely arrived in Chicago to be greeted by three new younger brothers and sisters. Life in an apartment and the business of a big city complicated by an expanded family of almost strangers created a new and different environment for Cely. That first summer in Chicago she was enrolled in a Headstart program in hope of facilitating entrance into an English-speaking kindergarten in the fall. Her teachers reported no gains were demonstrated from this experience.

Soon after entering the kindergarten class a personality change was noticed. Cely became quiet, moody, afraid, prone to tears and moping. She appeared to be still eager to learn, but afraid of school. Cely smiled and nodded "yes" to everything the kindergarten teacher said, but never uttered a word. There were never any attempts to complete assigned tasks. Cely was referred for a psychological evaluation, and placed in a classroom for educable mentally retarded children, where all efforts on the teacher's part to keep other children from verbally and physically abusing here were in vain. Her mother requested a different class placement.

Further investigation by a special education consultant found that there were two Celys. The docile, nonverbal, always smiling, and apparently retarded child that teachers saw at school was a very different child at home, where she behaved in a very mature fashion for a six year old. She was able to care for three younger siblings and run errands, and she possessed very good language and speech skills (both Spanish and English). Her recollections of life with her grandmother were very descriptive. She was able to prepare her own breakfast, as well as feed her brothers and sisters. Cely was re-evaluated by the psychologist and viewed to be not retarded, but having language and cultural differences significant enough to prevent her from adequately functioning in a regular classroom environment.

The special education consultant commented that "Cely's eyes and whole face totally changed whenever she saw me in school . . . the sad-looking expression would vanish momentarily and she would be eager to talk about a million things. One word, one concept learned since our last meeting was cause for great joy and excited sharing. She really wanted to learn."

After conducting a second evaluation and placement committee meeting, the decision was made to place Cely in a classroom for the emotionally disturbed. This decision was viewed as the best solution given limited community resources to provide the parents with counseling. It was noted that Cely's parents did not seem to be able to cope with the rigors of raising children, and certainly were having difficulty dealing with Cely's problems upon re-entering the family nucleus and going to school all at the same time.

CAUSES: A CONFUSING AND VARIED ARRAY

It is not possible to comprehensively discuss causes of mental retardation with any degree of accuracy or specificity, because fewer than 6 percent of the individuals identified as mentally retarded have known etiologies. Most discussions include an overview of pathological etiologies such as chromosome anomalies, abnormalities of gestation, maternal dietary deficiencies, metabolic disorders, virus infections of mother and newborn, blood-type incompatibility, lead poisoning of the fetus, or carbon monoxide, and other poisonous inhalations by the mother. Many of the 6 percent with known etiologies have diagnoses from the above list, but the majority of the mentally retarded (more than 80 percent) have no known diagnosed etiology and are classified as mildly retarded. Dunn (1973) used the terms nonpathological, aclinical, endogenous, and cultural-familial in discussing unknown causation.

The American Association on Mental Deficiency (Grossman 1973) offers six categories for describing causes of mental retardation: (1) infections and intoxicants, (2) trauma or physical agent, (3) metabolism or nutrition, (4) gross postnatal brain disease, (5) unknown prenatal following psychiatric disorder, and (6) environmental influences. Kirk (1972) has summarized the above in three categories: (1) organic causes, which are defects of the central nervous system, (2) genetic causes, which relate to hereditary factors; and (3) cultural causes, which relate to factors of psycho-social disadvantagement in etiological consideration of mental retardation.

A comprehensive overview of the causes of mental retardation is not warranted in a test of this nature. Readers seeking more information on etiology are referred to the Robinson and Robinson (1976) text.

EDUCABLE MENTALLY RETARDED

Characteristics

While some educable mentally retarded individuals have gross or fine motor impairments, as a group they are usually more like normal individuals in physical-motor characteristics than any other group of exceptional individuals. Those identified as familial retarded are usually superior to those with neurological impairments in motor and physical characteristics.

Educable mentally retarded children are not ready for the regular academic program of first grade at age six, since their mental age (MA) at that time will be 3.0–4.5. Educable mentally retarded children are characterized as having difficulties in memory, retention, and the ability to transfer learning. They usually learn at a slower rate—½ to ¾ of normal individuals. It has been estimated that individuals assessed as educable mentally retarded have the capacity to achieve between grades 3 and 7, those with IQs above 60 can be literate adults, and grade 4 achievement is not an unrealistic goal for those with IQs below 60.

Payne and Mercer (1975) elaborated on an earlier list of danger signs of possible mental retardation in the following manner:

> Delayed speech: No words by eighteen months; less than 100 words by thirty months; no phrases or simple sentences by thirty-six months; speech which does not approximate adult distribution of parts of speech by age six.
> Delayed motor development: Sits alone later than twelve months; walks later than twenty-four months; cannot hop by age four.

Delayed psychomotor development: Cannot pile five or six small blocks into a tower by age three; cannot hold a pencil and "scribble" by age two, draw a circle spontaneously by age four, or a square by age six, cannot write his name by age eight.

Delayed development of "common sense": Does not "come in out of the rain," literally or figuratively, or show caution toward strangers by age five or six; does not know enough to avoid common home dangers, such as matches or knives, by age four; cannot travel independently in immediate home neighborhood by age six; cannot handle small amounts of money accurately by age eight; is easily "conned" by others his own age or younger.

Delayed academic development: Cannot recognize most single letters of the alphabet by age seven; cannot recognize single simple words by age eight; does not understand concept of two objects by age four; or ten objects by age seven.

It is important to note that in early childhood and adolescence mental retardation is suspected and often diagnosed because of deficiencies in functioning in comparison to peers. With the educable mentally retarded this deficiency is usually most apparent in the academic work required in the school setting. More severe cases of retardation are usually detected at an earlier age. In adulthood, it is the individual's inability to adjust successfully to the community setting that might raise speculation about possible retardation. Many individuals diagnosed as mildly retarded in the school setting adjust successfully in the community setting as adults and thus are no longer labeled. With the mildly retarded this classification dilemma often occurs with children who score in the retarded range on a standardized intelligence test and have serious difficulty with academic school work, but perform normally in the neighborhood and in many ways are indistinguishable from their normal peers. Most definitions require that the individual demonstrate social incompetence in order to be classified as mentally retarded; thus the concept of adaptive behavior is important.

Models for Service Delivery

Special schools, special classes, regular classrooms and supportive services have been the major administrative arrangements used with educable mentally retarded children in public schools. Mainstreaming, the integration of the special child in a regular classroom, resource rooms, and itinerant services are program arrangements that have recently received increasing attention as program models for the educable mentally retarded. These models have gained in popularity largely due to the adverse publicity concerning special classes and the inappropriate labeling or mis-diagnosis of large numbers of poor and minority children. Each of the above administrative arrangements might have unique value for a specific child. Placement decisions should be made on the basis of which program model can provide the best emotional, social, and learning environment for the individual child.

Special schools or centers have a concentration of resources and specially trained staff as their primary value. The major criticism of this model is the isolation of children. Few educable retarded children require this sort of protective service.

Mainstreaming has been praised as an efficient and effective model of programing for children such as Marty and Cely, who have learning or adjustment problems in the school, but should not be labeled or classified as a special education student. The model also had been criticized as an attempt to maintain "special" students in regular classrooms without the benefit of necessary special services. In an attempt to bring some order to the confusion concerning mainstreaming, the Council for Exceptional Children (1975) published the following information:

Mainstreaming is:

—providing the most appropriate education for each child in the least re-strictive setting.

—looking at the educational needs of children instead of clinical or diagnos-tic labels such as mentally handicapped, learning disabled, physically handi-capped, hearing impaired or gifted.

—looking for and creating alternatives that will help general educators serve children with learning or adjustment problems in the regular setting. Some approaches being used to help achieve this are consulting teachers, methods and materials specialists, itinerant teachers and resource room teachers.

—uniting the skills of general education and special education so that all children may have equal educational opportunity.

Mainstreaming is not:

—wholesale return of all exceptional children in special classes to regular classes.

—permitting children with special needs to remain in regular classrooms without the support services that they need.

—ignoring the need of some children for a more specialized program than can be provided in the general education program.

—less costly than serving children in special self-contained classrooms.

It was expected that mainstreaming would be a model that could assist in achieving the goal of equal educational opportunity for exceptional children. Programs were to be designed based on the least restrictive environment concept, where the diagnosed needs of children are the focus of programming, and where both children and teachers are provided alternative and supportive services. Socialization and academic achievement will not occur just because a mentally retarded child spends a portion of the school day with non-handicapped children.

Several basic models have been developed over the past five years which have had an impact on the development of individualizing mainstreaming programs at the public school level. One is Deno's Cascade of Services, which contains seven levels of special education services from full-time regular class placement with or without supportive therapies, regular class placement with supplementary instructional services, part-time special class, full-time special class, special stations, homebound instruction, and non-educational supervisory services. Emphasis is on the wide variety of alternative services depending upon the needs of the child. She sees the highest level (maintenance in the regular class with or without supportive services) as containing the highest proportion of children, with decreasing numbers of children being involved in the lower levels of the cascade.

Lilley's training-based model focuses on teachers, not children directly. In this model, a consultant or instructional specialist instructs the teacher in ways of helping the child, who stays in a regular classroom. It is the regular class teacher that carries out the educational plan under the guidance and support of the special education personnel.

A third model which is referred to in many mainstreaming program designs is Adamson's and Van Etten's fail-safe model. After an initial referral from a classroom teacher, the child is observed and evaluated for ten weeks by a methods and materials consultant, who also gives the teacher recommendations for working with the child during the remaining time in a manner similar to the procedure described in Lilly's training-based model. At the end of the ten weeks, a conference, including the parents, teachers, and administrators is held, at which time decisions are made as to whether the child will continue with the designated treatment for another ten weeks or be placed in a combination resource room/regular class placement for ninety days. At the end of this time period, another conference is held, and other options are explored: intensive special class/resource room placement, continuation of the regular class/resource room program, etc. If special class placement is recommended, it will be for no more than nine months.

Mainstreaming has raised many questions that have yet to be resolved. To date there is very little definitive research on the topic. The major question waiting some response is, what effect is mainstreaming having on children? Many special education professionals have warned that programs should move into mainstreaming cautiously until this question has been resolved.

Special classes are usually housed in regular secondary and elementary school buildings. These classrooms have been criticized as being too segregative and of creating a "special" learning environment which does not promote academic achievement. Some educable retarded children require the semi-isolation of the special class as they have not yet and may not reach a developmental level sufficient to handle a great deal of academic integration with normal peers. The special class model does have the flexibility of efficiently including such supportive services as speech therapy and remedial reading in a child's program where needed and allowing the opportunity for individualized integrative activities where appropriate.

Historically, special education has been synonomous with self-contained classrooms, which were created on the basis of a series of assumptions about the "best" learning environment for handicapped children. Special classes were thought to provide a homogeneous group which would enable handicapped children to compete with children of similar intellectual abilities; with a specialized curricula designed to meet their specific needs for cognitive and affective development, and specially trained teachers to provide appropriate learning experiences. These assumptions have not been supported. Even with specially trained teachers, increased funding, smaller class size, and special curricula, special classes have not proven to be any more effective than regular education in providing for mentally retarded children (Johnson 1962). Dunn (1968) urged that a moratorium be placed on special classes. He was especially concerned about the over representation of poor and minority students in the special classes, and noted that regular educators tended to use the classes inappropriately as a depository for their problem children. Few support the total abolishment of special classes. There is general agreement that this is the best model of service delivery for some children. The task is to identify the children for whom this type of class placement is the most beneficial.

Resource rooms are an administrative arrangement that allows the educable retarded child to spend the major portion of the school day in a regular classroom. The child reports to the resource room for instruction in those academic areas where he is having the most difficulty. He also may receive additional assistance from some of the school's supportive service staff. Resource rooms have been used to provide the adjunctive supportive services required for many mainstreaming programs.

Many educable retarded children have the psychosocial backgrounds, experiences, and achievement drives for successful adjustment in a regular class setting. These children should not be recommended for placement in a special school or special class. However, the majority of educable retarded children do require special services in some form. Normalization must be approached individually, based on the strengths and assessed psychosocial and academic needs of the individual.

EMR SPECIAL EDUCATION CURRICULUM OVERVIEW

The broad goal of education for normal and educable mentally retarded individuals is essentially the same—the development of independent living skills. In subdividing this goal school programs attempt to develop skills in (1) personal adjustment, (2) family, social, and civic living, (3) necessary or essential academics, and (4) good work habits. The curriculum for the educable mentally retarded individual should be of a developmental nature. It is important that the skills and concepts to be taught are sequentially structured and presented to the individual when he or she has attained the appropriate level of readiness.

Preschool

At this level, ages four to six, much of the curriculum of regular nursery school programs is applicable for educable retarded children. Social living skills, sensorimotor and perceptual training, and oral communication activities are the major focus of the program.

Primary

Curriculum emphasis at ages six to ten is on a continuation of preschool activities with sensorimotor readiness experience, oral language, increasing vocabulary, listening skills, and the structuring of ideas given primary attention. It is important to remember that academic work must not be pushed too soon.

In the early school years both mental and physical health are important curricular areas. Many children will have experienced the frustrations of much failure prior to receiving special education services. Opportunities for success will promote feelings of self-worth and are essential for the development of good habits and attitudes. Personal hygiene should be given particular attention, and many classrooms at this level have regular routines for brushing teeth, grooming hair, and checking for body cleanliness and appropriate attire. Parents can be especially helpful in the development of skills in these areas. Social experiences to foster group and independent work habits and skills should be given particular attention. They must learn to work independently and cooperatively toward specified goals in the same social and physical environment. Of course, much of the instructional time in the preschool and primary levels are preacademic experiences in speech and language skills, concept development, and motor training. Writing, coloring, cutting, and pasting require a fairly high degree of eye-hand coordination. Other motor and visual coordination skills are necessary for both school and non-school activities.

Intermediate

At this level, ages ten to thirteen, the student is ready for formal instruction in basic skill subjects. The intermediate curriculum is more structured than the primary and should utilize group as well as individual instruction.

Reading, math, writing, and spelling are the academic areas given the greatest attention at this level. Specific reading skills should be taught at the various developmental levels. Approaches to reading instruction will vary from child to child. One student may learn best by a phonetic approach, another may need a sight or whole word approach, and yet another may best benefit from a combination of the two. Children must be instructed to read for understanding. Supplementary reading for recreation and in social studies, sciences, and math should be encouraged.

Spelling and writing should be taught as skills and developed in some meaningful relationship to the child's everyday world. In all skill development areas it is important for the teacher to remember the major educational goal of independent living. Instructional experiences should be structured so that the student becomes familiar with the use of money, telling time, using community resources such as the fireman, post office, policeman, transportation, and other social agencies and services. The teacher must structure these learning experiences so that they are appropriate for specific individuals, groups, and communities. Attention also must be continually focused on creating a learning atmosphere that promotes the growth of healthy emotional and social behavior.

Secondary

The major focus of the curriculum at age thirteen to seventeen is on life adjustment and occupational education. Curriculum emphasis is now on essential and practical skills in reading and math. Reading newspapers, banking, shopping, and using the telephone and public transportation systems are some of the activities of instruction. Many secondary programs include work experiences where the student is placed in the community on a part-time basis. Since mandatory legislation in some states require programming for retarded individuals to age 21–25, a number of post-school programs have been developed. In most instances these programs are for the more severely impaired.

An important feature of the manner in which secondary schools are organized is the wide variety of opportunities for academic and social integration with normal peers. In addition, students may be instructed by a larger number of specialty teachers as they have classes in vocational skills, physical education, art, music, home economics, as well as some academic areas.

It is necessary that the sequential or developmental nature of program activities not be forgotten. If remedial activities are needed they must be provided. The relationship of academic skill development to daily living and independent functioning must be clear.

Preoccupational instruction should include an intensive study of jobs, available job opportunities, and community services available to assist in securing employment. The student should be aware of community agencies and services that might aid in social and personal problems. Interviewing skills, filling out application forms and acquiring the habits, attitudes, and skills necessary for maintaining employment are some of the specific areas requiring instructional attention.

Work-study and on-the-job training experiences are a critical phase of the secondary program. The teacher must be skilled in finding work opportunities, supervising students in work situations, orienting employers to the abilities and disabilities of the students and working with other teachers to assure that the student is prepared for the world of work and has the type of job experiences that will lead to full-time employment.

Example of Program Planning

John is a ten-year-old white male currently enrolled in fourth grade in the public schools. He is an only child living with his natural parents in a modest home in an urban area. He has no apparent health problems. He is well coordinated. He was administered the Cognitive Abilities Test in first and fourth grades, attaining IQ scores slightly below the normal range of intelligence. He spent one year in a special classroom because of the depressed IQ score and consistent difficulty in reading. The Primary II Battery of the Stanford Achievement Test was selected because his reading level in comprehension was reported to be substantially below his word recognition ability. Results of the Stanford Achievement Test (SAT) are summarized in Figure 2.1.

John's total battery performance is comparable to that of an average third grader tested at the end of the school year. His performance is below the median of his class on the total battery.

He performed so well on some subtests that it is recommended that those tests be given him using the next higher SAT level (Intermediate I): Word Meaning, Word Study Skills, and Language (usage only).

Word Meaning

The words that John missed on this test are well above the grade level at which he is receiving instruction (3.1). For example, the words he missed were: capture, amazing, glance, unusual, scare, plentiful, cultivator, frequently, convenient. It is possible that he is sounding out words, without understanding their meaning. Therefore, it is suggested that his word recognition skills instruction concentrate on the use of the dictionary to find meanings of words as well as using them in meaningful context. He should use the dictionary to find synonyms and antonyms for words he is studying. Exercises such as the following might be used.

> Your word to study is *handy*. If a store is close to where you are, it is *handy*. Write some other sentences to use the word *handy*. Use the dictionary to find some other words that mean the same as *handy*; find some words that mean the same as not *handy*. After each of the following sentences, write a word or phrase which would make sense in the sentence in place of *handy*:
> 1. Is the bookstore *handy*?
> 2. A saw is a *handy* tool for cutting.
> 3. Keep aspirin *handy* when you are ill.
> 4. A carpenter is *handy* with a hammer.
> 5. Keep your pencil *handy*.

FIGURE 2.1

Example of achievement profile on the SAT

Name: John
Name of Test: Stanford Achievement Test, Primary II Battery Form W,
administered 5/25/73

Subtest Name	Grade Placement Score
Word Meaning	4.0
Paragraph Meaning	2.8
Science and Social Studies Concepts	2.0
Spelling	4.8
Word Study Skills	5.4
Language	3.9
Arithmetic Computation	3.8
Arithmetic Concepts	3.4

Paragraph Meaning

John began missing more items as the grade level of the paragraphs increased, when he must make inferences or apply information not directly stated. He will be taught strategies to find needed information in context. The teacher's guide to basal reading series at the third grade level may be used to locate activities to provide practice in making inferences and finding needed information. A third grade workbook associated with a basal reader may also be used to supply practice pages for paragraph meaning. In addition, the *My Weekly Reader* at third grade level will provide such practice (Xerox Educational Publications).

Science and Social Studies Concepts

John's poor performance on this subtest appears to be due to a lack of instruction. It is recommended that scientific and social studies terms be included in his word recognition practice, dictionary practice, and reading material content. A science or social studies text not in use by the class could be used to supply content for improving his paragraph comprehension skills. Care should be taken to select a text written on approximately third grade level which features experiments John can perform and write up. The teacher may prepare science teasers, questions which he may find answers to by using reference material specified. In addition, the *Reader's Digest* (Reader's Digest Services, Inc.) series for children has a science series which might be used.

Spelling

John performed so well on this test that it is recommended that he take the Spelling subtest on the next higher SAT battery. He is performing at grade level.

Word Study Skills

John performed generally well on this test. When a word was read to him and he was to find a word which began or ended with the same sound, he missed 33 percent of the items. When he was to make a visual match, he missed 5 percent of the items. Since neither of these tests evaluate whether or not a child can use word study skills to sound out unknown words, it is recommended that such skills be informally assessed.

However, observation of the items he missed on this subtest and the Spelling subtest indicated that he needs practice in using word study skills in the following situations:

1. Word analysis instruction in the use of the schwa, that this sound can be made by any vowel, and that which vowel makes the schwa sound must be learned by memory.

2. That some words have silent letters, which must be learned from memory (*answer*); however, there are some silent letter combinations which typically make a specific sound (*dg* sounds like *j*).

3. That the letter *c* sounds like both *s* and *k;* *c* sounds like *s* when the *c* is followed by an *i, e,* or *y (city, cents, cyst).*

4. His word study skills should include instruction in the study of root words, the meaning of suffixes and prefixes, and how the meaning of root words are changed by the addition of prefixes or suffixes. A survey test could be used to evaluate instructional needs and should include the following: finding the two words which make a compound word, finding root words, the meaning of the prefixes *dis-, en-, in-, re-, un-;* the suffixes *-er* (of agent), *-er* (of comparison), *-est, -ful, -ish, -less, -ly, -ness,* and *-y.*

Language

John correctly answered 80 percent of the usage items, while he correctly answered only 50 percent of the punctuation and capitalization items. He appears to understand that capital letters should be used at the beginning of sentences, person's names, places he knows (such as U.S.), days, and months. He missed items where internal sentences in quotations should be capitalized, and organizations with which he was not familiar. The format of this particular test is especially difficult, and a clearer understanding of John's capabilities to apply rules he knows would be tested for adequately by giving him another informal test which included punctuation when capitalization was being tested, and where he could make the corrections on the material. His language usage should be tested, using the higher level SAT (Intermediate I).

Arithmetic Computation

John performs simple and complex addition with good accuracy. He performs simple subtraction problems which do not require borrowing. He has learned some simple multiplication and division facts. He should practice borrowing in subtraction and mastery of multiplication and division facts.

Arithmetic Concepts

John had great difficulty with all story problems. He appeared to be unable to assess what process to use. First, he added the numbers in the problem to see if his answer matched any of the choices. If it did not, then he subtracted the numbers. He should be taught some problem solving strategies, such as restating the question, reviewing information given, and then selecting appropriate process.

John should be able to participate with the total group in many activities, especially if daily lessons are planned to include activities that provide John with an opportunity for practice. For example, his word recognition, word study skills, language usage, and written expression could be learned while participating in the reading group working at grade level (5th grade). He could participate in most group activities of the regular fifth grade next fall. Figure 2.2 is a sample daily schedule for John in a self-contained fifth grade classroom. Each content area period of instruction typically begins with a teacher-directed activity, followed by small-group or individual activities. Where individual activities are specified for John, such activities could be either teacher-directed,

FIGURE 2.2

Sample daily schedule for John, self-contained fifth grade classroom

Content Area	Instructional Activities	
	Group	Individual
9:15 Language Arts		
Vocabulary	X	
Word Study Skills	X	
Reading Comprehension		X
Usage	X	
Capitalization		X
Punctuation		X
Written Expression	X	
10:00 Arithmetic		
Skills Development	X	X
Oral	X	
Skills Practice		X
Concepts	X	X
Oral Story Problems	X	X
11:00 Social Studies		
Vocabulary	X	X
Concepts	X	
Written Expression	X	
Oral Discussion	X	
1:00 Spelling		
Oral	X	
Word Study	X	
1:15 Science		
Vocabulary	X	X
Oral Discussion	X	
2:00 Art, Music	X	
2:30 Physical Education	X	

	Student-Tutor	Teacher	Individual
3:00 Learning Options			
Science Project			X
Prefixes and Suffixes	X		
Multiplication facts	X		
Division facts	X		
Borrowing in Subtraction		X	
Leisure Reading, Science,	X		
Social Studies			X
Reading Comprehension		X	
Capitalization	X		
Punctuation	X		

student-tutor-directed, or self-directed. John should have a copy of his schedule so that he will be able to help carry it out. The teacher may work out such a schedule with John, so that he will know who his student-tutors are for each activity, where his work materials may be obtained for individual practice, and where to seek help in such individual work. The teacher must be able to effectively utilize the valuable tutor resources of other students, parents, and teacher aides.

John's parents could participate in a number of activities which would help John make academic gains. The parents should be fairly informed of current educational goals and their assistance sought. Areas where the parent's assistance would be of benefit are:

1. Parents could help in developing word concepts and word meaning. A list of words could be given the parents so that they provide casual practice by using such words in daily conversation.

2. Parents could be provided materials for improving reading comprehension. The teacher should demonstrate to the parents and child how such skills are taught, and the parents should be provided with appropriate text materials, a teacher's guide, and study sheets. The teacher would ask that parents help the child to remember to bring his or her completed homework to school. Such a procedure is a good follow up on daily activities, and it gives the teacher an opportunity to provide feedback to the child and parents that improvement is being made.

3. Parents could be provided with daily practice materials for the child to use in mastering the multiplication and division facts. Parents could record on a chart at home the number of multiplication and division facts the child correctly remembers. Such a chart provides information to both parents and children that gains are being made.

Care must be taken by the teacher that the parents do not attempt to do too much with the child in each tutoring session. Parents should be informed that daily practice in a few skills will produce greater gains than less regular practice in many skills, even though the amount of time spent may total the same.

An end-of-the-school-year assessment allows the teacher to spend some time working with parents to implement a tutorial program during the summer to continue after school starts. If such activities are anticipated, the teacher should plan to make regular contact with the parents or child so that the tutoring program proceeds as planned and mutual feedback is provided.

John is not typical of many retarded children. His low IQ score and reading problems were the primary consideration in special class placement. This case summary was included because it represents an excellent example of a mildly handicapped child who should receive instruction in a regular classroom.

TRAINABLE AND SEVERELY MENTALLY RETARDED

Characteristics

Trainable mentally retarded individuals are identified for special education purposes as having IQ scores in the 30–35 to 50–55 range. Their intellectual development is at a rate of about ⅓ to ½ that of normals. At age six trainable retarded children will express the cognitive behavior of a normal two or three year old. Adults usually will not exceed an academic achievement level greater than grade three. They are not likely to attain the fourth grade reading level required for functional literacy. While most of them are not able to read newspapers or use money wisely, a good number can develop sufficient skills to read simple materials for recreation, safety, or information.

In a sheltered, protective, or familiar environment trainable retarded individuals can perform simple and sometimes complex chores of a work nature, guard themselves against common dangers, travel short distances with minimal supervision, and acquire the social skills necessary for visiting public places. Although verbal skills are limited in the preschool years, they can attain sufficient proficiency to carry on simple conversations and have sufficient ability to develop self-care skills in eating, dressing, and toileting, with proper instruction. Trainable retarded adults rarely develop beyond a stage of semi-independence. Care and supervision by family or some public agency will be necessary all of their lives.

Severely retarded individuals are identified for special education purposes as having IQ scores between 20 and 35. Intellectual development is at a rate of only 1/5 to 1/3 that of normal individuals. At age six their intellectual performance will be at a one to two year age level. Adults usually do not exceed a preschool level of functioning above age five. Walking, toileting, dressing, feeding, elementary speech, and the performance of simple chores in a restrictive environment are behaviors within their range of abilities. Severely retarded individuals will be dependent upon others for support and protection all of their lives.

Trainable and severely retarded children usually possess physical and psychological characteristics that are observable at a very early age. Most of the children in these categories are identified either at birth or during the early preschool years. In addition to the medical symptoms associated with some of the major disorders such as Down's syndrome, a lack of coordination and slowness in learning to walk, sit, and talk are signs that may be apparent during the first year.

Dunn (1973) reports that these children generally fall into three classification categories: (1) one-third clinical types, with the vast majority identified as Down's syndrome; (2) one-third have diagnosed organic brain damage; and (3) one-third miscellaneous or undifferentiated (metabolic, biochemical, and genetic defects are the probable etiological agents in this group). Surveys of the 1970s may show that medical advances have caused these proportions to shift.

Programs

Special programs for the instruction and care of trainable and severely retarded individuals include (1) public and private residential facilities; (2) special day schools and classes; (3) child care centers; (4) halfway houses and community homes; and (5) sheltered workshops. Prior to the 1940s parents of trainable and severely retarded children had the choice of keeping their child at home or placing the child in a public or private residential facility. Optimistically, the early residential schools were organized to educate the mentally retarded to be self-sufficient citizens. The optimism faded with the reality that a high percentage of the students were unable to attain the goals of self-sufficiency and the schools became custodial care facilities, where many individuals became segregated from society for life.

Since community-based programs appear to be the focus of the future, public school programs will be the emphasis of the discussion in this section. Three program levels are usually identified—preschool (age six and below); school age (seven to seventeen); and adult (age eighteen and over).

Four curricular objectives are usually cited as the major goals of instruction for trainable and severely retarded individuals: (1) self-help and independent or semi-independent living skills; (2) language, communication, and cognitive skill development; (3) socialization skills and personality development; and (4) vocational, recreational, and leisure skill development (Dunn 1973). Feeding, dressing, toileting, washing, grooming, and other behaviors related to controlling one's physical presence and action in the environment are all areas of self-help skills. Both trainable and severely retarded individuals are capable of a fairly sophisticated level of skill development in this area, but specific instruction is necessary. In the following section the case summary of Kay is reviewed to provide a representative sample of instructional techniques used with severely retarded individuals.

A Partial Curriculum Review

Kay is a fourteen-year-old severely mentally retarded girl. She has an IQ score of 22 and a mental age of 1.7. It is suspected that she suffers from tubular sclerosis, and her full-term life expectancy is estimated at thirty years. Kay's classroom teacher describes her as nonverbal and low functioning. She is severely withdrawn, has little interaction with peers or teaching staff, and spends a great deal of time in self-stimulating behaviors. She seems to lack trust in social processes and relates to staff momentarily as she sees it necessary, on her own terms.

Kay has been a resident in a state institution for most of her life. For the past six months she has been a student in a special school program outside of the institution. All of her classmates are residents of the same institution. Her new school program is a direct result of Michigan's mandatory special education legislation. In the community where her school is located the residents petitioned not to have Kay's school program located in their neighborhood. They did not want those "crazy" kids running loose. A ten-foot chain link fence surrounds the school property as a concession to their demands.

The educational goals for Kay are to get her to participate in classroom activities, to establish social relationships with the teaching staff and peers, to increase her attending behaviors (attending to a task, improving work and training tolerance), to improve her ability to follow verbal commands, and to encourage speech and improve receptive language.

Teaching strategies include imitating Kay's behavior in appropriately similar situations. For instance, in the gymnasium during sessions in gross motor training, imitation of her scooting, rocking, running, and hitting behaviors are encouraged. Staff verbalizations describe the activity which her behavior approximates: if she is running the teacher says, "Kay, that's good running," or "let's run to the wall and touch it." In this way praise is used as a reinforcer in conjunction with a verbal description of the behavior with the expectation that an association is formed between her behavior, in this case running, and the descriptive term "running."

In the classroom the teachers have been imitating Kay's sitting on the floor behavior and her touching behavior. Kay will sit in a corner of the room and stimulate herself by bouncing a ball, or more recently, turning the pages of a book in an appropriate fashion. She crouched when approached at the beginning of the term, but now looks forward to being approached and imitated. Her teachers have begun to use the periods of mocking her behavior as a reinforcing time for periods of cooperation or participation in teacher-oriented behaviors, because her seatwork activities are interrupted by periods of her covering her head with her skirt and withdrawing from the activity. The teachers attempt to ignore inappropriate behaviors, such as her covering her head with her skirt, at other times they bribe her into participating by saying that they will not spend time with her unless she takes her head from her skirt. If she removes her head from her skirt, they attempt to encourage her. If she does not, they go on to the next student with the understanding that she will receive attention when she is attending to her tasks appropriately. At other times the teacher demands that Kay remove her skirt from her head and attend to the tasks, saying that this behavior is not acceptable and what is acceptable is the completion of the assigned activity. In some instances the teaching staff designates the task, explain what is expected and ignore Kay until she initiates appropriate responses to the task. Sometimes at lunch Kay will wait to be manipulated to the table. The staff will say it is lunch time, and "when you are sitting at the table appropriately (with hands in lap), we will serve your plate. Will you join us at the table?" Until she sits at the table appropriately, her behavior is ignored.

Although we have not described the complete curriculum for Kay the summary should provide the reader some understanding of Kay, a severely retarded person, and the careful and tedious program planning which is required for successful instruction to improve her skills (see Johnson and Werner 1975, 1977).

In the past institutions provided the primary source of special services for trainable retarded individuals. It was not until the early 1960s that the numbers of students enrolled in public school services surpassed that of students enrolled in public residential facilities. Most trainable retarded individuals received instruction and training in a community day treatment center. In order to provide the reader with a representative overview of the behaviors and teaching strategies employed with individuals in the trainable-to-severe retardation continuum, two additional case summaries are reviewed. In each of these cases, principles of behavior modification were utilized in order to change specific behaviors.

Brenda is a very endearing but stubborn ten-year-old girl. She was more an observer than a participant, and encouragement to join in group activities usually resulted in limited success. In Brenda's previous class, she had been allowed to lie on the floor most of the day, because of her tantrums and other disruptive behaviors whenever there was an attempt to force her into class activities. As a result, her skill and knowledge levels did not reflect her abilities.

Finding something with which to motivate Brenda was essential. She was required to join the class, even if she would not participate. When her retaliatory tantrums were ignored, she consistently had bowel movements in her underpants. This happened at least twice a week and often more frequently.

A two-fold behavior-modification program was established for Brenda. The first stage was designed to eliminate her retaliatory excretions, and the second was an attempt to have Brenda participate in class activities. The first objective was reached by finding a commodity desirable enough to Brenda that she would forego her retaliation in order to earn enough tokens to buy it.

She would not play with toys, and although she loves music, eating, going outside, and communicating with her teacher in her own special sign language (she has no speech), none of these were sufficient to motivate her. Her love of observing people provided the key. She received ten tokens at the close of each day spent with clean underpants, and these she used to buy time to sit in the hall. This commodity also provided the motivation for her to participate in classwork, since by doing so she could buy more free time in the hall.

When Brenda's skill and knowledge levels increased, she began enjoying the classwork and relating to her classmates to some degree. Brenda has since learned to hold and use a crayon and scissors, to print a B, and to count up to ten objects on her fingers, all of which make Brenda and her parents very proud. After token intervention, Brenda had clean underpants for four days, for two weeks, and then for five months, etc. The tokens were gradually eliminated during this time, in favor of teacher praise.

Brenda's case is an example of the need for interstaff communication on goals for certain children. Sitting in the hall became even more reinforcing for Brenda when it became general knowledge among the staff, via a sign on the wall above her head, that Brenda was being rewarded, not punished. The staff had been ignoring or chastising her in passing, assuming that she was being punished.

Robert is a nine-year-old Down's syndrome boy. He is alert and shows a high potential for skill development, but his inappropriate behaviors, as well as his relationship with others, hindered this. He displayed such behaviors as exposing his penis and urinating in the classroom and on anyone near him; vomiting intentionally; hitting, biting, pinching, and kicking other children; and stealing and eating food from the other children's lunches. His behavior at home was similar, and his parents were considering institutionalization.

After intervention (tokens given for nonaggressive behavior), Robert's aggressive behavior lessened a great deal. Formal data was not collected after the middle of the school year, but the teacher's anecdotal records show that by the end of the school year, Robert's aggression, as well as his other attention-seeking behaviors, had almost disappeared, even though token reinforcement had been reduced considerably.

After one year of operant programming, Robert is one of the gentlest and most constructively involved children in the class. Tokens are now being concentrated in reinforcing the academic behavior of printing his name, and Robert has so far mastered printing an *R*.

The individual programs used with Brenda and Robert yielded gradual behavior changes and weaned to more intrinsic forms of motivation. In neither case was there any particular magic involved in changing behaviors. These case summaries illustrate that goal identification and specification of strategies to achieve changes in targeted behavior can result in positive variations in student performance.

Another Human Experience

The positive impact that public school programming can have on the profoundly mentally retarded is clearly illustrated in Anne McClure's (1978) story of her son Mike. After years of doctors, testing, diagnostic clinics, and rejection from all schools, Mike's family was informed that a class would be started in their county for the profoundly mentally retarded. Mrs. McClure reported:

> I submitted Mike's name with skepticism and determined not to get my hopes up as I had experienced disappointment too many times before. I had already accepted Mike as a person who could not benefit from a classroom education. We love him as he was and we thought that was enough for him.
>
> The class did become a reality in the fall of 1977 and after two weeks of dragging Mike out of the car and into his new classroom that he did not think he liked, many times I wondered if it would ever work. He did begin to experience new experiences that he liked and showed a new interest for his new life. He experienced new ways of independent living and was able to master and comprehend much more than I had ever dared to hope for.

He was able to find his own classroom without help from his family, pick up things he had finished with and put them in the proper place, and develop coordination we had thought impossible. I cried one day as I saw him use his strong legs and arms to walk behind and push the wheelchair of another classmate, taking her to her room.

I began to hear rumors from school that Mike (my Mike who was thought totally dependent) was carrying a tray full of milk for all of his classmates. After having been helped in and out of a car for 16 years, he surprised us by opening car doors to get in and out. He began to take responsibility for returning his own coat and lunch box to the car and then to the proper place at home. If he knocked something over, he bent down to pick it up. He learned to put his own tapes on his tape player and enjoyed selecting his favorite tapes.

Mike continued to take on a new look, with improved self-esteem he smiled more and walked straighter. He became more assertive and would defend his right for possession of a selected toy. He progressed from understanding and two words to comprehending sentences. His attention span increased and he would listen for directions.

Mike's mother continued her story:

The summer came and he began to fall back into his old routine at home with TV and music, secluded from a lot of activity. Then one day we noticed something different with Mike. A spark of something very normal. We saw what we dared not dream. Mike was bored. Yes, after years of complacent anonymity our son, after just nine months of constant challenging by stimulating teachers and contact with active elementary children, was no longer satisfied with endless hours of music and television.

The first day of a new school year confirmed all of the previous thoughts as Mike literally bounced up and anxiously cooperated with school preparation. After hurrying through breakfast and practically snatching his snack box from the kitchen counter, walking to his school transportation was not fast enough. He ran all of the way. After his first summer away from his first school year, he entered the doors of his school building and went straight to his room remembering what he had learned the previous year. With smiles and loving gratitude to his dedicated special teachers, who would dare to believe there was more there than even his parents and friends would dare to hope for, he continues to enjoy school.

If anyone doubts that all of the time, expense, and endless efforts are really worth it all, let me say that at last a number of families can look at their children in Fayette County who have been termed profoundly retarded for their entire life and now see them with a new perspective. And these children who have been considered hopelessly helpless can now be known as children with new possibilities every day. Speaking as a parent who has been jarred loose from my limited ideas of what these special children can accomplish, I can no longer sit by and accept anything less than a full challenge of their potential.

There are thousands of school-age children like Mike all over this country. We hope their human experiences are as rich and rewarding as Mike's. This must be special education of the present, not the future.

HAROLD COOPCHIK

Harold Coopchik was for four years assistant director of the League School, and he became director upon the untimely death of Carl Fenichel in 1975. The League School is a day school program for children diagnosed as very seriously disturbed. Parents were part of the program from the start. Some twenty-five years ago the idea that parents could be constructive assets in the education of these children was a radical view. The professional community was convinced it would not work, since many believed parents were the problem. The success of the League School proved the reverse was true. Furthermore, the League School pattern has spread to other cities.

A general introduction to the field by William C. Morse precedes a case prepared from Dr. Fenichel's work by Harold Coopchik. Before coming to the League School, Coopchik was a special education teacher and on the faculty of the Department of Special Education at the University of British Columbia. During his tenure there, he developed the diploma program in the education of children with behavior disorders. The story of Ted covers the type of seriously disturbed child about which the United States federal government is particularly concerned because such children are so often given up. Many members of the League School staff contributed time and talent to this project: Joyce Borkin, Joan Fenichel, Rose Jones, Wendy Rosenblum, Tomannie Walker, and Vivian Yale.

3

Socioemotional Impairment

WILLIAM C. MORSE AND HAROLD COOPCHIK

THE OVERALL PROBLEM

IN MANY WAYS THE CATEGORY of socioemotional impairment is the most complex of all in special education. There is no clear definition and the variations are many. Also, as indicated in Chapter 1, being "different" in any category is accompanied by adjustment risk; hence, emotional impairment is found in combination with other difficulties. This creates a treatment issue since programs tend to be focused on a single category. One of the few books which addresses the components of disturbance combined with other special education problems is by Balthazar and Stevens, *The Emotionally Disturbed Mentally Retarded* (1974). This contains a review of the research about the emotionally disturbed–mentally retarded. Much more attention to special education category combinations is needed.

Regardless of the definition one uses, decisions come down to a *judgment* of a teacher or clinician. Unfortunately, adequate diagnosis is expensive, and even between well-trained personnel there will be disagreements. Hence parents shop around. Also there is a persistence of moral attitude about misbehavior. Children who act out are still sometimes considered "bad," and it is implied they misbehave on purpose. They could stop if they wished. No one judges the behavior of other disabilities in this way, though it does sometimes happen with learning disabilities. The idea that socioemotional impairment is in the child and what he does is "his fault" recedes very slowly since we all assume we have some degree of free will.

Recent evidence has shown that blaming the child or adolescent is

57

wrong on two counts. First, certain socioemotional behavior is believed biological in origin. When that is not the case, the child has learned to behave so because of how he or she has been managed. A pattern may be so well learned that the child cannot change the habitual behavior without a great deal of help. Second, whatever a youngster brings, the child is also reacting to external conditions of the moment: behavior is a product of the interface between person and environment. As the ecological psychologists have emphasized, both are involved. We all know children who behave one way with a particular teacher and another way with another. Classroom groups differ in what they induce in different children. Johnny blows up at math time but has no problem in art. This raises the question of the consistency of behavior style. Individuals may develop various degrees of *intra*personal impairment, but they are also always *inter*acting with an outer world.

Unfortunately special educators in this field tend to take polarized positions of either seeing the problem in the pupil or in societal forces, with little attention to the balance of both. This disagreement in turn rests upon more profound differences regarding the nature of the human organism and the role of learning through experiences. Dynamic psychologists see motivations and human drives as the wellspring of behavior while behaviorists are prone to describe a more passive organism, with stimuli from outside being the dominant force. The self-evident truth of both sides should make us realize that the real problem lies in how these two sets of forces interact and resolve. Maintaining one's self-esteem is of primary importance. The environmental forces which are arranged—rewards or punishments—do not exist in a vacuum. They impinge upon a child. On the other hand, the individual does not respond without being to some extent influenced by external stimuli. It is interesting to note that some children are relatively impervious to anything but stringent external forces. An autistic child, for example, may not stop watching a record spinning around and around on the turntable until great efforts at diversion are made, and then the child may rush back to watch it again. Other youngsters are keenly aware of differences in the environment, showing fear before strangers but not with a mother, or by giving up when a task is difficult but attending when it can be accomplished easily. One delinquent may steal only from those he does not know while another may concentrate on those he seems to care about. Minimizing environmental provocation is a significant tool in helping disturbed youngsters.

Special educators have a practical turn of mind; they want to discover the interventions which will alter unacceptable or unsatisfying behavior. When one oversimplifies the human dilemma, interventions also become oversimplified. One modifies behavior by external manipulation on one hand or one rectifies motivations and perceptions of the individual on the other. Since neither approach is a universal treatment for all the manifestations, a false choice is implied if one concentrates on a given methodology rather than on the nature of the child.

The term "disturbed child" includes a multitude of captions: behavior disorders, emotionally disturbed, the psychotic, the autistic, or the socially maladjusted to name only a few. It is interesting that definitions themselves have been a major problem in the design of state programs. The extent of this special education category depends upon the definition and the degree of severity included. It has been estimated that 10 to 12 percent of the child population have socioemotional problems of sufficient severity to need professional help. Theoretically the needs of these children are met by mental health personnel either from the community or directly from the school. But much evidence indicates this area is one of the least adequately served categories. It is important to remember that many children with socioemotional problems do not fit the special education definitions in various states because their behavior is not severe enough. Special education resources are seldom available for crisis intervention or prevention. This is the source of much friction between regular and special education—the inbetween child who may be more difficult to manage in a regular classroom than certain of the categorized children.

At least 3 percent of the total pupil population are very seriously disturbed and in need of intensive help. Here the role of special education is not always clear. Many such children do not constitute a learning or behavior problem in school: their grief may be focused elsewhere. When a family breaks up, there are predictable child and adolescent problems, but perhaps not acute enough to warrant special education. Certainly children who are depressed or face impossible odds due to family stress are a legitimate concern even if they do not act out or fall behind academically. Of course the majority of the pupils who are disturbed do give signs of their plight in school behavior or achievement.

Subcategories of Socioemotional Impairment

Regardless of manifest behavior deviations, 6 percent of the 2–3 percent of the school population needing help were found to have the primary diagnosis of mental retardation. This means that they would be classified as MR even though there were secondary (and severe) behavior aberrations. Another 7 percent were classified as organic and would be classified as physical disabilities. We now are down to the true socioemotional disturbance, 87 percent of our original serious group. They fall into four categories.

Reactive

When the children and their lives were studied intensively, it was found that 26 percent were reacting to a crisis or sustained stress situation but that they had not yet incorporated a set pattern or style of behavior. With the disintegration of social supports (family conflict, divorce, movement, tragedy of economics, war losses, and violence), these potentially normal youngsters were producing deviant behavior. They acted out, regressed, became depressed, suffered self-esteem losses, could not do their studies—the same behaviors which will be found in subsequent categories. As the ecological psychologists pointed out, this was reasonable behavior given the conditions. The precipitating condition might be in the school but was more often in life situations external to the school.

Interventions for these reactive children depended upon removing the source of the overwhelming stress so that the child's innate coping strength could be activated again. Two methods can be utilized. One is to change the environment—a reasonable first choice if it can be done. A second and also very useful way of helping is to change the youngster's perception of the external events. Reinterpretation sometimes makes events less frightening. For example, a divorce is seldom easy for a child, but therapy may reduce the necessity to take sides or hate a parent—which produces guilt. An adolescent may come to recognize that parents are restrictive out of their fear of society today, not because they are punitive and hostile. Since we react to the world as it seems to us to be, there is room for alteration of damaging effects in some instances. Of course, the preference would be family therapy, a more hygienic attitude on the part of a teacher, or teaching the pupil how to make friends—whatever would help to provide normal growth.

Such reactive children need crisis help until they have managed their world adequately or the provocations have been altered substantially. In contrast to the next categories, the prognosis for reactive behavior is favorable: with relatively little investment we can prevent the pattern from becoming fixed. One of the major school interventions is the crisis or helping teacher who can deal with failures to cope. It should be emphasized that the nature of the behavior, often coming on rather abruptly, does not differentiate this group from the others. The difference is in the resiliency of the organism to recoup with crisis support. By all odds we are obligated to move rapidly before unfortunate patterns become fixed.

Neurotic Pupils

This group comprises some 26 percent of the seriously disturbed. While they have internalized values and have a conscience, their impulses and controls are in conflict. Sometimes the conflict is real, but often the difficulties stem from the unconscious. It is not that the children do not know how to behave but that they lack the skills. While they may test and act out, they do have the capacity to relate and care.

The strong emotional components in the behavior of these children are related to problems around such basic feelings as acceptance-rejection, love, fear, anger, despair, and hope. It is common for such children to assume blame for conditions well beyond their control, such as personal failure or family tragedy. Sometimes the child will subject the environment to continual testing. Many behave in ways which are self-defeating and provide strong negative reactions. Most often these children suffer from very low self-esteem and try to defend themselves against further personal devaluation. Common subpatterns include: children who act out in ways which are destructive to property and person, often to the point of seriously endangering others; children who turn in upon themselves, giving up and becoming depressed, sometimes to the point of doing self-destructive acts; children who resolve their conflicts through psychosomatic symptoms such as headaches and sickness; children who present combinations of behavior patterns such as the passive-aggressive alternation.

School achievement may be reduced, unaffected, or even at times used as a compensatory avenue. The quiet, depressed, lonely, and withdrawn child is often overlooked while the acting out child forces attention because the behavior cannot be ignored or even tolerated. Assistance for these children should combine therapy (sometimes from mental health or private agencies), teacher counseling using life space interviewing, and modulation of the curriculum. The provisions of the mainstream crisis teacher, special class, and day school will be discussed below.

Inadequate Socialization

Some 27 percent of the seriously deviant children have been variously classified as having character disorders or sociopathic and psychopathic disorders. Often these youngsters are delinquent, but in a separate section it will be pointed out that not all delinquency stems from this difficulty.

In these children, the core defect in values produces many and diverse behaviors. Common symptoms are an extremely short time perspective, much self-serving behavior, a distinct lack of empathy, and an absence of the recognition of the rights and feelings of others. Should anxiety be present, it is related to the possibility of apprehension and punishment, not to guilt. Conflict with social requirements and constituted authority are typical. Their guilt-free violations often touch their peers. Such individuals constitute a most difficult social management problem to the schools.

In the most extreme cases it has been found that such children substantiate their very identity by inflicting themselves on others. They feel they actually exist only when they impinge upon adults or peers; random aggression and craving for excitement substitute for genuine pleasure and satisfaction. The behavior is often unbridled impulsivity, aggression, and even self-defeating defiance which stems from serious limitations in both affective and cognitive controls.

Not all such children are violent or aggressive. Those with milder limitations are often pleasant though impulsive. Basically the difficulty stems from an inadequate primary group experience in the family which has not engendered trust, the start of an acceptable identity through interaction with the family members. There has been a failure to give the child enough care, love, and attention to his or her physical needs while at the same time patiently requiring reasonable age-appropriate social conformity.

For such children, the significant conflict is with the external world and especially the school with its usual curricular expectations and behavior codes. Their abrasive behavior produces a hostile, rejecting response. The occasional misbehavior which one expects in the normal course of development, or the reactive misbehavior described before, should not be equated with the persistence and depth of the behavior resulting from severely retarded socialization. Since aggressive behavior is the prime cultural problem of our times, these children and youth should be a major concern of special education. In matter of fact, they have been pushed out or referred to delinquency programs. More girls are joining these ranks, unfortunately. Inadequate and malignant family situations which engender this behavior occur at all socioeconomic levels.

Treatment is most difficult, and only recently has it been recognized that there are shortcomings to surface conformity forced on such children. A carefully designed and controlled milieu with benign but enforced limits (non-punitive), adult figures for identification, utilization of group processes, significant curricular alterations, and a high level of gratification are necessary. Time investments are high. Control of environmental conditions after treatment and opening ways for young people to participate gainfully in the social order are necessary for long-term improvement. Teachers who themselves have high ego strength and yet do not resort to hostile behavior are hard to find but essential. Group life space interviewing has been found a basic technique.

The Psychotic Group

The most seriously impaired comprise only 8 percent of the total socioemotionally impaired population, but the attention they require is only beginning to be recognized by special education with mandatory legislation. They present severe and comprehensive disability which includes communication limitations, distortion or misreading of reality, and the failure to learn as other children do. They do not relate to adults or peers as normal children do.

While there is increasing professional interest and research concerning these children, there is little agreement on etiology, treatment, or prognosis. Most authorities recognize two conditions.

1. Some children evidence severe disability from birth or early years, a condition often called infantile autism. There are three essential characteristics in diagnosing this category: (1) total lack of language or appropriate language; (2) inability to relate to adults, peers, or objects in an appropriate manner; (3) the presence of these conditions before the age of three. In addition, there are idiosyncratic sets of atypical behavior including such things as gestures, gait, fixation on given objects, screaming, and gross handling of food. These children are unable to cope with the social or physical environment in an adequate fashion for their age and are presumed to lack any sense of identity. Some show clinging behavior and panic at the absence of the mother. Others appear inert and do not notice the presence even of their primary caretakers. They appear unable to relate to other human beings, even in cases when they attach themselves in a symbiotic manner.

Reactions to common stimuli vary from passivity and withdrawal to fixation, hyperactivity, and destructiveness. While some are lethargic, others are driven and impulse ridden. Continual rocking and self-mutilation may occur; bizarre motor behavior and sounds are often present. Differential diagnosis is very difficult since there are often interrelated factors of a neurological nature. Their severe developmental lag is indicative of biogenetic causation. Unevenness of performance must be scrutinized for there are those with intact areas of function which could go unnoticed.

Unable to respond to minimum expectations in schools (usually at the preschool level), these children are often excluded from school, when in fact the opposite is indicated for their treatment. They need early and extensive educational provision since they learn so slowly and require such detailed assistance, step by step. Once the overlay of the usual poor prior handling is eliminated, consistency and warm patience are brought to teach the rudimentary living skills. Even to modify the child's behavior to obtain his attention is painstaking. Parents need a great deal of support and training to extend the changes needed into the home. While the prognosis varies, continued effort to help them is in order. After minimum self-care is learned, the educational program is expanded to provide the children with as many school skills as possible. Effective programs include a combination of deep relationships with systematic behavior modification. The teacher-pupil ratio must be high, for a good part of the work is one to one, at least in the early stages.

2. Some children, after what appears to be reasonably normal development, experience a gradual or precipitous break, lose their contact with reality, and escape into a world of their own. Labels of childhood or adolescent schizophrenia are given. Identity becomes confused and developmental growth is arrested. They can no longer cope with life tasks appropriate to their age. Withdrawal is characteristic. Inappropriate responses may induce scapegoating by peers. Severe phobic reactions, paranoid reaction, fearfulness, and morbid preoccupation reflect the underlying disorder in their perceiving and thinking. Withdrawal into phantasy is often seen; outer reality is ignored or made to fit the inner complex. In some instances delusions and hallucinations occur.

Intervention includes intensive therapy, milieu care, and special education where efforts are maintained to reinforce reality without punitiveness and to call the child back to the tasks. Many of these children can be taught the rudiments of social behavior. Some have particular abilities in mathematics, art, or other areas which can be worked into the curriculum. Adolescence is often a most trying time for them. While some recover and lead normal lives, others will need a life-long protected existence.

The Special Problem of Delinquency

Delinquency is both a legal and psychological phenomenon. As a legal condition, delinquency is behavior which violates a legal statute ranging from staying out late to murder. These days one does not have to detail the increasing amount of juvenile crime, the increasing seriousness of the type of crimes including much violence and aggression, and the gang nature of juvenile behavior. It is interesting that delinquency is not a special education category, but the condition cannot be ignored, especially since the schools are now mandated to provide for all children. Delinquency is a major social deviance category, with 5 percent of youngsters coming before the courts each year. And this represents only those apprehended, not the full tide of the children.

Our concern in this book is to recognize that the symptom of delinquency does not repesent a single syndrome or psychological pattern. In fact, delinquent acts are motivated by such a range of causes as love and hate; sometimes they steal for love. Many delinquents do fit the value-deficient syndrome indicated earlier. These undersocialized children and youth have never incorporated the social codes upon which the legal system operates. In the extreme cases these youngsters lack not only a value system but a sense of being as well. A report on child murderers reveals not only that they lacked empathy and had virtually no cognitive skills (like reading) but that they felt most alive when destroying someone or something. At that point they existed, so to speak. This is akin to those who steal for thrills and excitement and who do not feel alive when they are not risking. The danger creates a challenge which makes them feel powerful at the moment. With normal and marginal youth delinquent acts often take place in a group where dares are made until all, fearful or not, join in to do something they would not otherwise do. No one wants to be chicken. The gang also will punish recalcitrant members. One facet of their behavior is a magical belief that next time they will not get caught or that they have ways of beating the game.

Quite a different genesis of delinquency is found in subculture values which condone certain types of behavior not accepted by the society at large. Often such youngsters will have one set of behaviors for the outside group victimized, but another for their family and friends.

Underlying considerable delinquent ideology is a "might makes right" attitude. This results in a fixation on power and who is the toughest, and is described in detail in the book by Foster, *Ribbin', Jivin', and Playin' the Dozens* (1974). One sees it in institutions for delinquents where there is a culture within a culture. The youth have their own governing society, laws, and leaders apart from the official operation. These youngsters often throw out the challenge of "you can't make me." The adult may then use physical force or gamesmanship, in effect joining the poser ideology. In recent times less primitive methods have evolved, such as the reward system in an institution where a delinquent earns all except his right to minimal care by acceptable behavior. It pays to participate. If this is done in a system without primitiveness or hostility and by secure, strong adults who are not naive, it is one useful method. But the whole milieu must be so ordered, as one finds in the educateur program in Boscoville near Montreal. Here the adults work through all the problems with the adolescents, from rules and allowances to their schooling and recreation in a totally integrated milieu. Less sophisticated and based upon a confrontation model is the positive peer culture approach, group work model something like the Synanon and other peer interaction styles.

But there are still other patterns which produce delinquent behavior. Some few psychotic children will become preoccupied with fire, for example. Certainly a youngster of this type needs psychiatric care and treatment, not incarceration with sociopathic delinquents who would scapegoat him.

There are also neurotic and reactive children who become delinquent. Some youngsters who have guilt and anxiety are beset with hopelessness. They feel they have gotten a bad deal, and their frustration generates anger and hostility. They would get back at those who have what they cannot have. Anger may be directed at those who punish them in ways they feel are unjust. Such retaliation differs in kind from the wanton aggressive behavior mentioned above. It is also worth noting that many youngsters experiment with mild delinquency in one form or another as they grow up, but it does not comprise a career.

Teachers who have delinquent youngsters in their classes will need help to clarify the pattern involved because what one does depends upon the pattern and not the symptom. Life space interviewing is again the major interactive tool. Teaching these youngsters academic skills is not easy and seldom is accomplished by traditional means. The youngsters have too low a frustration tolerance and want instant accomplishment with little effort. In *Hooked on Books* (1968) Fader has described the necessity involving them in language development. Many ashamed of their low skills are defensive and reluctant to start where they must. Through newspapers, paperbacks, and personal journals plus charismatic teaching, this failure can be reversed, as Fader shows. Academic skills such as reading, writing, and math are not to be taught as subjects: they are taught around things the adolescent wishes to know—even to how to deal with his court situation. Getting a driver's license and learning about cars may be the channel. Much more work experience, vocational education, and money earning—these learning procedures are useful. It should not be thought that work experience is a cure in itself, however. In *400 Losers* (1971),

Ahlstrom makes it evident that, while real world experiences are important, these must be arranged carefully and difficulties worked through, or their behavior will destroy the opportunity there as well.

There is a limit to what can be done in a hide-bound traditional school even by moving in this direction if youth values are totally alien. The schooling these children need may only be available in an alternative form. Often this must be combined with a group-home situation; it is generally conceded that large-scale institutional designs cannot be managed effectively. Whatever the program, remedial educational work is essential since the typical delinquent shows gross failure to acquire academic skills (see the entire issue of *Behavior Disorders*, Summer 1975).

For the serious student the publications of the National Assessment of Juvenile Corrections is recommended (Sarri and Hasenfeld 1976; Vinter 1976). The country is undergoing a major revision of laws, and it appears that schools will have greater responsibility and less coercive support from the courts.

We have reviewed the special education condition termed serious social, emotional, and psychotic maladjustment in childhood and adolescence. Now these patterns are abstractions of how children really look: very seldom does one find pure cases. The importance of the subcategories has been to take us behind the scene so that we may look beyond the symptoms and gain a conceptual understanding of various patterns of maladjustment.

But each child grows up with a highly individualistic profile of problems and assets. We have also indicated that social and emotional problems are often found in company with other special education categories. What is it like to be seriously disturbed? What is it like to teach such a child? We turn now to the real life world of these children.

The central example of this chapter is typical of the youngsters who were, until recently, thought to be virtually uneducable. Carl Fenichel never thought so. He did not accept a zero prognosis for any pupil. His diligence, clinical knowledge, and educational expertise made him the outstanding leader in this field. The program of the League School is built around positive parent involvement. He recognized that only through the total family could a child's potential be maximized. Parents are allies rather than enemies or the cause of difficulties. Fenichel was mindful of the devastating pressures on both parents and children.

Ted is the type of seriously disturbed child who is a particular concern of the federal government. These youngsters are the responsibility of the public educational system whether or not the actual programs are conducted in public schools. It is easy for teachers to think that the neurotic and sociopathic pupils they often encounter are very disturbed until they know of children like Ted. Then the difference is evident. If progress can be made for such pupils are we not all the more responsible to attend to the needs of those with less to overcome?

The function of a continuum of intensified treatment services for disturbed children is evident in this case report. What teacher could have mainstreamed Ted when we first see him? Would we ever expect him to function in a regular school setting?

TED: THE CASE OF A VERY SERIOUSLY DISTURBED PUPIL

When Ted Jordan* was six years old he sucked his thumb, banged his head, and rocked incessantly. He was hyperactive, had temper tantrums, spoke unintelligibly, and used a secret language no one could understand. His withdrawal from the world was almost total. His mother was anxious and tearful—distraught at her inability to help her child. His brothers and sisters, unable to compete with Ted's behavior, were quietly well-behaved; all were tense to the point of explosion. Ted had been expelled from kindergarten as hopelessly uneducable. His diagnosis: "Childhood schizophrenia."

The Psychoeducational Approach

In this chapter we will follow Ted Jordan through the ten years, from the age of six to sixteen, that he spent at the League School, a day school in Brooklyn, New York, for the most seriously disturbed children. However, the lessons learned from Ted, and from other severely disordered children, have applicability to children whose disturbances are less severe, and even to children considered "normal." Even as with normal children, teachers must learn to assess and work with an individual child's strengths and weaknesses. As we shall see, Ted had many interrelated

* All names are fictitious. Case material herein is drawn from situations and problems of various children who have been students at League School, combined into a cohesive case presentation.

problems. Before we return to Ted, we will describe the psychoeducational approach as it is generally practiced.

Upon entering League School every child is seen by the full psychoeducational team (psychiatrist, psychologist, language therapist, special education, and social worker) which evaluates his or her strengths, disabilities and deficits, lags and limitations in the many basic areas involved in the learning process, including sensory and perceptual intactness, neuromotor development, spatial relations, body image, visual and auditory discrimination and retention, and the child's ability to use symbols, understand language, and form concepts. The team and the teacher then develop specific remedial, training, and educational techniques and activities that attempt to reduce, correct, or remove these disabilities, if possible, or to work around them and compensate for them if the disabilities are irremediable.

Tasks are carefully tailored to keep pace with the child's capabilities, no matter how minimal these may be at first. This affords the child an opportunity to achieve, a prime factor in his development. Achievement can do for the disturbed child what it does for any other human being: make the person feel more self-confident and motivate that person toward further achievement. By teaching a helpless child to perform a small basic task—to wash his or her hands or tie a shoelace—we are helping the child to develop motor skills that may facilitate other more advanced skills and activities. The child's mastery of any of these simple tasks will often increase feelings of adequacy and self-esteem.

A psychoeducational assessment encompasses four major areas of development: (1) self-care skills; (2) socialization; (3) communication; and (4) academics. For any child, functioning in each of these areas can be described in terms of developmental age. Of course, each area can and must be broken down into many smaller components, but it is important to remember that we are assessing a child's levels of development in all four. For young or severely delayed children self-care skills include the very basics of toileting, feeding, and dressing. An assessment of self-care skills for older children may also include such age-appropriate abilities as traveling alone or buying one's own clothes.

Communication is an extremely complex subject, and a very large percentage of the children who are severely emotionally disturbed also have some degree of language disability. Teachers of all children should be well versed in normal language development and deviations from the usual patterns. Courses in language development should be a mandatory part of the training of special education teachers.

The three following general areas are assessed:

1. Receptive language—does the child hear and process what is being said? When you ask the child to get something, do the words communicate the idea, or are gestures needed? Many parents and teachers have described children as "willfull" and "stubborn" only to discover later that the child was unable to process information auditorily and thus "obeyed" only when there were enough nonverbal cues.

2. Expressive language—what sounds, words, and phrases does the child emit? Can the child put his or her ideas into words? Can the child organize thoughts and make himself or herself understood? Is the child intelligible?

3. Inner language—does the child show evidence of inner cognitive organization? For example, a child who plays with a doll house—putting furniture in appropriate rooms, placing people on the chairs, cars in the garage—can be described as having inner language. Although they may have neither receptive nor expressive language, children with this ability clearly must be seen as having learned a sense of order from their environment.

In the assessment of socialization skills, there is again a wide range of age-appropriate levels. Very young infants would be expected to recognize and smile at their mothers; adolescents are expected to be able to maintain a variety of complex conversations and social interactions.

Specific academic abilities and disabilities are, of course, a major part of any psychoeducational assessment. Later in this chapter we will describe in detail Ted's reading disability in order to give the reader an example of a common problem area and the many methods of remediation that can be employed.

Originally we assumed we could successfully isolate and dissect a child's mental processes into distinct abilities and disabilities that could be identified and then trained or remediated. We have learned that the available observational and testing instruments do not enable even the most skilled and experienced professionals to separate and measure many specific motor, sensory, perceptual, verbal, and all other mental functions. The many complex components of a child's mental processes do not function in isolation, independent of one another. A strength or deficit in one area is likely to affect other areas as well. Every mental task or activity in which a child engages involves a combination or integration of many of these functions. Every function that one works with can and must be coordinated with others. This is especially true in programming for disturbed children, since the majority of them have serious deficiencies in the little-understood process of integration.

We must try to find out how a child uses his or her sensory equipment —eyes, ears, fingers, nose, and mouth, the entire body and central nervous system—to incorporate data from the outside world; we must discover how the child selects, organizes, stores, and interprets these data; we must observe how appropriately the child responds and reacts to what he or she has organized.

As we describe Ted Jordan, we shall focus on various aspects of a special education program during different periods of our almost ten-year contact with Ted. Case material about Ted is presented in three major sections—Ted's "home training" year; Ted's first three years as a day student; and Ted's development from ages of ten to sixteen.

Ted's preschool special education experience focused largely on his behavioral problems, which affected not only his future school career but also intimately affected the members of his family. Ted's first three years as a day student encompassed many concerns, but we shall focus here on his reading program, as an example of the detailed planning and work that go into the remediation of a disability of such severity.

Ted Jordan's Early Childhood Special Education

When Ted was referred to League School at the age of six, he was not ready for a full-day program. He had to acquire some skills before he could tolerate and be tolerated by a group of children. Initially Ted and his mother were enrolled in the early childhood special education program, which at League School is called the Home Training Program.

In home training we work one hour a week with the child in an individual educational and training program with the parent as a participant observer. The parents then meet in a group to discuss the bases from which we work and to generalize the principles. Through group participation parents join forces and resources so that they may develop an understanding of the individual training and educational programs to be used at home to help prepare each child for life and growth within the family, school, and society. The group also provides the opportunity for parents to share anxieties and feelings about their child with other parents who are experiencing life with a disturbed child.

The value of early intervention for seriously emotionally disturbed children has long been recognized, and many states have early special childhood programs. Most of these programs begin to work with children at three years of age.

When Ted entered our early childhood program at the age of six he was already toilet trained and could undress himself. Although he was able to take off his clothes, he rarely exhibited this skill appropriately; he would frequently shed his clothes in a tantrum, but his mother had to undress him for bed and dress him daily. He could feed himself, but threw food and spilled it if he was made to sit at the table. As a result, Ted frequently ate his meals while marching around the table, occasionally grabbing food off other people's plates. Ted had two reactions to any kind of social demands—screaming tantrums or total withdrawal. Ted had the ability to shut out the world. His face would go perfectly blank and he would appear neither to see nor to hear.

Ted's mother treated him in a kind and gentle manner. In fact, during the course of home training, it became clear that Mrs. Jordan was extremely reluctant to punish or restrict Ted in any way. She was afraid of damaging him further. As a result, Ted had never been asked to conform to the normal routines and restrictions required of most children. Ted's mother needed a great deal of support, encouragement, and instruction before she could deal with Ted in a more appropriate manner. Her fears that he would not understand or that he would not know she loved him caused her to behave in ways that reinforced and maintained some of Ted's bizarre behavior.

In home training, Ted's initial psychoeducational assessment avoided psychiatric diagnostic categories. Our first impressions were: "emotional immaturity, severe articulation disorder, fine motor incoordination, and language retardation in a behaviorally disordered youngster who exhibited retardation in many areas." A severe malformation of the jaw was also noted. This diagnosis was functional, planned in order to suggest the general design for Ted's habilitation. Further observation soon indicated moderate to severe difficulties in both auditory and visual perception. Ted did not understand the concepts of past, present, or future. Basic functions needed for language development in all its forms seemed to be impaired or poorly developed. Ted also proved to have problems in correctly perceiving speech sounds. At six and one half his acquisition of sounds was below the three-year level.

It would have been very difficult for a teacher in an average kindergarten to understand his speech. Even in one-to-one situations, it took concentrated effort to understand what Ted was saying. Mrs. Jordan was able to see that Ted was aware of, and exceedingly sensitive to, his unintelligibility. She also noted that if he were asked to repeat a phrase, he put his thumb in his mouth, his open eyes shuttered like a camera lens and his face lost all expression. She was taught to encourage short sentences not by asking, "What did you say?" but to respond in a conversational manner, modeling proper articulation. For example: When Ted wanted to go out to ride his bike and asked for his *gaecool,* she would give him the bike saying, "Here's Ted's bicycle."

And yet this child had a sense of language. When he used his private language, his voice pattern was highly communicative with seemingly meaningful changes in inflection. In his spontaneous talk, his mother, the language therapist, and his teacher, all of whom were familiar with his speech, began to hear language structures which included complex questions, statements, and correct use of personal pronouns.

During his training sessions, using dolls to acquire dressing skills, he was heard to say: "The boy's bigger than the girl. But the baby's the littlest. Papa's bigger than mommy, the boy, the girl and the baby. And I'm the very biggest." The number of individuals accurately reflected the makeup of his family.

It became clear to Mrs. Jordan and the staff that Ted's communication problems were exceedingly complex. Because speech (the production of sound) was impeded by his severe jaw malformation, Ted was referred for evaluation and correction of this disability to a local specialized dental clinic. Language (the communication of ideas) was impeded by a combination of neurological, behavioral, and experiential deficits. These deficits required a program of specific, intensive remediation techniques for each problem area.

We were able to use positive verbal reinforcement to ease his temper tantrums, rocking, and head banging, as well as to encourage greater independence in self-care activities. Socialization was encouraged within the family as Mrs. Jordan became aware that Ted was able to participate in normal family interaction. One by one, realistic demands were made on Ted, and there was a modest gain in developing more acceptable behavior. For example, when Ted refused to go to bed at a reasonable hour, Mrs. Jordan learned to lead him quietly and firmly to his room and go through bedtime preparations while ignoring his temper tantrum. Ted began to understand it was expected of him and to conform to the family's bedtime routines. At the end of a year, Ted's tantrums had been reduced from several a day to two or three a week. He now sat at the table for meals and accepted bedtime routines calmly.

Ted had demonstrated that he was able to benefit from his first year of special education. In that year it had become clear that the many problems based on his extensive disabilities would require long-term individual programming.

Ted Jordan's Beginning in a Special Day School Program

At the age of seven, Ted became a full-time student at League School in the entry level unit for children who are ready to learn to function in a peer group. Classes consist of groups of six to eight children with two teachers, supported by a full psychoeducational team, all coordinated by an educational supervisor.

Ted was seen by staff members as very vulnerable, dependent, and helpless. He made clear his sense of difference from other children and his feelings of worthlessness. He showed controlled anger and a guarded negativism. Yet Ted was not merely a passive victim of his disabilities. Within a short time his behavior changed, revealing some significant strengths. His understanding of language was better than one would have expected. He had interesting bits of information and considerable intellectual curiosity. He showed strong motivation and persistence in learning specific skills. He had a sense of humor and an empathy and tolerance for other children, particularly those who were less mature than he. The balance between strengths and weaknesses became the critical factor in his psychoeducational treatment program.

Ted also brought certain strengths to his participation in a group of children. He was obviously aware of all the children in the class and chose a mothering role toward the less capable younger children. He had a winning smile when happy and was generally alert when involved with tasks in which he achieved success. He was receptive to language, was avidly involved in stories read aloud by the teacher, and was able to grasp information from these stories. He was superior to many of the children in the class in that he knew his age, could name common objects and body parts, and had number concepts up to six. He understood prepositions of position and comparative words for size.

However, his liabilities often overpowered his ability to use his assets. His language disabilities were profound and pervasive. In addition, his short-term memory for sounds was very poor. Aware that his jargon was usually incomprehensible, he was reluctant to speak and withdrew when not understood. He expressed his anger in violent play, and tested teachers through teasing and provocative statements. He sucked his thumb constantly and ate voraciously. He still preferred to play alone and was unhappy if younger peers performed better than he in play skills. He trusted few people and remained guarded with his teachers. When under stress he still "clicked-off," much as a TV set stops when the switch is turned off.

Discipline and Structure in the Classroom

Structure, controls, and limits can be used in the classroom to create an atmosphere which will allow children like Ted to grow and develop.

Disturbed children, like young infants, are generally oriented toward the here and now; they must learn to give up, postpone, or limit immediate desires and gratifications for the greater satisfactions that can later be theirs. All children must learn to wait their turns on the slides and swings in the playground. They must learn to sit at table for snacks and lunch in school before their teacher can take them for a pizza treat in a neighborhood restaurant. They must learn how to lower their voices and speak softly before they can go to the public library. They must learn to remain quiet in a darkened room in order to go to a movie. They must learn to control the impulse to touch, throw, or drop every object before they can go shopping in the supermarket.

Discipline and structure are neither good nor bad in themselves. Like any rule or regulation, their value can only be judged and measured in terms of the purpose they serve and how helpful they are in achieving that purpose. Discipline means channeling a child's energies and drives toward constructive goals. It means reducing the child's confusion and disorganization by setting up clear and reasonable limits that help a child understand exactly what is expected of him or her. It means supportive controls that help a child respond more effectively to the world by more appropriate and more adequate looking, listening, and attending. It means guidance and direction that facilitate learning and functioning.

Structure means putting things in meaningful and purposeful order. It means planning and organizing all tasks and assignments and each day's activities and learning experiences to meet the specific needs and problems of the child and the particular aims and objectives of the teacher. It means setting up realistic educational goals and behavioral standards that are in line with the child's comprehension and capacity to achieve. One must know and work with each child's unique behavior and learning disabilities, levels of functioning, interests and deficits, as well as strengths, skills, and potentials. One must constantly re-examine and modify the program and procedures in order to help the child move toward greater achievement, maturity, and self-direction.

There is no fixed formula for prescribing controls. Nor can they be imposed indiscriminately on any and every disturbed child. The quality, quantity, and timing of controls require as much flexibility, insight, sensitivity, and understanding as any other element in a therapeutic program. Controls and limits do not preclude the child's freedom of expression. In fact, every one of these children needs help and guidance in experiencing and coping with the give and take of human feelings. Teachers must be able to identify with a child's feelings of anger, fear, confusion, frustration, and aggression. We must not only know when to permit such expression but how to deflect, dilute, or control it before it becomes too overwhelming.

The teacher must know how much control to impose on a particular child, what specific purpose it serves, and when and for how long it is to be applied. Limits and controls cannot be imposed all at once, any more than one would try to teach the entire alphabet at one sitting. At the beginning the teacher must carefully evaluate and give priority to those situations where controls are most needed. The child must be made fully aware of the exact reasons controls and limits are being set.

Ted's Program and Progress

A reading readiness test was administered to Ted when he was seven, at the time his reading program began. He achieved a very high score, the 96th percentile. Since chronologically he should have been in the second grade, the score was inflated, but hopeful. The problem was that the test tapped concepts and assessed visual perceptual tasks already mastered, but could not show how profoundly his deficits in auditory perception and his articulation disorder would affect further acquisition of reading skills.

Reading requires an active use of language. Ted's language deficit was one we thought he could overcome. The average child comes into school in possession of some 6,000 words and their meanings. Although Ted did not appear to possess such a large receptive vocabulary, he did come from a highly verbal home. Because of financial difficulties, the children's cultural experiences were severely limited; his lack of experience interfered with Ted's understanding and interpretation of some of the stories he read.

A favorable prognosis for reading was based on his great interest in listening to stories and his fascination with books. He would hoard them in his desk and pore over the illustrations. He would take some home every day to "read." His school behavior had become much more appropriate in every way.

Since structure and predictability are liberating organizers for younger handicapped children, the daily schedule was put on the blackboard and reviewed each morning, and when changes had to be made these were discussed by the teacher with the children in advance. Ted seemed to pick up the words in this activity by sight. Since this seemed a strength, we decided to develop a functional vocabulary of sight words. His choices included *kick, punch, kill, hate, eat you up, ugly*—words and phrases which he used in free-time play with dolls, cars, and blocks.

Pre-primers using an urban environment were introduced, again with seeming success. Ted loved the mischievous antics of the children and he read, somewhat slowly, but with relish. In retrospect, this first success might be explained by the very easy vocabulary, the short sentences, the constant repetition, and the simple cues provided by the clear illustrations. By the end of the school year Ted had a sight vocabulary of about fifty words. Over the summer he forgot most of them.

A year later, Ted was just completing the *second* primer and the optimism of his teacher was giving way to consternation. The deficits in his understanding and production of speech were having their effect on his reading. He absorbed none of the phonic attack skills that he had been taught, and his sight vocabulary was unreliable. The total process was painfully slow and Ted once again began to speak of himself as "dumb."

A year after Ted's admission to the full-day program, the psychologist noted that Ted was socially adept and self-critical but low in his fund of knowledge about the world. Although Ted tried to be cooperative during testing, there were strong indications that he would give up when he found the test difficult. Much of his mental energy seemed to be devoted to developing the facade of a sweet, lovable child. On one of the standard IQ tests, he achieved a score within the borderline range, equivalent to a "slow learner."

Despite this apparent improvement, our experience with other children had taught us to suspect that this might only be a surface change. The child is now armed with sufficient skills to present a mask of competence to the world; he trusts us enough to relax a little and wants us to like him. For Ted, a special day school offered the initial security he sought— enabling him to grow. But his severe physical, communicative, and cognitive disabilities had resulted in emotional damage which required years of consistent, positive, and supportive relationships before it could be repaired in some measure.

Arithmetic was less troublesome for Ted. At first he had problems in writing the numbers, then he reversed two-digit numbers and, as expected, the reading of story problems caused him difficulties at first. He could now compute in all four basic mathematic operations (addition, subtraction, multiplication and division) but sometimes needed a model for special situations.

At the age of ten, Ted's IQ score was low normal; later tests showed him to have reached an IQ score of slightly above average. His intellectual growth, substantiated by this evaluation, coupled with his increased social and emotional adjustment, raised the question of his readiness for a special class in the regular system. However, we decided to retain him at League School, since he was still grossly impaired in his communication skills and was still fragile emotionally. At the age of ten it appeared to the psychoeducational team that Ted had made enough social and emotional progress to consider the possibility of summer camp.

The social worker introduced the idea to Ted's mother. Although Mrs. Jordan had made great strides toward treating Ted more like a normal child she was still extemely protective. She worried about how he would react to being away from home. Mrs. Jordan also worried about the other children whom she could not afford to sent to camp. Again, the social worker worked closely with Mrs. Jordan; Ted's teacher worked closely with him; the result was an extremely successful camp experience for Ted. For the next several years Ted returned to camp and to new and different success experiences. Ted's camp experience was also a success for Mrs. Jordan. She was finally convinced that Ted could and would survive. Ted's success encouraged her to enter a job training program and eventually to obtain a new and much more satisfying job, although it meant she could not spend as much time with Ted as before.

The Teacher as a Member of the Psychoeducational Team

The educational as well as therapeutic value of a daily program depends on how effectively the teacher employs individual and group tutoring and remediation. Each program must be based on an ongoing assessment of each child's learning and behavioral problems and deficits, and on how well each child's individual skills, interests, and needs can be integrated into the program and group processes of the classroom.

The teaching process attempts to modify behavior and promote growth within an interpersonal relationship. It does this by presenting new learning situations and experiences aimed at correcting and gradually replacing inadequate habits and patterns of behavior with more appropriate and effective ones. In working with seriously disturbed children the differentiation that is often made between education and therapy is largely a matter of word usage. Whenever one human being helps another, something therapeutic is taking place. A teacher who fosters self-discipline, emotional growth, and more effective functioning is doing something therapeutic. Any educational process that helps to correct or reduce a child's distorted perceptions, disturbed behavior, and disordered thinking, and that results in greater mastery of himself, is certainly a therapeutic process.

Few would question the importance of the relationship between therapist and patient or between teacher and child. We recognize that in relating to a teacher, children are reacting not only to that teacher's methods but to the teacher's total personality.

A child who can identify with his or her teacher and gain satisfaction from that relationship is more likely to be motivated to learn, to change, and to grow. A relationship, however, must offer more than love, understanding, and acceptance. The teacher must use this relationship not to make the child dependent, but to help the child become a more organized and autonomous human being.

Essentially all forms of child therapy and special education are corrective processes. They involve unlearning old patterns of behavior and learning new ones. They try to help the child develop the capacity to postpone immediate gratification and accept limits and controls. They seek to fill or narrow the gaps in a child's maturation which, if left unfilled, would impair future learning and social development. They discourage the child from perpetuating poor, inadequate functioning and help the child meet expectations and demands appropriate for his or her capacities. They strive to help the child emerge from a world of confusion and withdrawal and begin to accept a world of order, purpose, and reality.

Ted and his Teacher

When Ted was ten years old, he was moved into a unit of older children, a cluster of classes designed for children who have normal intellectual capabilities but severe social and emotional problems. Ted's behavior had to conform to the unit's criterion—the ability to be a participating member in group instruction even though he could achieve only at a minimal level of interaction. He was placed in a room with seven other children and two teachers.

A child like Ted, who has a long involvement with the school and who is treated in the ways described above, develops a positive relationship with particular staff members. We have found that many staff members are able to assume more intensive therapeutic roles with individual children. Teachers, psychologists, educational supervisors, language therapists, and members of the administrative staff have all worked with individual children. Confidentiality is explained to the child and observed when he or she requests it, except in instances where the child may be in grave personal danger.

Because Ted's school has a small population, it often happens that a teacher and child who remain for a long time have a long-standing class-room relationship. Ted had one particular teacher as co-teacher of his homeroom team for six and a half of his ten years at the school. She was sensitive to his needs and moods and available when he needed her attention.

While many people consulted and helped pinpoint the direction of the interventions, it was this particular teacher's closeness to Ted and her continuous recording of his behavior which facilitated all our work, as she recounts in the following section.

Ted's Teacher's Viewpoint

During the 6½ years that I worked with Ted, I attempted a wide variety of supports. Of course, as he grew and our relationship changed, the supports became more complex and varied. Because of the nature of his learning disabilities, much academic support was given; because of the nature of his emotional problems, much emotional support was necessary through the years. I will deal with academic and emotional supports separately, but because of the interlocking of the academic and emotional problems, academic supports were necessarily emotional supports as well.

As Ted's trust in me grew, he would whisper answers to me during lessons. I would then encourage him to present his responses aloud. At the beginning, he would need to have me state the answers; he gradually became able to speak for himself. He needed this encouragement, to a lessening degree, for several years. During the next to last school year, his attitude seemed to change. After many discussions, he finally could accept the fact that he knew as much as or more than his classmates. At this point he frequently began to participate in lessons.

In his last year at school, he began to resent his classmates' lack of knowledge. He expressed boredom and exasperation. I continued to encourage his participation, so that he could teach his classmates what he knew and get much-needed practice in formulating his thoughts and expressing them clearly. Although he felt he knew more than his peers at school, I think he was still frustrated with his continuing difficulty in expressing himself. Throughout his career at school, Ted was dependent on adults to write responses for him. The speed and facility of his handwriting improved with the years; however, his inability to spell and to retain the visual memory needed for efficient copying always hindered him. When he was ten and eleven, it was frequently necessary for the adult to rephrase Ted's ideas, fleshing them out, before they were written. By the time he was twelve, it was usually possible to write down exactly what he said, making him more responsible for his answers. He was then urged to write as much as possible for himself (usually the first letter of each word). The same progression was seen in verbal intervention required in lessons. During his first years in my class, I spent much of the lesson time as support teacher, rephrasing, interpreting, expanding, and filling in information during lessons. In the later years, I felt it was necessary and possible to withdraw this support. It should be mentioned that at this stage it was necessary for me to explain and enforce this withdrawal, since he was comfortable with the support and gave no indication that he would like it to terminate. At times, specific topics or skills were taught, tailored to Ted's needs. This was done individually or in the whole group. Over the years such topics included figure and object drawing, current events, measurement, and scale drawing. As he became more assertive and more conscious of his own needs and desires, I encouraged him to ask for changes in schedule and program that he thought would benefit him. This proved effective in giving him both a sense of control over his life and experience in approaching other adults without my direct support. A few times he attempted to manipulate teachers to help him avoid competition and evade his disabilities. I explored with him (or for him) what I thought were the motivations behind his requests. He understood and dropped his demands.

I used methods developed by many experts in the field and found value in ideas from a wide range of approaches. I would frequently catch Ted's eye when things were being said in class that I knew would make him uncomfortable; when topics came up on which I knew he had private, important thoughts (which he had shared with me); when criticisms were being leveled at the group which I knew did not apply to him; or if his behavior (silliness, wildness) was getting out of control. He utilized this support more frequently than necessary, because he judged his actions more harshly than I did.

When something was troubling Ted, he would withdraw with thumb in mouth, head down, shoulders hunched. He couldn't initiate contact, nor could he say more than monosyllables at these times. I would press him to answer questions, which he would do with nods or shakes of his head. By guessing what was on his mind, I would eventually ascertain his problem by a process of elimination.

Language arts periods were sometimes used to explore things that were troubling him and blocking his thinking. He could relate troubling incidents, which I would write down and discuss with him to clarify his misperceptions. At this time, I believed he was not able to talk about what was bothering him but was conscious of the problem; I later realized this was not true.

My first clue that my early analysis of his thinking was incorrect came when he was ten years old, after his psychiatric conference. Each child has a full-scale conference every two years in which the full team presents its findings; the child and the parents are interviewed, and the psychiatrist develops a current diagnosis. Ted was immobilized during the psychiatric conference, unable to respond to even simple questions about the class schedule. I expected him to be devastated by his failure. When I saw him at lunch, he behaved normally. I asked him what had happened to him at the conference, but he did not know what I meant. I described his behavior and asked him what he had been thinking about. He replied, "I just wasn't thinking." From this point on I tried to help him understand what this blankness looked like to other people and encouraged him to think actively about his problem.

The next qualitative change in Ted's style of thinking and relating his thoughts was brought about by his impending oral surgery when he was eleven. This prospect was extremely frightening for him. He was sure he would die on the operating table and, if he did not die, he would certainly be horribly disfigured and unable to speak at all. The doctor's lack of sensitivity in presenting the information that Ted needed, combined with Ted's blocking out of the little information presented, led to extreme anxiety. In order to be able to explain to Ted what would really happen, I accompanied him on visits to both the oral surgeon and the consulting dentist.

As the time for the surgery neared, Ted began approaching me daily, initiating conversations about his fears. We generally sat together at lunch and talked about whatever topic he suggested. My role was to give continual reassurance that he would not die, would not be disfigured, would not suffocate when his mouth was wired shut, etc., etc. We talked about what he could expect during the operation, the hospitalization, the recuperation. Although this was a daily occurrence for many weeks, the conversations were not just anxious repetitions. Ted used the information I gave him each day, interpreted it, and the next day he presented new questions or new frightening fantasies. The surgery was spectacularly successful in improving his appearance, his speech, and his self-image.

I saw Ted only four times a week in language arts during his second year in my class. We talked about his learning disabilities to some extent and maintained our relationship, although it was not as intense as before. Several times during the year, Ted procrastinated during the lesson until it was obvious he had things on his mind he wanted to share with me. We used the class period to talk over his worries about the future and problems with kids in his neighborhood. I would also explore specific problems with him and discuss what he could do to solve them. If the solution entailed speaking to another teacher, we would rehearse the conversation, and I would generally go with him to provide support. If it was impossible for him to communicate with other adults because of his unrealistic fear of their responses, I would intervene and discuss the problem with them in his presence.

As he entered adolescence Ted began to take a more assertive role in our talks. We met on a weekly basis and had topics he wanted to discuss and he frequently told me to wait if I interrupted his train of thought. He began asking me questions about my life in terms of his own concerns. He would ask how girls and boys teased each other when I was his age, whether kids stole when I was a teen-ager, or how I let my husband know when I wanted him to kiss me. If nothing particular was on his mind, I would suggest topics and he would choose one.

As the time approached for Ted to leave the school, he became more resistant to going to our meetings. He began to complain more about my wasting his time and about not having anything to say. During this time, however, some of his most serious, depressed communications came out. I never let him avoid our meetings. However, I did say he could decide how long he wanted to stay—he could leave after 10 minutes. He rarely left before an hour had passed.

I called him several times during the summer following his departure from school at age sixteen, but was unable to get in touch with him. He did not return my calls. I arranged a meeting with him at school. He came in with two friends who remained in the lobby, while he rather unwillingly came upstairs with me. He was angry and not overly communicative, but did some talking. I arranged to meet him the next week nearer his new school. He came late. Although initially he seemed quite uncomfortable, he warmed up when I looked at his books and honestly sympathized with him about the difficulty of his homework. I gave him specific suggestions about how he could get help at his new school. By the end of the session, he was obviously glad I had not given him up, and we agreed to meet again. It became very difficult to reach him by phone, so I began making appointments by letter. After he missed two appointments, I invited him to meet me at my home. He did not call to confirm this arrangement and did not show up.

As we have seen from this teacher's report, a special education teacher must realize that as the children grow and improve their functioning, personal contact may be lost. A great deal of effort in the education of disturbed children is focused on helping them to become independent of the need for special supportive environments. Success in helping the children to become more normal members of the community often means that they no longer need or want the supportive therapeutic relationships that were crucial to their earlier development.

Ted Jordan Today

For the six months prior to his discharge from League School, Ted attended both League School and his neighborhood high school on a part-time basis. In this respect he was luckier than many of the children growing up in urban environments where schools are uniformly over-crowded. Ted's new school had a remedial program where the student-teacher ratio was small, and the teachers were aware of their students' special needs.

At the time of this writing, two years have passed since Ted entered a regular high school. He is approximately a year older than his class-mates, and the special remedial program is no longer available to him. We see Ted as a success. He can communicate with his peers and adults. De-spite his weaknesses in reading, writing, and spelling, he can participate in learning a vocational skill to equip him to become self-supporting. He is a healthy, attractive young man, shy, quiet, and friendly. He has an aware-ness of his areas of disability, and he has learned socially acceptable ways of defending himself from exposure. He does not have to withdraw or hide or shut out the world, living as an isolate. He knows that his vulner-abilities are more apparent to him than to his friends and the community in which he lives.

His mother understands his problems and can offer support when he needs it. She too has grown emotionally, for her struggle to help her child reinforced her own strengths. She has new dignity, stature, and re-spect as a productive, functioning, self-supporting widow raising her family alone. Both she and Ted hardly resemble that distraught mother and helpless child who sought our help ten years ago.

INTERVENTION PROGRAMS

As was clear in Ted's case, a significant treatment or intervention plan follows individual diagnostic study. Since in most instances there is such deep interlocking of personal impairment with provocative environmental conditions, it is obvious in some cases that the environmental situation deserves equal attention with attempts to alter the child's perceptual world. Again, we saw this with regard to Ted's mother the environment is no easier to change than a child in many instances. A family which scapegoats or rejects or overprotects a child is seldom able to change upon request, or even accept responsibility for the problem. A teacher who baits a particular type of pathology may not be amenable to change. At once it becomes obvious that the task is complex. There are certain steps to be taken in the sequence of special education for the socioemotionally disturbed.

1. *Identification.* While the disturbed infant and toddler must be recognized and referred by the parent, pediatrician, or some other professional worker, the school constitutes the basic cultural screening agency for the pre- and adolescent child. If—and these are big ifs—the teacher is reasonable (adult authority relationship), the peers are accepting (social relationship) and the curricular task expectations are suitable (school work), this represents a reality test of potential adjustment. When a child fails in one or more of these areas and these conditions are hygienic, the child is screened for further study. A sensitive teacher will recognize not only the aggressive but the unhappy, depressed youngsters even though they may be compliant.

2. *Diagnosis-Planning.* The diagnostic study includes contributions from school personnel, parents, the psychologist, social worker, and psychiatrist. Sometimes the path for assistance is clear at an early stage. At other times family history, psychological tests of ability, achievement, and adjustment, as well as psychiatric interviews may be needed.

3. *Mode of Assistance.* Different stages may be considered in the delivery of assistance. The first is provision of individual or group therapy outside of the school. This mode is often combined with the others which follow. Alteration of the school situation may not be required. Second, the pupil may be accepted in special education, but mainstreamed where we know 80 percent of the total categorical number are already. Here the criteria start with the needs of the child or adolescent and the question of whether or not these can be met in the regular classroom or any set of courses for the junior and senior high. Can the teacher give the pupil the necessary toleration with stability at the same time? Can the teacher accept an individualized program to fit the capabilities of performance? Will the teacher be able to communicate with the youngster about the child's difficulties? Above all, is there teacher time for the psycho-

social and academic program proposed? Is the mainstream peer culture a hospitable one which will assist or at least not exacerbate the pupil's difficulty? If not, can acceptance be cultivated? Is the curriculum as flexible and individualized as the special pupil needs? Finally, since with most disturbed pupils there will be times when the behavior cannot be accepted in the classroom, is there immediate, nonpunitive back-up when the teacher needs it? Other staff members will need to be positively involved, especially at the junior and senior high level. While it has been truly said that many disturbed children and youth do not need something different from that needed by any child, it is also critical to note that they need the proper relationships more intensively at a more sophisticated level and consistently for long periods of time. Regressions and struggles are to be expected. Mainstreaming for the emotionally disturbed means finding and cultivating the many potential resources any good school will have. The mainstream may have the needed assets but a good mainstream may require ancillary outside therapy or school-related therapy from social worker, guidance person, or psychologist. Parents will need to be involved. Tutors, big brother-sister help, and recreational groups (athletics, Scouts, etc.) will need to be included. The teacher will usually need considerable consultative help, and often there are new skills to learn such as behavior modification and Life Space Interviewing.

The next service delivery stage is more or less a balance of mainstream and special service, a shared responsibility, at times of crisis or a regular planned resource room for given times and experiences. The teaching team of regular and special teachers work together with the pupil to provide the best of both educational worlds. The junior or senior high school student may be able to function in only part of the mainstream, and even here the special teacher may be spending a great deal of time in mediation. Often the extracurricular or special activities (such as drama, shop courses, music, and art) are denied these "troublemakers," though the therapeutic values of these media are pronounced.

There are disturbed children and youth who need a more protected and specialized environment in order to maximize their education. They need the stability of one teacher and very few peers with a vastly altered curriculum for survival. In fact, this represents a primary group condition, a family simulation, with the potential for the much more profound human relationships which are needed for those who have much past experience to unlearn and replace. As soon as they are able, integration with the mainstream is introduced, usually by degrees. It is obvious that calling a class a special class for the disturbed just because it has a trained teacher and a small number is not accurate. Classes range from highly constructive environments to the mundane and even chaotic. Since not all schools can afford a special class, there is usually a busing problem which may be more counterproductive than the class is productive.

The style of classes ranges from strict behavior modification to dynamic and humanistic; in practice one usually finds eclectic procedures. One of the best-known programs has been developed by Hewett (1968) in his engineered classroom format. By including various types of special children together, he anticipates one classroom for an elementary school. Rich in self-directed curricula and divided into subcenters for various levels of learning, this style is highly profitable. Since mandatory legislation in most states includes ages from preschool through twenty-one or more, attention must be given to special programs at both ends of the usual public school.

There are more seriously disturbed and disturbing pupils who need a totally planned design: this is the day school. Some such schools extended into the late afternoon to provide more controlled time. Usually there is close work with parents. For very difficult-to-handle children, this also provides respite care, giving the family relief. Most of the day schools are multidiscipline and focus on an intensive, carefully planned set of interventions for basic academic and social skills as in Ted's case.

When the whole environment needs to be controlled (either for short or long time periods) to insure treatment, when a child may be a danger to self or others, when the family is ineffective or absent, total life care is provided. Special education is a critical part of the milieu, but there is the simulation of family in learning living skills as well. Some institutions are called schools because the educational program is the core of the operation. Even here the most seriously handicapped may not get much beyond living skill levels. Institutions are most difficult to operate and tend to get perfunctory, but there are examples of those with highest standards which show what can be done. Round-the-clock care is astronomical in cost and few children need such help, but for those who do there is no alternative. Effective work with parents is not always easy because of distance. While intensive treatment for some disturbed children and youth leads back to the mainstream, for others the future is more constricted. The many levels of intervention are clearly depicted in the life of Ted. Unfortunately few of our very seriously disturbed children are given the multidisciplinary help which is required.

JOHN G. FRAUENHEIM AND JOHN R. HECKERL

John G. Frauenheim has been a learning disability therapist in the language clinic at Hawthorn Center, Northville, Michigan, a state psychiatric resident and outpatient center for emotionally disturbed children and youth. Special education is a major component of the program. Frauenheim saw how LD children who had made significant improvement could be devastated by unsympathetic public school programs. Frequently neither the professional nor the student really comprehend what must be done for survival in the mainstream or in the public school special program. Some of the literature implies that children either outgrow or can be remediated out of their learning disability problems—and even go on to become doctors. Since this did not seem to be true of the seriously limited children Frauenheim had studied, he undertook an extensive followup study. Some of the most fascinating case material is included in this chapter. Frauenheim is now Assistant Director of Administrative Services for the Livonia, Michigan, public schools, and he is responsible for special education programs.

John R. Heckerl, co-author of this chapter, had many similar experiences at Hawthorn in the Language Clinic. A school psychologist as well as a certified teacher, Heckerl directed a public school Learning Improvement Center, and was later on the staff of Oakland University, where he taught courses and supervised students in the areas of emotional disturbance and learning disability. He is now Assistant Director, Neuro-Education Center, William Beaumont Hospital, Royal Oak, Michigan. He has published articles in the *Journal of Learning Disabilities* and *Academic Therapy* as well as other journals. He is an expert in developing the evaluation aspects of grant proposals and demonstration grants, and serves as a consultant to many schools. Heckerl's research interests focus on the integration of bisensory data in dyslexic pupils.

4

Learning Disabilities

JOHN G. FRAUENHEIM AND JOHN R. HECKERL

THIS CHAPTER PROVIDES A BRIEF OVERVIEW of the learning disability field to-day and should help the reader begin to appreciate the developmental problems learning disabled children face both educationally and personally.

A case study of a person who experienced a moderately severe learning disability will be presented. The case study information is taken from clinical records at Hawthorn Center in Northville, Michigan. Hawthorn is a state mental health facility that provides comprehensive residential, day care, and out-patient services to children and adolescents. Children who experience learning problems have been the subject of extensive clinical and educational research at the center for approximately twenty years.

At this time learning disabilities is perhaps the least well-defined area of special education, especially with regard to professional agreement regarding definition, the causes of the disorders, and remediation/treatment procedures. William M. Cruickshank addressed this issue in his opening remarks at a conference on learning disabilities examining the "decade ahead." He stated that "when I look at the field of learning disabilities . . . having been in and working in this area for a good number of years, I find the total field confused and in an almost unusable condition. . . . I have not lost hope in any sense, but I see the field of learning disabilities muddled, confused, and misunderstood by a great number of people who are actually functioning in it, and certainly by those who are functioning in the ripples around it." This remains the case today.

In recent years, three broad approaches to the study of learning disabilities have emerged, each with distinctly different philosophies. The first and most thoroughly pursued is the neuropsychological approach or

89

view. Here learning disabilities are attributed to basic neurological deficits, which affect the psychological processes required in "normal" learning activity. The second approach, emphasizing social environmental phenomena, sees learning disabilities as the result or product of a child's disordered environment. In the third view, focusing on instructional and broader educational factors, learning disabilities are considered to be the result of our present educational system. The fundamental difference between these approaches lies in the area of cause and, subsequently, in views regarding learning potential and remedial procedures for dealing with the problem. For example, in both the socioenvironmental and educational views, the cause of learning disabilities is attributed to conditions outside of the child. The psychological processes for learning are seen as intact, but the realization of their potential is inhibited by external factors such as educational opportunity. The neuropsychological view, on the other hand, holds that the term "learning disabilities" should be reserved for those persons in whom the learning difficulty stems from an identified or suspected neurological disorder which affects the "processes" required for normal learning.

The neuropsychological approach to the study of learning disabilities is by far the most prevalent view in the field today. This chapter will focus upon children who experience this type of learning disability.

DEFINITION

Presently the most widely accepted definition of children with learning disabilities is the one developed by the U.S. Department of Health, Education, and Welfare as part of the Education of All Handicapped Children Act of 1975 (PL 94–142), which defined learning disabled children as follows:

> Specific learning disability means a disorder in one or more of the basic psychological processes involved in understanding or in using language, spoken or written, which may manifest itself in an imperfect ability to listen, think, speak, read, write, spell, or to do mathematical calculations. The term includes such conditions as perceptual handicaps, brain injury, minimal brain dysfunction, dyslexia, and developmental aphasia. The term does not include children who have learning problems which are primarily the result of visual, hearing, or motor handicaps, of mental retardation, or of environmental, cultural, or economic disadvantage.

Considerable dissatisfaction has remained with this definition, especially on the part of educators, as the inclusion of terms such as "minimal brain dysfunction" and "dyslexia" are viewed primarily as medical in nature and generally include behaviors or symptoms that are also found in children with normal learning ability. Also there is little agreement regarding the meaning of learning process "disorders" and the procedures for diagnosing such. In general it has been difficult to translate this definition into meaningful educational practice.

PL 94–142 requires that the determination of a learning disability be done by a multidisciplinary evaluation team which must include the following personnel:

1. The child's regular education teacher.
2. If the child does not have a regular education teacher a regular classroom teacher qualified to teach a child of his or her age must be included.
3. A local school district must appoint a teacher qualified to work with preschool children for those who are less than school age.
4. A member of the team must include a person such as a school psychologist, speech and language teacher, or remedial reading teacher qualified to conduct individual diagnostic examinations of children.

In determining that a child has a learning disability the team must consider the following:

1. That the child does not achieve commensurate with his or her age or ability levels in one or more of the areas listed in the definition.
2. That the child has a severe discrepancy between achievement and intellectual ability in one of those areas.
3. The team may not identify a child as having a learning disability if the severe discrepancy between ability and achievement is primarily the result of other sensory handicaps, mental retardation, emotional disturbance, or environmental or cultural and economic disadvantage.

At least one member of the multidiscipline team, other than the child's regular teacher, must observe the child's academic performance in the regular classroom setting. In the case of the child of less than school age or out of school a team member should observe the child in an environment appropriate for that person's age. As part of the eligibility process the team prepares a written report of the results of their evaluation. This report addresses the question as to whether the child has a learning disability and the basis for making the determination. Part of the determination of eligibility for special education is that the severe discrepancy between achievement and ability is not correctable without special education and related services.

CHARACTERISTICS OF THE LEARNING DISABLED CHILD

An examination of the learning disabilities definition presented above suggests three basic characteristics that LD children have in common:

1. The learning deficit is attributable to neurological impairment.
2. The learning deficit exists despite average or above intellectual potential.
3. The cause of the disability is not the result of sensory deficit, other handicaps, or environmental disadvantage. These factors, however, may be present.

Numerous behavioral symptoms have been associated with LD children. Perhaps the most exhaustive list of such behaviors was compiled by Clements (1966), who listed approximately a hundred specific behaviors under sixteen general headings (such as disorders of attention and concentration or disorders of motor function). The ten characteristics of such children in order of frequency cited, were:

1. Hyperactivity
2. Perceptual-motor impairments
3. Emotional lability
4. General orientation defects
5. Disorders of attention (short attention span, distractability)
6. Impulsivity
7. Disorders of memory and thinking
8. Specific learning disabilities in reading, arithmetic, writing, and spelling

9. Disorders of speech and hearing
10. Equivocal neurological signs and electroencephalographic irregularities

As with other complex conditions, continued experience with learning disabilities in children may reveal more specifically identifiable symptom complexes. At present we find few characteristics that are shared by all children identified as having learning disabilities. In fact, many of the behaviors noted may also be found in children who do not experience learning problems.

DYSLEXIA

The following sections of this chapter and the case study data address more specifically the disability of dyslexia. The terms "primary reading retardation," "specific reading disability," "specific language disability," and others have been used in describing this condition.

Briefly defined dyslexia is a disorder in which the capacity to learn to read is impaired despite adequate intelligence, appropriate education and sociocultural opportunity, and basic intactness in those sensory functions associated with "normal" learning. The problem appears to reflect a basic disturbed pattern of neurologic organization.

Studies of children with a developmental dyslexia have been reported for many years and certainly precede the formal establishment of the LD field. Some of the early cases reported refer to such children as experiencing "developmental wordblindness" or "strephosymbolia" and very accurately describe children with severe learning problems.

It is only natural that developmental dyslexia or specific reading disability in children receive much professional attention in the LD field. Reading is a basic communication tool underlying practically all of our educational experiences. It is a necessary skill if a person of any age is to function satisfactorily in a society that depends so heavily upon literacy. Someone who cannot satisfactorily acquire these essential skills deserves special attention. The ramifications also reach far beyond the limited realm of academic functioning, touching upon life-long personal and social adjustment needs.

Developmental dyslexia is considered one of the most serious types of learning disabilities. As the definition indicates the defect centers in the ability to learn to read normally, which on a broader level may extend to other symbol systems such as arithmetic, the learning of a foreign language, musical notation, etc. In fact, the term "dyssymbolia" has been used to describe the basic disturbance.

The incidence of developmental dyslexia reported in the literature ranges from about 2 to 10 percent. Those who have worked extensively with the problem believe that approximately 2 to 5 percent of children of school age with reading problems suffer from this disability (deHirsch 1963; Critchley 1964). At the same time it has been noted that dyslexia is found more frequently in boys than in girls, with a reported ratio of about 5 to 1. In clinics that work extensively with severe cases of dyslexia the referral ratio of boys to girls is about 15 to 1.

There is no satisfactory explanation for the fact that dyslexia is found more frequently in boys than girls. Clinical data suggest a genetic factor in that the disability may be a sex-linked male characteristic. Another explanation has been that boys are more prone to act out and call their problems to the attention of the authorities while girls simply sit in school and fail quietly year after year. It is unlikely, however, that this accounts for more than a small fraction of the sex difference.

The severity of developmental dyslexia varies from person to person. Less severe cases will evidence the same types of learning problems as severe cases but to a lesser degree. A specific defect in the ability to deal with symbols is involved, the complete resolution of which is doubtful. Even though the extent of reading disability may vary, a specific deficit is present and some residual problems may persist throughout life.

LEARNING DISABILITY: A CASE EXAMPLE

Paul, who experiences a developmental dyslexia, was first seen at Hawthorn Center at the age of eleven, having been referred by his special education teacher and the director of a perceptual development pilot program in Oakland County, Michigan. This program provided a self-contained special education classroom for children who evidenced perceptual deficits. The small teacher-pupil ratio (1 to 10) allowed for highly individualized instruction.

At the time of referral, Paul had been in the perceptual development classroom for three and one-half years. The school was especially concerned that he had made only minimal progress academically during that period despite average intellectual potential. Paul's teachers and parents were also concerned about increasing behavior problems such as frustration with insufficient provocation, impulsivity, and some aggression directed toward peers.

On initial screening at Hawthorn Center, Paul was seen for psychiatric evaluation and psychological testing. A social worker interviewed Paul's mother in order to obtain pertinent developmental and family history. Within a two-week period following initial screening, a neurological examination was completed and additional language and reading testing was done.

In conference on the diagnostic findings, the professional team involved in the evaluation felt that Paul presented a case of developmental dyslexia with some reactive behavior problems. The test data obtained and the developmental information agreed with the symptomatic pattern normally associated with dyslexia or primary reading disability. These diagnostic findings are reviewed below.

Developmental and Family History

Paul is the third child of three, with one brother seven years older and a sister five years older. The family is intact and lives in a middle-class suburban Detroit community. The family tone as noted in initial and subsequent interviews was one of warmth and acceptance, with both parents expressing sincere interest in and concern for their children. With regard to Paul's problems the family had actively sought professional help from the time difficulties were first noted early in Paul's school years. At the time of Paul's evaluation at Hawthorn Center, they were willingly following the referral initiated by the public school's special services department.

Birth history as reported by Paul's mother appeared to be uneventful. Delivery with Paul was normal and progressed so rapidly that he was almost born en route to the hospital.

Developmental milestones for the most part were within normal limits—sitting alone at six months and walking at approximately thirteen months. Language acquisition, however, was reported to have been delayed. Paul was described as being late in saying words and apparently did not speak in sentences until about three years of age. Toilet training during the day was completed without difficulty, but Paul remained enuretic at night until he was close to ten years of age.

Paul's mother reported that his preschool years were generally uneventful. Paul was an active youngster but responsive to parental demands. He played well with other children in his neighborhood and looked forward to starting school upon reaching kindergarten age.

Paul's parents first became aware of his potential learning problems when he did not acquire the appropriate readiness skills in kindergarten and the school suggested that Paul repeat kindergarten. They were further concerned because Paul's older brother was experiencing a fairly severe reading problem in elementary school and had been held back a year.

Paul's father was also reported to have a reading problem, and for several reasons did not go beyond grade eight in school. One of the father's brothers was similarly handicapped and did not complete school. Paul's mother also acknowledged that she had a younger brother who had great difficulty learning to read and had finished school only with the assistance of special education classes.

Sharon, the only female sibling, was reported to be a good student in school and well-adjusted in general. Developmental data and family information reveal two variables that are often associated with the diagnosis of dyslexia. The first of these relates to language development. It was reported that Paul's speech was delayed and that he was slow in beginning to talk in sentences. This is one of the most frequently noted conditions with children who later develop problems in reading.

The second variable is the occurrence of reading problems within the family. Paul's older brother experienced a similar kind of difficulty. The father and a maternal uncle are also reported to have had reading problems of some duration. This strong familial incidence suggest the possibility of a genetic factor in Paul's case. Positive familial incidence has been noted often in families of children with learning disabilities. Murphy (1970) assessed the records of 2000 school children who were considered "perceptually handicapped" and found that "70 percent had a familial trait for learning disabilities. That is, either a father, uncle, brother, male cousin, or grandfather had a learning disability or difficulty in learning language skills."

Other behavior patterns that have been noted frequently in preschool children who have later experienced learning disabilities include hyperactivity, poor impulse control, over-all poor coordination in large and/or small muscle areas, and emotional lability. These behavior symptoms have been associated with minimal brain dysfunction; if they are the result of this condition they will likely be present into the school years. One caution, however, is that many "normal" children may exhibit one or more of these behavior symptoms and not evidence subsequence learning problems. This may be attributed to a variety of circumstances such as normal developmental variance, parental expectations and management techniques, cultural influences.

Psychological Assessment

The Stanford-Binet intelligence test was administered to Paul when he was 7 yrs. 5 mos. of age. He was midway through the first grade, having repeated kindergarten the year before. Reading progress was extremely slow at that time and referral was made for psychological testing, with further consideration of placement in the pilot program for perceptually handicapped children. The test results were as follows:

Binet Test: Mental Age: 7–4; IQ: 98

The examiner noted that Paul was a "tall, polite, cooperative child who is currently capable of functioning with average intelligence. His greatest weaknesses appear in the areas of small muscle coordination and handling two abstract concepts simultaneously. Major strengths include vocabulary and social comprehension. . . . Paul is able to count but he cannot associate objects with the number unless he handles each object and counts out loud. On the basis of observation and test results it is felt that Paul manifests the psychological concomitants of a neurological dysfunction." At that time Paul was functionally a non-reader.

At the age of 10½ Paul was given the Wechsler Intelligence Scale for Children (WISC). This evaluation was prompted by the concern that Paul had made minimal academic progress even with special education placement. At the time of this testing the Bender Motor Gestalt Test and the Wide-Range Achievement Test were also administered.

On the WISC Paul scored as follows: Verbal IQ, 87; Performance IQ, 97; Full Scale IQ, 91.

On the Bender, which is a visual-motor perception test, the examiner felt that Paul's performance suggested some lag in perceptual development. It was also noted that he was anxious about his performance and "really squeezed his pencil, face close to paper."

Reading ability was assessed at grade 2.0 as measured by the Wide Range Achievement Test.

Based upon mental age according to Performance IQ (MA 10–11) and reading age (RA 7–0) Paul was retarded approximately 3½ years in reading. This is a significant discrepancy between actual achievement and that expected based upon intellectual potential.

All of the intelligence test data obtained on Paul indicates basically average intellectual functioning and potential. He typically does rather poorly on the verbal section of the WISC and somewhat better on the performance section. This test pattern is noted frequently with dyslexic children, often more pronounced. "Verbal" types of tests generally call for responses that are closely associated with educational learning experiences, and dyslexic children experience a basic problem in reading and symbol skills which inhibits normal learning activity. On the other hand many dyslexic children have adequate perceptual motor skills which, when coupled with good general intelligence, aids in achievement on performance type tests.

Because functioning on IQ tests, especially those which stress verbal skills, is related rather directly to educational experience, a young dyslexic child may do better on the verbal section of the WISC, for example, at age 5 or 6 and do less well as he or she becomes older and more fully entrenched in the educational process, one in which the child experiences a disability.

Children with minimal brain dysfunction may exhibit more significant problems in the area of visual-motor perception and integration. These difficulties are often noted on performance types of tests which require such skills.

Educational Assessment

Paul demonstrated difficulty with academic tasks from the very beginning of his exposure to school. He demonstrated a certain slowness even in kindergarten that prompted the school to recommend repetition of that year.

Slow progress in the presence of apparently adequate potential was again noted early in grade one. Fortunately, a special education program was available and Paul was quickly identified as a candidate. Special class placement followed midway through grade one.

During Paul's second year in the perceptually disabled room several tests measuring perceptual functioning were administered. They indicated that visual-motor functioning was not particularly deficit: "Using Kephart's tests of motor coordination we found Paul to be adequate in all areas. The Frostig test of visual perception showed him to be low only in form constancy, and this was not significant. His auditory perception is poor, although our school tests revealed no hearing loss. The eye pursuit test was good in all directions." Paul was eight and one-half years old at the time.

Paul's scores on the Stanford Achievement Test, administered at age ten, showed severe academic retardation. A grade score of 1.7 was obtained in reading areas with 1.0 on spelling, and 2.7 on arithmetic.

As part of the initial evaluation at Hawthorn Center Paul was noted to be achieving at the following levels academically: reading, 2.2 grade level; spelling, 1.2 grade level; arithmetic, 3.8 grade level.

On the oral reading test the examiner noted the following: "Slow, laborious, word for word; initial phonics with no follow through; some confabulation and word reversals." One word reversal was recorded on the test itself and this involved the misreading of *no* as *on*.

To summarize public school assessment data, from kindergarten on, Paul evidenced learning difficulties although his potential for learning was average. Problems in the language area and poor motor coordination were observed as part of the deficit pattern. Formal visual-motor perceptual testing, at least by the age of 9 however, did not demonstrate deficit functioning that would significantly inhibit learning progress. Auditory perception was noted to be poor without further elaboration. Specific academic progress remained limited overall.

Many dyslexic children demonstrate the academic achievement pattern that Paul evidenced; that is they usually experience greatest difficulty in spelling, next reading, and then arithmetic. All three areas are usually affected. There seems to be some consistency in this pattern and it has been noted into adulthood with moderately severe dyslexics.

Psychiatric and Neurological Evaluation

The results of Paul's neurological examination through Hawthorn were negative. The physician reported that there was "no apparent neurological abnormality." In psychiatric interview Paul was seen as an average, intact youngster who related warmly with the examiner. The most striking characteristic noted was the variability of his performance intellectually and in language functioning. General language usage was poor and there were major deficits in the areas of reading and spelling. Motor coordination appeared intact although it was noted that Paul could not sit completely still for any period of time.

The diagnostic impressions formulated by the psychiatrist upon complete review of the record were: (1) primary dyslexia, probably with a hereditary basis; and (2) secondary neurotic reaction; his behavior is probably reactive to his perception of his learning deficits, which are intensifying with age and maturity.

It was recommended that Paul be admitted to the Hawthorn Center day school program in an effort to assist him both emotionally and academically. Residential treatment was not considered.

Children with specific learning disabilities often present concomitant behavior problems, at times to the extent that they may also be considered emotionally disturbed. These children do not experience the success with learning that their peers encounter, and they quickly realize that they are not meeting the expectations of significant others in their lives such as teachers and parents. Deficient self-concept and repeated frustrations and failures in learning situations may be present and manifest in acting out or withdrawn or depressed behavior. The affective or emotional components of learning disability must be given considerable attention in any treatment effort.

EDUCATIONAL PROGRAMMING

Elementary Years

Paul's learning difficulties were recognized early in his school career. Midway through grade one he was placed in the special self-contained class where intensified individual instruction and remediation could be provided.

Speech therapy was also provided on a twice a week basis and was continued for two school years. Paul's history of slow language development and apparent difficulty in expressing himself in school situations made him eligible for such assistance. Paul's parents felt that this help was beneficial, although an official record of change or progress was not available.

Paul's inclusion in the special education classroom lasted through his elementary school years. This was advantageous as his difficulty in academic areas would have prevented him from functioning in a regular class setting. The special program, however, did not extend beyond the elementary level, and school authorities became concerned about educational planning for Paul as he reached junior high. His learning difficulty, even within the special class, was seemingly having an adverse effect on him after a 4½-year period. Paul was beginning to act out his frustration with learning and gave evidence of a rather poor self-concept.

On two occasions during his elementary school years Paul was involved in private tutorial work related to motor training and improvement of coordination. At age seven he worked on large muscle coordination problems with a local optometrist. Below-average functioning had been noted in this area with follow-up by the parents of private help. The extent to which this special tutorial help was of benefit to Paul is not known. The transfer of improved coordination to academic achievement was not realized.

The second period of private help occurred at age nine. Paul worked for approximately one year with an occupational therapist to help with his poor handwriting and small muscle coordination. Again, there seemed to have been minimal progress in this area, at least in the transfer to academic achievement.

The early interventions and overall educational plan provided Paul during his elementary school years would seem to be more than satisfactory despite limited academic gains. The awareness of potential learning difficulty in kindergarten and early availability of special education help probably served to lessen the overwhelming frustration that Paul might have otherwise experienced in a larger, competitive regular classroom.

The severity of Paul's learning problem necessitated a basically self-contained small group setting with a specially trained teacher; an environment that would realistically reduce academic demands, providing for an individually directed diagnostic-prescriptive learning approach and yet stressing success experiences within individual capability.

Ideally, a self-contained classroom for learning disabled children should also provide some opportunity to mainstream or integrate the student into those regular educational activities where he is able to function. These opportunities might occur in non-academic areas such as physical education, art, or music or in an academic subject area where the child might function satisfactorily.

Paul's special elementary program did not provide for integration even though he could have functioned satisfactorily in several "regular" curriculum areas. One reason for this was perhaps that the philosophy of the program stressed intensive remediation in all areas with return to a full regular classroom setting as soon as possible.

The benefit to Paul from the two tutorial experiences in motor control improvement, both with large and small muscle groups, is questionable. It is possible that such training improved functioning in these areas, but the relationship of coordination improvement to academic learning seems to have been negative in this case. Paul's visual-motor functioning, when tested at age ten, was essentially satisfactory yet learning problems persisted.

The speech therapy that Paul received for two years stressed vocabulary development and verbal expression. This was reported to be of help to him.

Elementary Years in Retrospect

Paul's adult feelings toward his elementary school years are somewhat ambivalent. He recalls that his teachers and parents were supportive of him in his learning difficulties but that he was frustrated by his problem and strong feelings of failure which were continually reinforced by limited learning progress. He felt isolated from his peers who, in some instances, considered him to be retarded. Paul could not understand why he had such a severe problem with reading in relation to other students while knowing or sensing that he was as competent as his peers in many activities.

Paul acknowledges that he was very embarrassed when others discovered his difficulty and did everything he could to keep it a secret: "I became angry with myself and others too much, but at that time I really didn't know why."

Children in elementary school who experience learning problems similar to Paul's and those with a less severe disability should be provided with various special education alternatives. The self-contained classroom that Paul experienced and the support services available to him are an example.

To provide comprehensive service for the learning disabled student at the elementary level requires that there be a careful assessment of each child's strengths and weaknesses. Appropriate instructional objectives for each child should be initiated. The strategy selected for the delivery of service will also depend upon this assessment. In addition to the type of self-contained classroom provided for Paul, alternative programs are implemented by a teacher certified to work with learning disabled children. Two of these are the resource room or learning center and the itinerant teacher program. These two program approaches are more suitable for those children with mild to moderate learning problems who can be successful in some areas of regular education.

The resource room program provides assistance to the learning disabled student who is assigned to a regular classroom. The student attends the resource room for special individual or small group instruction as needed, perhaps one or more periods of instruction each day, depending upon the child's needs. The special education resource teacher also works closely with the child's classroom teacher and other building staff members to better understand the unique needs of the learning disabled student and to plan cooperatively in meeting those needs.

The itinerant teacher usually serves two or more schools providing a support service for LD students. The special teacher, for example, might work with a student two or three times per week while at the same time providing consultation to the student's classroom teacher regarding the child's learning needs and methods of coping with them. This generally includes instructional and behavior management techniques.

Ideally, an attempt should be made to provide or maintain as much regularity or mainstreaming in a learning disabled student's program as possible, while dealing with his specific educational needs. One factor to be dealt with here is the school itself and the program flexibility it can provide in addition to its orientation toward exceptional children. A child who can function with his peer group in various activities will be better off doing so rather than being maintained unnecessarily in a special class for the entire day.

The LD teacher, along with social workers and psychologist, must be extremely sensitive to the emotional impact of a learning disability upon elementary children. Much counseling and reassurance is needed both for the child and the parents. LD children do not experience success in academic areas as do their more "normal" peers, and they can easily become frustrated and defeated. In the course of their struggle to succeed they soon realize that they are for some unknown reason not meeting the expectations of their parents and teachers. They need support in understanding their disability and compensatory learning experiences that will realistically challenge their potential.

Secondary Years

As Paul completed his elementary school years it was obvious that continued special education programming was needed. He was a puzzle to the public school special services' staff; they were at a loss to provide appropriate educational experiences for him in junior high as there were no LD programs available.

The existing special programs were basically for the retarded or emotionally impaired, neither of which could satisfactorily meet his specific educational needs.

Paul's junior high years were spent at Hawthorn Center in the day school program. This program initially provided Paul with a comfortable and partially self-contained classroom with nine or ten other students. In addition, daily special reading was provided by a trained specialist on an individual basis. This continued through his stay in the program, although group special reading experiences were introduced.

A psychologist and social worker were also active with Paul's case and provided the necessary individual support and family counseling. This intervention stressed acceptance and understanding leading toward realistic goal planning.

The seriousness of Paul's learning problem, along with indications that complete remediation of the disability was unlikely, suggested that in addition to remedial academic work, pre-vocational experiences be introduced early in his junior high program. This goal was interwoven with his curriculum by various means. Remedial work in specific content areas such as reading and math began to focus on activities of a prevocational instructional nature. Paul's reading class stressed skill development utilizing material such as job application forms, tax withholding statements, names of tools, career exploration information, and driver's education text material, etc. Math work emphasized functional and prevocational skills including money management, vocational math measurement, and the practical application of such skills in other curriculum areas.

In the latter half of Paul's eighth grade year through grade nine he was involved in an intensified prevocational program which provided substantial periods of time each day to participate in various industrial arts and related vocational experiences.

Paul was quite skillful mechanically and in woodworking, areas in which he found much success. Toward the end of his stay at Hawthorn Center he performed part-time work in the community in a service station while also spending some time in school each day.

Paul's junior high program was growth producing and beneficial within the limits posed by his disability. Ideally, similar programming capabilities should have been available in public school which would have provided a more natural educational setting or environment, thus focusing less attention on his "difference" from others.

Paul left Hawthorn Center at the age of fifteen, entering his local public high school in the tenth grade. Extensive planning with Paul's family and the special education staff in the local school district was done prior to his entrance.

Unfortunately, the special education department in Paul's school system did not provide a program for his type of disability. There were no specific programs for learning disabled students at the secondary level, although school authorities readily acknowledged that they had other students with similar problems, Academically, Paul was still functioning at approximately a fourth grade level in reading despite his average intellectual potential. In reviewing his continued needs it was obvious that he, as a minimum, needed specific skill instruction in reading and math, adjusted academic requirements in general curriculum areas, and extensive vocational programming.

The public school staff were willing to plan individually for Paul to the extent possible. It became apparent that in order to meet his needs some type of special education involvement would be necessary. The only available program at the high school was a special program for the educable mentally retarded. Paul of course did not qualify for this program due to tested average intelligence but it was felt that the services of the special teacher could be helpful in monitoring an individually tailored program for him. This was the program plan that was initiated.

Paul felt a little uncomfortable being identified with the program for retarded students, but at the same time knew that he could not compete, or achieve, in most of the regular classes offered by the school, especially those required for graduation. Instruction, therefore, in certain content areas such as social studies and language arts was taken with the educable mentally impaired group where the work could be adjusted relative to his reading skills. Some individual reading instruction was also provided.

Paul was fortunate in the vocational area. He had developed excellent woodworking skills which were emphasized in his school program. He was allowed to take two related woodworking classes and in his twelfth grade year served as a woodshop assistant. Other vocational areas were also available to him which included auto mechanics, small machine repair, and welding. This was accomplished through the efforts of the special education teacher who worked closely with Paul and his vocational instructors in managing the reading and written requirements of such coursework.

Paul graduated with his expected class group and felt proud of his accomplishments. The successes he experienced in vocational activities, often surpassing those of other able and competent students, were reassuring to him that despite his learning disability, he was capable of high achievement in certain areas. In fact, in his last year of school, he won first place in a state-wide competition for individually designed and crafted industrial arts projects.

Secondary Years in Retrospect

In discussing his secondary school experiences, Paul as an adult generally expressed positive feelings. He recalled with pride his successful accomplishments in the areas of industrial arts and vocational education activities which often surpassed those of more academically competent peers. He has fond memories of the special education teachers who provided extensive support and understanding during these years.

Reading and math skills continued to be problem areas for him, and he could not understand why these learnings were so difficult. He acknowledged strong feelings of inadequacy which often raised questions in his mind as to whether he was just "dumb." He did arrive at the realization that this reading disability would probably always be with him, but he was never comfortable in dealing with it. For the most part he did not believe that people adequately understood his disability, and there were times when pressure was placed on him to perform beyond his ability.

Paul's disability continued to cause him embarrassment and he would go to extremes to prevent such instances and in general to keep others from knowing. He stated as an example that he rarely dated in high school for fear of having some girl discover his inadequacy. This influenced peer relationships in general.

Paul also recalls being uncomfortable with some of his high school special education classes and more general identification with the mentally impaired program. This reinforced feelings of inadequacy even though he knew he could not make it in some of the other classes.

Education goals for the learning disabled student at the junior and senior high level are addressed through the development of the Individualized Education Plan (outlined in PL 94-142). In addition to the specific programs and services recommended several specific instructional/counseling areas should be considered. These can be summarized as follows:

1. Basic Academic Skill Development
   A. Specific skill instruction. Here special teaching in areas of learning difficulty or deficit is stressed. This may be in reading or math or some other area.
   B. General subject area content. The LD student must be provided opportunities to learn in broader academic and nonacademic areas within the general curriculum. Specific content instruction, for example, in science and social studies should be made available through modifications in materials and techniques of presentation. Nonacademic learning experiences must be structured similarly.
2. Prevocational/Vocational Education
   Prevocational and vocational skill instruction must be infused into the secondary curriculum for the majority of LD students. Such experiences must be structured and organized to lead toward occupational skill development and self-sufficiency.
3. Personal Counseling/Adjustment
   There is a pressing need for ongoing counseling for the learning disabled student to help an individual's understanding of the student's problem and in developing ways of adapting or ad-

justing to the total environment. This may be provided through individual contacts or group sessions with various supportive professionals such as social workers or psychologists.

4. Parental Counseling
   There also exists a pressing need for parents to receive information and guidance regarding the educational and life adjustment needs of the LD student. This informative counseling may also include parent group sessions where common problems are reviewed.

The organizational structure associated with the delivery of service to LD students becomes much broader at the secondary level. The elementary intervention designs are in some cases discontinued while in others they are modified and expanded to meet the needs of older students and the demands of a secondary school curriculum. For example, the strategy of placing secondary LD students in a self-contained classroom setting is, in the opinion of most authorities, one of the least desirable alternatives, even though implied within this concept is integration into some regular or general education activities. Segregating LD students for the major portion of their school day reduces opportunities to associate with the "normal" school environment and may perhaps reinforce or foster self-deprecatory concepts. The self-contained room does not resemble the traditional curriculum structure at the secondary level, where students normally participate in many different classes and activities. Self-contained placement may also limit access to broader educational experiences found in the general curriculum which may be both necessary and beneficial.

The unique needs of secondary LD students suggest that delivery of service be considered through a special education support team. One LD teacher cannot be expected to deal adequately with the educational complexities and personal needs faced by the older LD student. Additional support must be available from other special education professionals.

The special education support team should be comprised of the following professionals: special education LD teacher, special education vocational needs coordinator, school psychologist, and school social worker. The latter three team members would also work with other categories or types of special education students. This does not mean that the LD teacher would not work with other special education teachers where programming dictates but that this teacher's primary responsibility is for LD students.

The interaction of the special education support team should be flexible and depend upon the given needs of the program and students. Some of the contributions and responsibilities of each team member can be summarized as follows:

1. The service role of the LD teacher may be designed and implemented in several ways. The intervention strategies that are encompassed in this role, however, should include direct academic support to the LD student, consultation to general education, curriculum management in general and special education, and personal adjustment counseling.

    A. Direct academic support for the LD student at the secondary level must be directed toward both specific skill instruction and general subject matter areas. Specific skill areas such as reading or math, where the LD student demonstrates significant deficits, will have to be dealt with on a special remedial basis either individually or in small groups. The goal of such instruction must be at least to achieve a functional performance necessary to meet the demands of daily living.

        Instruction in certain general education subject areas might also need to be provided by the LD teachers. This may involve such areas as English, language arts, or social studies. For the seriously disabled student it is unrealistic to attempt via the regular classroom teacher to individualize instruction in all subject areas. A tenth grade student reading at a second or third grade level for example, should not be expected to struggle to participate in a regular or even low average English class. Often such attempts at individualization produce only frustrating accommodation within the class as opposed to a sound learning experience. For a small group of students, then, the LD teacher must provide the course content instruction stressing individual and group needs.

    B. Consultation to general education. The LD teacher must be skillful in working with general education staff to assist those teachers in planning for LD students who can benefit from general education class instruction with slight modifications in materials and/or content. The relationship established by the LD teacher with the regular education teaching staff is of ultimate importance in achieving this level of intervention. The special teacher must be able to interpret in manageable terms the unique needs of the LD student and offer concrete suggestions and specific help to the teacher in meeting those needs. The extent of the interaction will vary depending upon the class and the student. It may be, for example, that in an experimental science class the reading assignments might have to be placed on tapes with the help of the LD teacher who might also administer required tests orally.

C. Curriculum management. The LD teacher with full understanding of the disability and needs of the LD student must provide guidance in both the direction and selection of curriculum alternatives. This includes specific classes within the general curriculum and the overall curriculum design leading to successful vocational accomplishments. The LD teacher must be in a knowledgeable position to aid in choosing classes and teachers as well as helping to modify content in specific courses. Assistance in this area of intervention can be sought from other team members as a total curriculum plan is articulated.

D. Counseling. Appropriate counseling is essential in order to assist the LD student in realistically understanding his handicap and how it affects him. All too often LD students persist in thinking of themselves as retarded or "dumb" and do not have an appreciation for the etiological basis of their disability. These self-deprecatory feelings can affect total adjustment and often lead to a withdrawal from educational experiences that may be beneficial and growth producing. There seems to be a natural tendency to keep others from knowing of their difficulty and thus avoiding situations where their problem might become detected or embarrassing. It has been reported, for example, that many such adolescent boys refrain from participating in coed activities or dating for fear of being embarrassed by their disability.

Personal understanding and adaptation to the problems posed by a learning disability must be of ongoing concern for those working with such students. The impact of the disability upon vocational choices must be dealt with realistically. Such understanding must also be imparted to parents and other family and community members. The task is not small.

2. The special education vocational needs coordinator serves a vital role in helping to plan and implement vocational programming for secondary handicapped students. With LD students in particular, this person might coordinate vocational assessment, assist both the LD teacher and the vocational education teacher in the management of this curriculum area, coordinate community vocational involvement either through procuring and monitoring appropriate work study experiences or coordinating planning efforts with other agencies such as the Department of Vocational Rehabilitation.

   Vocational counseling of the LD student is also an important aspect of this role. The student and his family must be guided in the realistic appraisal of skills and abilities leading toward vocational decisions.

3. The psychologist and social worker can assist in providing the much needed counseling both to the LD student and his parents. The secondary LD student must be aided in understanding and dealing with the impact of his disability as it affects all areas of functioning—personal, social, academic, and vocational.

   The roles of the psychologist and social worker are complementary and at times they may team together in dealing with specific problem areas. For example, both staff members might periodically meet with a small group of parents of LD students to deal with a variety of issues.

   The psychologist also plays an important role in ability assessment and in the interpretation of such information as it affects decision making in all areas.

Good pre-vocational and vocational planning for the majority of secondary LD students is an essential part of programming at this level. Realistic experiences in academic and vocational areas are necessary if the student is to encounter success in school and prepare himself for a satisfying adult life. This is no easy task as it requires extensive effort and creativity on the part of many professionals to assure that such goals are reached. The traditional school posture of only providing remedial work in certain academic areas is far from satisfactory for the LD student.

The stress upon good prevocational and vocational programming must be considered for the majority of secondary LD students. There are others, however, with moderate disabilities and high educational aspirations who will want to attend college after high school. Students for whom this goal is realistic must be assisted to develop compensatory techniques which will help maximize strengths and compromise for learning deficit areas.

Adult Status

As an adult at the age of 24, Paul still experiences residual problems in reading and related academic areas. He participated in a lengthy interview discussing his disability and the extent to which specific problems persisted in reading, spelling, and arithmetic. Retesting in these areas was done utilizing basically the same tests that had been administered when Paul was first seen at Hawthorn Center.

At this time in his life, Paul might be considered functionally illiterate. He scored grade 4.0 in reading and grade 2.9 in spelling. Arithmetic was somewhat higher with a grade score of 4.8 obtained.

Paul's performance on an oral reading test demonstrated poor word analysis skills and a limited sight vocabulary. Context clues were relied upon extensively for word identification. Interestingly, several word reversals were also noted. In regard to this, Paul acknowledged that he still has difficulty with small similar appearing words such as "on" and "no," etc. He further stated that he has absolutely no trouble seeing the words correctly but that their correct identification is not automatic, resulting frequently in misreadings.

Spelling remained the most severely impaired area of functioning. The problem seems to reflect a poor visual memory for words and difficulty with sound-symbol association, which makes spelling very hard especially in the absence of visual clues.

Paul attributes his poor writing to the fact that he writes very seldom and has always been intimidated by such tasks because of his disability. Fine motor coordination in general is not the problem.

It can readily be imagined how serious the impact of this disability is in Paul's life. He said that he is still extremely embarrassed by his problem and goes to great lengths to keep it hidden from others. Daily activities such as the reading of newspapers, TV guide, and menus are difficult. It is almost impossible for Paul to fill out a job application, and when such occasions arise he attempts to take the forms home for assistance.

Overall, Paul appears to be a fairly well adapted and stable young man. He has worked for several years now as an assembler in a snowmobile factory and repair center. His mechanical skills have enabled him to become one of the most valued employees. He is not married but dates occasionally and has become more comfortable with informing new friends about his disability. Paul's future is still uncertain and of concern to him as he tries to deal realistically with the limitations imposed by his dyslexic condition.

Paul's case is not unique. There are many others like him and perhaps more with similar, though less severe, disabilities. In the majority of such cases, however, some residual problems will likely persist into adulthood.

A recent follow-up study conducted with forty adult males who had been identified at Hawthorn Center as dyslexic in childhood found that the symptoms associated with the disability persisted into adulthood in all cases. The length of interval between initial diagnosis and follow-up contact exceeded ten years yet the problems in many instances were similar.

The subjects of the study all had average or above intellectual potential and were basically from middle-class backgrounds which assured reasonable educational opportunity. Upon retesting it was found that as a group they remained seriously retarded in reading with a mean grade score of 3.8. Similarly, arithmetic and spelling were also deficit areas with spelling being the most severely impaired area of academic achievement. They also evidenced many of the same performance characteristics as they did as children. The entire group, for example, still has trouble with word reversals, and they continue to demonstrate deficiencies in both the visual and auditory skill areas required for adequate reading. This persisted despite the fact that all had had a significant amount of special reading assistance. The impact of their disability left no area untouched: personal, social, educational, or occupational.

All of the subjects acknowledged that they attempt to keep hidden the fact that they have a reading problem. Some had developed masterful techniques to avoid reading situations and to compensate for their difficulty. One subject, for example, stated that when he has to write something he intentionally writes very poorly so that his spelling handicap will avoid detection. When questioned regarding the response he gets to his writing, he stated, "Many people tell me I should have been a doctor because my writing is so bad."

Another person who was a master jeweler and manager of a central repair shop for sixteen jewelry outlets read at a beginning second grade level. When asked about some of the problems his reading handicap presents, he stated that he likes to travel and eat out and that he has been embarrassed on several occasions when seeking the restroom in "fancy restaurants" that may label their doors with such names as "King's Lane" which he is unable to read. At those times he has had to wait and watch until someone enters the correct door. With regard to travel this person stated that he was fairly comfortable. His wife handles all the details, and when he meets people, he knows that the relationship will be sufficiently transient that they will not discover that he has a reading problem.

All of the adults had to compromise occupational and educational goals. Some had continued to hold aspirations in these areas which seem unrealistic. One person who reads at a beginning fourth grade level was determined to go to college. When interviewed he had just recently failed his first semester at a local university. He was partially encouraged however, as he had receive an "A" in a bowling class. On the other hand, he had failed several academic classes, one labeled "Developing College Reading." Another man at age 26 wanted to be an art teacher. He was being tutored in one class taken at a local community college.

Social and heterosexual relationships had been influenced and in fact seem to have been limited in many instances because of the reading problem. The tendency to want to keep others from discovering their problem automatically limited many social contacts. Unmarried subjects acknowledge that they were reluctant to date for fear of having their reading problem detected, and subsequently, being embarrassed and perhaps having the relationship terminate because of this. In some cases girls were dated only once or twice and then dropped before the reading problem had a chance to surface.

The pattern of maintaining distance in heterosexual relationships seemed to be longstanding and was evidenced in early high school years. According to the study participants, this was fostered not only by discomfort with the reading problem but also by the fact that opportunities for meeting girls were limited. Several subjects stated, for example that they were unable to participate in extracurricular activities such as the drama club or science club even though interest might have prevailed. In addition, compensatory interests and school successes were usually focused in industrial arts areas where few coeds participated. This remained the case into adulthood.

The daily demands of a literate society posed numerous problems for most of the study participants. None of the unmarried men, for example, maintained a checking account because it was almost impossible for them to write checks. Additional frustrating problems such as reading menus, the newspaper, TV guide, theater marquee, advertisements, road signs, and maps were frequently mentioned. But every subject had developed some compensatory interest and skill in performance or manual activities such as art, mechanical and automotive activities, and woodworking. These interests were generally incorporated into hobbies, although several persons were utilizing their skills occupationally.

One of the most surprising findings was that approximately 90 percent of the adults had a relatively poor understanding of their learning disability and persisted in projecting blame to secondary or external factors, often of a self-devaluating nature. They tended to blame themselves (poor motivation, attitude, not smart enough) or teachers and parents.

TEACHING STRATEGIES IN LEARNING DISABILITIES

For many years, issues concerning the identification and diagnosis of learning disabled children were given much more attention by professional workers than the development of teaching procedures and techniques. Ideally, a comprehensive evaluation of a problem learner that leads to the diagnosis of a learning disability should suggest specific teaching strategies. During the past three decades, two major strategies have evolved. Each strategy was strongly supported by those professionals whose philosophy it represented. Each strategy was intended to develop or remediate those symptoms found on examination thought to be associated with, or the cause of, the learning disability. These two major strategies, each representing numerous teaching techniques, are frequently referred to as the perceptual-motor approach and the modality approach.

Perceptual-Motor Approach

The terms sensorimotor and perceptual-motor are often used interchangeably and refer to the process of organizing information received through the senses (visual, auditory, tactual, kinesthetic). Early perceptual-motor learning is viewed as a foundation for later, more complex perceptual and cognitive development. For example, a young child who is offered a toy first sees it (visual) then reaches (motor) for it. This process of input-organization-output becomes increasingly complex.

A number of professionals believe that inadequate perceptual-motor functioning in children may underlie their learning problems and that training in these areas is important if not essential to academic success. The assumption here is that adequacy of performance in perceptual-motor areas is necessary if the child is to attain higher level skills, such as reading. Proponents of perceptual-motor theory have developed training programs ranging from highly sequenced instruction to loosely structured collections of activities.

Among the sensorimotor theorists who have influenced the field of special education are Getman (1965), visuomotor theory; Barsch (1967), movigenic theory; Kephart (1967), perceptual-motor theory; and Delacato (1963), the patterning theory of neurological organization.

There has been considerable disagreement among various professional groups regarding the effectiveness of motor training procedures for LD children. Some acknowledge that lags in basic sensorimotor development may lead to subsequent difficulties in other areas of learning, but question the basic assumption that improvement in sensorimotor skills will lead to improved functioning in cognitive and academic skill areas. Lerner (1976) has summarized the situation:

> Research with exercises to develop motor skills and thereby improve academic learning is currently in progress, but thus far there is little conclusive evidence to indicate that motor programs result in significant academic gains. As a group, children who have difficulty learning appear also to have difficulty with motor performance. One hypothesis for this high correlation is that the motor problem is not the direct cause of the learning problem, but, rather, a concomitant difficulty that children are likely to have. According to this view, training in motor skills leads to improvement in motor learning, but it does not necessarily lead to improvement in academic ability and learning. A further consideration is that the role of language development in learning is relatively neglected in most motor theories. Finally, the correspondence between motor growth and learning can be questioned by the observation that some children with superior motor skills are unable to learn to read or to succeed in other academic areas, while some children with excellent academic skills are inferior in motor performance and physical activities.

A strong reaction to visual training practices used with LD children prompted several medical groups to review the role of the eye and learning disabilities. A position paper was subsequently adopted by the executive committees and councils of the American Academy of Pediatrics, the American Academy of Otolaryngology and the American Association of Ophthalmology. This joint organizational statement includes the following:

The problem of learning disability has become a matter of increasing public concern, which has led to exploitation by some practitioners of the normal concen of parents for the welfare of their children. A child's inability to read with understanding as a result of defects in processing visual symbols, a condition which has been called dyslexia, is a major obstacle to school learning and has far-reaching social and economic implications. The significance and magnitude of the problem have generated a proliferation of diagnostic and remedial procedures, many of which imply a relationship between visual function and learning.

The eye and visual training in the treatment of dyslexia and associated disabilities have recently been reviewed with the following conclusions by the American Academy of Pediatrics, the American Academy of Ophthalmology and Otolaryngology, and the American Association of Ophthalmology:

1.   Learning disability and dyslexia, as well as other forms of school underachievement, require a multi-disciplinary approach from medicine, education, and psychology in diagnosis and treatment. Eye care should never be instituted in isolation when a patient had a reading problem. Children with learning disabilities have the same incidence of ocular abnormalities, e.g., refractive errors and muscle imbalance, as children who are normal achievers and reading at grade level. These abnormalities should be corrected.

2.   Since clues in word recognition are transmitted through the eyes to the brain, it has become common practice to attribute reading difficulties to subtle ocular abnormalities presumed to cause faulty visual perception. Studies have shown that there is no peripheral eye defect which produces dyslexia and associated learning disabilities. Eye defects do not cause reversals of letters, words, or numbers.

3.   No known scientific evidence supports claims for improving the academic abilities of learning disabled or dyslexic children with treatment based solely on:

     a.   visual training (muscle exercises, ocular pursuit, glasses);

     b.   neurologic organizational training (laterality training, balance board, perceptual training).

Furthermore, such training has frequently resulted in unwarranted expense and has delayed proper instruction for the child.

4.   Excluding correctable ocular defects, glasses have no value in the specific treatment of dyslexia or other learning problems. In fact, unnecessarily prescribed glasses may create a false sense of security that may delay needed treatment.

Teaching strategies based upon a perceptual-motor approach should be considered carefully in working with LD children. There is little evidence at the present time to support those theories that recommend development of sensorimotor skills before working with academic tasks. Further, the assumption of transfer of improved functioning in these areas to academic skill learning has been severely questioned especially for school-age LD children who are beyond the early readiness level. On the other hand, very young children with delays in sensorimotor functioning should have attention directed to those specific needs. This, of course, is common practice in preschool and kindergarten programs.

Modality Approach

A modality or channel refers to those sensory avenues through which information is received—the visual (sight), auditory (hearing), tactual (touch), kinesthetic (muscle feeling), olfactory (smell), and gustatory (taste).

The problems experienced by learning disabled children are generally noted in the visual and auditory modality areas. Visual processing skills include visual discrimination and recognition, visual memory and association, and visual sequencing. Auditory processing skills include auditory discrimination, auditory memory and association, auditory blending, and auditory sequencing. Deficits in these skills or processes in one or both modalities may result in a learning disability.

It is also recognized that children may learn better through one modality than another. Evaluation of these processing skills, in addition to assessment of academic or readiness skills, will determine the strengths and weaknesses of the learning modalities. Once this assessment is complete several alternative teaching strategies are possible (Lerner 1971):

1. Teach through the intact modality. In this approach, once the modality of strength is determined, materials and methods that utilize the intact modality are selected. For example, if the child is high in auditory, but low in visual perception, then an auditory teaching method would be selected.

2. Strengthen the modality of deficit. In this approach, the teaching procedure is designed to improve performance in the poor modality. The goal of this approach is to build the ineffective modality so that it can become a productive pathway for learning. The child who manifests a deficit in auditory perception would be taught with methods designed to improve his auditory processing.

3. Combination approach. This is a two-pronged approach to teach-

ing; the stronger modality is initially used, but meanwhile separate lessons are also used to build the deficit modality. Care must be taken so the child is not overtaxed in the tasks that require processing within the weak modality. For example, in the case of a child who has a strong visual, but weak auditory modality, the clinical teacher might teach him to read using a visual method, while strengthening his auditory skills in separate lessons.

Another alternative is to teach academic skills through a multisensory approach using the visual, auditory, kinesthetic, and tactual modalities (VAKT). The techniques developed by Fernald (1943), and Gillingham and Stillman (1966), to teach children with severe reading disabilities are examples. The premise here is that stimulation or utilization of as many sensory avenues as possible will reinforce the learning of specific reading skills.

Currently, objective-based instruction is being implemented in all areas of special education, including learning disabilities. Following a formal or informal assessment of a child's strengths and weaknesses in cognitive, affective, and psychomotor areas, the teacher determines or selects from published materials specific objectives or goals to be accomplished. The teacher is usually asked to state the objective, the materials or techniques to be used in accomplishing the objective, and the period of time in which the child should attain the skill. In addition, the teacher determines a criterion of success, usually 80 percent correct response on a formal or informal posttest.

The teacher is not limited in the choice of instructional materials or teaching techniques to be used in reaching the objective.

In the area of learning disabilities, a task-analysis approach may be helpful to the teacher in determining how a specific objective skill might best be taught.

Task-analysis refers to an approach whereby the teacher structures the skill to be taught from its most simple to its most complex aspects. The teacher might begin by asking, "How can I present this skill at a level to assure success and avoid confusion?" "What additional steps can be introduced in a logical sequence leading to mastery of the objective?" The teacher must also constantly have in mind two additional questions while instructing the child: (1) To which modality am I presenting the material —visual, auditory, or combined visual-auditory? (2) How am I asking the child to respond—nonverbal (pointing), verbal, or written?

These are important questions to ask oneself in order to adjust the task so that the student experiences success.

DONALD J. TREFFINGER

Donald J. Treffinger is Professor of Creative Studies at the State University College at Buffalo, Buffalo, New York. He is also Editor-elect of the *Gifted Child Quarterly*. Treffinger has previously taught at Purdue University and at the University of Kansas, where he was Chairperson of the department of Educational Psychology and Research from 1972 to 1978.

He is author or co-author of three books and more than 70 journal articles dealing with creativity, problem-solving, and education of gifted and talented children.

His particular interest in this area goes back many years and extends in several different directions. Not only does he teach courses in this area but he has been much involved in curricular programs and workshops in addition to the psychological constructs which are pertinent.

Treffinger brings to this chapter another particularly important focus: his attention to the parent-family influences. He has also been interested not only in talented children and how they function but the possibility of enhancing such special functioning in all youngsters. Thus there is a crossing of the regular-special education line which is essential for mainstreaming. The author has also studied classroom processes with the consequence that what he suggests will be within the realm of actual possibility. The author describes how the emotional conditions, home and school provisions interact with the child's innate potential. The implication for regular school programs cannot be ignored.

5

Gifted and Talented Children

DONALD J. TREFFINGER

SOME SPECIAL EDUCATION STUDENTS are surprised when a text includes a chapter on the education of gifted and talented students. You may share some of the feelings and beliefs that have frequently led to overlooking the special educational needs of gifted children. Your attitudes have been influenced by some of the misunderstandings that persist quite commonly in our society. Some people believe, for example, that truly gifted individuals are so rare that we really cannot plan special programs for them. Others believe that, unlike many handicapped children, the gifted will take care of their own needs and problems, and thus do not require special, differential education. Still others fear that efforts at special educational programming for the gifted will encourage the creation of a privileged, elite group, contrary to our democratic ideals. And even another group is convinced that our current efforts at individualizing instruction adequately meet the needs of gifted and talented children.

This chapter presents some of the unique personal, motivational, and learning characteristics of gifted and talented children, as well as some of the very serious problems they must confront both in and out of school. From this first-hand knowledge, as well as the information provided by research, we hope that you will reach the conclusion that special, differentiated educational attention is important for these students. You may also identify some practical steps you can take for working with gifted and talented students.

The goals of this chapter can also be stated somewhat more formally. We shall attempt:

1. to illustrate how superior talent in many areas can be observed in typical settings in and out of school;

2. to illustrate the complex, multiple selection and identification procedures that must be used to locate outstanding talent;

3. to illustrate the unique personal and educational characteristics of gifted and talented students, and to describe their implications for teaching;

4. to review factors which facilitate and inhibit the effectiveness of parents and regular classroom teachers in working with gifted and talented students; and

5. to identify and review significant unresolved issues and current national trends in education of the gifted.

There are a few preliminaries to which we should attend at the very start of this chapter. First of all, it is reasonable to ask, "Who are the gifted and talented? What do you mean by these terms?"

Gifted and talented students are those who have been identified by qualified professionals as having the potential for consistently outstanding performance or accomplishment in any area of endeavor. By virtue of this exceptionally great potential, these students display personal and learning characteristics that cannot be served adequately without special instructional provisions.

Traditionally we have defined the gifted only in relation to high scores on IQ tests (such as IQ of at least 130). Today, as indicated in our definition, we recognize that the traditional narrow definition is quite inadequate, and sometimes it provides a misleading or inaccurate label for a student. We now realize that an IQ score gives us only a partial picture of the nature and extent of human abilities. Recent research suggests that the nature and measurement of intelligence is much more complex than we have traditionally believed.

For example, Guilford's (1967) *Structure of Intellect* Model proposes that intelligence comprises many specific abilities. Each of these can be described as a specific combination of three factors: *operations, products,* and *contents.* The *operations* include memory, cognition, convergent and divergent production, and evaluation abilities. *Contents* involve processing information in *figural, symbolic, semantic,* or *behavioral* forms. The *Products* involve *units, classes, relations, systems, transformations,* and *implications.* Technical information concerning these abilities, and the tests developed to assess them, may be obtained from Guilford's book, *The Nature of Human Intelligence* (1967); a more introductory explanation of Guilford's model has been provided in his book, *Way Beyond The IQ* (1977).

Guilford's work implies that, rather than defining intelligence as one single ability, we should consider a whole constellation or profile of different factors—perhaps more than a hundred unique "kinds" of intellectual abilities. For our purposes, it is not necessary to learn all of the factors proposed by Guilford's model, but simply to use the model to illustrate one contemporary view of the complexity of human intelligence. When we talk about the gifted student, then, it is possible that we should consider students who display exceptionally great aptitude in many different areas.

Another researcher who has expanded our notion of the nature of giftedness and exceptional talent is Dr. E. Paul Torrance, now at the University of Georgia. For many years, Dr. Torrance has focused upon the nature, identification, and encouragement of creative talent. He has been instrumental, through several books and hundreds of articles, in helping us to realize that our traditional measures of intellectual ability and scholastic achievement may cause us to overlook some of our most creatively gifted students. In fact, there is very little doubt that selection of "gifted" students on the basis of IQ scores alone would result in overlooking many students with exceptionally great creative talent.

Dr. Calvin W. Taylor, of the University of Utah, has also been a pioneer in helping us discover students of exceptional talent who might be overlooked or under-represented if selection were based solely on IQ scores. Dr. Taylor's "multi-talent" approach (1968) has given us valuable insights into the complex diverse nature of human talents. Taylor's model suggests that *all* students' strengths should be recognized and encouraged. The several talent areas described by Taylor include *academic, creative, planning, communicating, forecasting,* and *decision-making.* Every student possesses these talents, in varying degrees. The teacher's challenge is not simply to determine whether or not a child is talented, but instead to identify and nurture the child's strengths. One child might naturally be outstanding in academics, planning, or communicating, whereas another might excel in decision-making or creativity. Taylor's work urges educators to build upon the positive attributes of each person's talents.

These expanded views of human talent do not render the IQ concept useless or obsolete, of course. The kinds of academic aptitude that are measured by IQ tests *can* give us valuable information about one potentially important aspect of giftedness. Newer, broader definitions serve, therefore, to enrich or supplement our earlier view. Although many special programs for the gifted and talented still focus primarily upon academic aptitude, as it might be reflected by IQ scores, the future direction will certainly be toward the utilization of a broader, expanded concept of giftedness.

IDENTIFICATION PROCEDURES

A more comprehensive definition of giftedness or talent means that it is not possible to locate gifted and talented children in our schools simply by examining their scores on a single test. Information from many different sources must be taken into account in searching for multiple talents; tests may provide some useful information, such as use of symbols, verbal and quantitative reasoning, memory and vocabulary, or creative thinking skills. But it is also necessary to utilize other, nontest assessment procedures, such as behavior checklists, rating scales (self- and peer-ratings; teacher, parent, and peer nominations), observation schedules, and biographical inventories. Data from many sources can be combined into a comprehensive case study and used to obtain a more thorough portrait or profile of a student's talent. Some useful instruments and procedures for identifying the gifted and talented have been presented by Martinson (1974).

We must remember, however, that it is not sufficient to define giftedness and identify students using multiple talent procedures. We must also ensure that the students selected will be offered an educational program that will be consistent with the criteria used to define and assess talents.

Students selected on the basis of mathematical talent, for example, should be provided with programming in mathematics and related topics, whereas students selected for musical or artistic ability should receive opportunities to work in those areas. It would not be desirable to select the mathematically, artistically, and musically talented students and then decide, "This year our program will stress writing novels." Although this may seem very obvious, too many schools have provided only a single program for all gifted and talented students.

The use of a variety of different screening and identification procedures also facilitates the recognition of superior talent among minority, culturally different, and disadvantaged students (Renzulli 1973; Sato 1974). In the last decade, we have made substantial progress in developing fair identification procedures for culturally different gifted and talented students, even though the controversy over the nature and extent of "cultural bias" in intelligence testing continues to be unresolved. It is incumbent upon professional educators to make every possible effort to identify superior talents among women, minority students, and culturally different learners, and to insure that such students are not discriminated against in educational programs.

NUMBERS

Under the usual assumptions we make about the distribution of IQ scores in a school-age population, a traditional definition (IQ of at least 130) would involve the uppermost 2–3 percent of our population. Thus, on the basis of the current population, we would be concerned with 1.5–2.0 million students. Under an expanded definition, such as Taylor's multi-talent approach, it is quite likely that the number of students identified would at least *double,* and some estimates of the total number of gifted and talented students, using a very broad conception of human talent, suggest figures as great as 10 percent of the total school population.

Martinson (1974) contended that, no matter how conservative a definition is employed, only a small percentage of these pupils are currently receiving any systematic special educational provisions. Twenty-one states offered no special educational services for the gifted and talented. Martinson concluded that fewer than 15 percent of our country's gifted and talented students are receiving special educational services. This is a smaller degree of service than has been provided for any other handicapped population in our schools.

CONSEQUENCES OF FAILURE TO PROVIDE PROGRAMS

Contrary to a long-standing belief among many educators, it is not true that we can assume that the gifted and talented will take care of themselves. There are instances of gifted persons who have survived an inadequate school experience with apparently undiminished talents, as evidenced by the great contributions of such people as Einstein or Edison. Marland (1972) has reported, however, that "studies show that gifted children in our schools today are locked in by structural and administrative restrictions that inhibit their development. They are denied open access to advanced materials, a cruel kind of censorship of the mind. They are unsatisfied in their mature concern about ethical and moral questions as well as in their intellectual pursuits." But who can predict with confidence what great advances might have been made possible had the school environment been more adequate for gifted people? Who can feel certain that, despite those whose genius survived despite their schools, the talent of countless others has not been denied? We must also recognize, of course, that the goals of education properly involve recognizing and encouraging the optimum development of every person's talent, not merely permitting that talent to survive if it is hardy enough.

The great problem in inadequate educational provision for the gifted and talented is the advent of boredom and frustration. Without adequate educational provisions, many gifted and talented students become so bored that they lose interest, not only in formal schooling, but in the very process of learning. It is impossible to calculate with precision the cost to society of such a waste of talent, but the magnitude of the problem is very great.

In addition, the frustration of the gifted child whose talent is unrecognized and unrewarded in school sometimes leads to the development of social and behavioral difficulties in the classroom, or to psychological withdrawal from the group. Confronted with boredom and the inability to utilize his or her talents constructively, the child may become a recluse, shunning contacts with teachers and age mates, or an unpleasant, and sometimes even disruptive, influence in the classroom.

IS INDIVIDUALIZATION THE ANSWER?

While individualized learning is a desirable goal, and can be advocated for all children, we must recognize that it is not an end in itself. "Individualizing" is a process, not a result; it is necessary, therefore, to ask, "individualization of what? For whom? How?" in order to assess its value. In some classrooms, individualizing means that all children eventually learn the same things, but at their own rates. While this may at least provide gifted and talented students some relief from the "hurry up and wait" ritual of group instruction, it will still be inadequate. We must also be concerned with individualizing other aspects of learning, in addition to *rate*. For example, it is important to provide students with instruction that involves the use of complex thinking and problem-solving processes, provides for examination of attitudes and values as well as facts and concepts, emphasizes interrelationships of content areas, and provides opportunities for the development of independence, self-direction, and self-evaluation. Individualized learning that takes into account all those factors *would* be valuable for the gifted and talented, without question.

We must also remember that individualized learning is not necessarily "learning alone." It is important for gifted and talented students to have independent learning experiences, in which they can actively pursue their own areas of interest. But it is also important for them to be able to have school experiences in which they have ample time to be with their intellectual peers, working in groups with other gifted students, and time to spend with their age-mates who may be less talented, too. Such a blend of individual and group experiences will help students develop their own talents, but will also protect against unnecessary isolation of children from their peers.

Individualizing instruction does not guarantee, then, that the needs of the gifted and talented learner will be adequately met, although it can be an effective way of organizing instruction for them. Its value depends upon its content, the thinking and feeling processes that are involved for the students, and the effectiveness with which individual and group activities are balanced.

IS CONCERN FOR THE GIFTED UNDEMOCRATIC?

One other common misunderstanding warrants discussion: that educational programming for the gifted and talented results in an undemocratic, specially privileged elite group of pupils. However, we do not believe that recognition of individual differences is undemocratic. Indeed, it seems more reasonable to assume that, in providing all students with the best possible education, we must acknowledge the differences that exist among individuals, and plan for their differential education accordingly. Special educational programs for the gifted and talented are best viewed, then, not as rewards for specially privileged students, but as our best efforts at providing students with instruction that has been designed to take into account their unique goals, needs, and characteristics.

Any view of human abilities that emphasizes multiple talents (such as the Guilford, Torrance, or Taylor approaches described earlier) implies strongly that education must center on the identification and development of an individual's unique abilities. To do less, by treating all learners as if they had the same talents and needs, seems not only to be less "democratic," but also unsound educationally.

An interesting problem. Are all students potentially gifted or talented? Certainly Guilford's *Structure of Intellect* and Taylor's *Talent Totem Poles* suggest that we may find some areas of considerable talent among all of our students. Is this, as some critics contend, merely an unrealistically romantic view that makes people falsely feel better about themselves? Is it impractical to implement in the classroom? We believe that the multiple talent approach does represent a very positive description of the human condition, and we find its implications challenging and constructive rather than naively idealistic. The implementation of a multiple talent approach to teaching has been described very well by Taylor (1973) and by Lloyd, Seghini, and Stevenson (1974).

NATIONAL TRENDS

Through the years, there have been several periods of rising and waning interest in education of the gifted and talented, although the field has never commanded as much attention as other special education areas. Much attention developed in the United States, for example, in the wake of the Soviet Union's successful launching of Sputnik I in 1957. At that time, our greatest concern was for the identification and nurture of talent in science, mathematics, and technology-related fields. The concerns of the late 1950s were very specific, largely "crisis-centered" issues, and thus did not lead to the development of long-standing programs or major shifts in educational priorities. Since then, as we have mentioned, educational and psychological research on the nature and development of talent has increased, and our contemporary concerns involve a much more comprehensive analysis of giftedness. Consequently, during the last decade, there has been another period of growing interest in educational programs for the gifted and talented. The current status of this field in the United States is marked by many questions, rising interest, and only very modest federal, state, and local support. There is an Office on Education of the Gifted and Talented in the United States Office of Education, which has made available some funding for new programs since 1976 (with total funding of slightly more than two million dollars for all programs). National organizations, such as the National Association for Gifted Children and The Association for the Gifted are growing in membership and conducting programs throughout the country. The National/State Leadership Training Institute on the Gifted and Talented has provided training programs and other services for educators, parents, and administrators throughout the country. Many states are developing legislation including provisions for special programs for the gifted and talented, and numerous local school districts are initiating programs on their own. Fellowship and internship programs have been developed, with support from the U.S. Office of Education, to identify potential leaders in the field and provide them with field experience and advanced graduate training. Thus, there are many signs of a significant growth of interest and concern for improvement of educational services for the gifted and talented; whether the results will be long-lasting and dramatic in their impact on our schools, or merely another swing of the pendulum, cannot yet be predicted. We can at least note that interest in this area is as strong as it has been in at least two decades, and that there is promise that the current interest is more stable, and educationally more systematic and comprehensive, than in previous years. Appended to this chapter is information about organizations concerned with educating gifted and talented children.

SUSAN: A GIFTED CHILD

It is one thing to talk about identifying and educating gifted and talented children, referring to "them" in the abstract, but quite another matter to consider the real, live children you will meet in your own classroom. In order to bring the test of reality to bear on our discussion thus far, as well as to illustrate the nature and extent of special educational programs for the gifted and talented, we shall look closely at the actual case history of a gifted girl. It is impossible to illustrate in one case all of the many talents we have described thus far. For illustration, the child in this case is one who would be considered "academically" gifted. That is, her exceptional ability is seen readily in traditional criteria (high IQ) and in her ability to master quickly and easily the kinds of learning outcomes that have traditionally been emphasized in our schools. The case is based upon the life of a real child, now in an elementary school in a small city. We shall consider her current condition, the background of the case in relation to home and school influences, and both short- and long-term planning for special educational provisions.

Current Condition

Susan is a seven-year-old Caucasian female who is small in stature (at the third percentile in height for children at this age), but very attractive. She is in good health, seems calm and pleasant, and appears to have no general physical limitations or disabilities. Contrary to the largely erroneous stereotype of the gifted child as a frail, puny person whose intellectual ability is a compensation for other deficiencies, Susan is a very ordinary, healthy child, if somewhat small for her age. Her case illustrates that most gifted and talented persons do not stand out visually from other less talented individuals. There are the same variations among them in height, weight, health, and physical appearance as will be found among most children at any age level, rather than any unique physical characteristics that provide a basis for instant recognition.

Her home is in a small urban community, and both parents have advanced education beyond the undergraduate college level. Susan's father has completed his doctorate and is currently a staff member at a university in the community, and her mother is taking graduate coursework. The family has one other child, a girl six and one-half months of age. They live together in a comfortable single-family home in a residential area of the community.

Susan attended a local nursery school for three terms prior to kindergarten enrollment. She was five years of age when she began attending a public school in the community, and she remained in kindergarten for the entire school year, although her intellectual talent was observed by the school, particularly in language and reading. In the following school year, she began in a regular first grade classroom but was moved into a combination first and second grade room at mid-year, in the belief that she would be able to work easily with the second grade children. For the current school year, Susan's parents have transferred her to another local public school, an open-space building in which a pilot program for gifted and talented students is being developed. At the new school, Susan was placed in a unit comprised primarily of third and fourth grade students.

Susan's exceptional ability has been shown in her performance on the Stanford Binet individual intelligence test (IQ = 160) and the Slosson Intelligence Test (IQ = 146); these tests were administered when she was six years old. In addition, the Peabody Individual Achievement Tests were administered at the end of the first-second grade school year, with Susan's scores all being exceptionally high:

> mathematics (grade level 6.0, 99th percentile); reading-recognition (grade level 6.2, 99th percentile); reading-comprehension (grade level 6.8, 99th percentile); spelling (grade level 5.8, 99th percentile); general information (grade level 5.1, 98th percentile).

Susan began talking within a normal development range, but her use of language accelerated rapidly. She had a small vocabulary by 16 months, and was using sentences between 18 and 20 months. During the period of 20–36 months, her parents noticed that she used complex language easily and with originality. She also began reading early, and became a very enthusiastic independent reader at home. In general, Susan's rapid development in these areas illustrates a common set of characteristics among academically or intellectually gifted persons. She learns quickly and easily, remembers well, applies what she learns in productive thinking, works easily and effectively with symbols (numbers and language), and has a very strong base of general knowledge and information.

In social settings, Susan's ability enables her to communicate easily and comfortably with older children and adults, and she discusses her interests and ideas freely with her parents and in regular visits with her grandparents. She also converses easily and maturely with adults at school. Her contacts with age mates are usually satisfactory, but some problems arise. She was liked by children at her first public school, but was occasionally impatient with others and merely tolerant of their interests and activities. She prefers to play and work independently, or with a single playmate, rather than to participate in group activities. In the new school setting, partly because of her small size for her age and partly because of her acceleration and movement into a new social setting, she was initially subjected to some teasing and name-calling about her size (calling her "shrimp" or "midget"). This has not caused any major difficulties, however, and as she is adjusting to the new school, her teachers report that the other children accept her and appear to like her. Susan does not actively seek social approval or interaction, however, and still remains somewhat apart from the peer group. She is concerned, according to her parents, about not being different from other children in school, and anxious about seeming to be unusual. Her teachers give no reports of any severe problems in getting along with other children. She seems shy and hesitant in groups, however, seldom volunteering to respond (even for routine matters like counting heads for cafeteria). Both her parents and her teachers have observed that she is somewhat reluctant to discuss her attitudes and feelings about school and learning.

Susan has many interests outside of her school experiences. She has participated in a Brownie troop, taken ballet at a local community center, and participated in children's programs at the university. She participates in a variety of activities at home, playing games with her family, walking, and bicycling. Her father gives her piano lessons regularly, and she enjoys music very much. She also enjoys a variety of childhood play activities, such as making "tents" and playing "dress up" with clothes donated by her mother. Susan is a very avid reader, and regularly amuses herself with reading; she reads on her own for about an hour daily outside of her school responsibilities. She particularly enjoys fiction and humorous writing. She has already read a wide variety of books including *Alice in Wonderland* (when she was in kindergarten), science fiction, several children's series, *Huckleberry Finn, Tom Sawyer, The Wizard of Oz,* and several biographical books and animal stories (particularly about horses). She collects birds' feathers, rocks, and a variety of "miscellaneous things." Susan also enjoys doing her own art projects at home, making a variety of different pictures and abstract drawings for display in a "gallery" on a wall of her bedroom. She also makes her own books, writing brief stories and illustrating the pages with her own drawings. Her teachers from her first school reported, however, that she did not seem eager to participate in independent projects in science or social studies, although occasionally she did accept some projects and share them with her classmates.

In many ways, Susan illustrates the commonly described characteristics of the gifted child. She displays a wide range of interests, and participates in many activities. By examining the quality of her writing, the variety of written products she creates, and the complex level of the language in her stories, it is easy to forget that Susan is only seven years old. Her very great talent is readily apparent in her activities and accomplishments outside her school experiences. She also displays some very typical problems and concerns, such as her concern for being like other children, and for getting along in school without being labeled as "different." Exceptional talent places many burdens upon a child, and Susan, like many others, needs to learn how to accept and use her talents without guilt, embarrassment, or vanity. Some of the current challenges which must be met at home and at school in Susan's case are summarized in this list, to help review clearly her current status:

*Susan learns very rapidly and easily, and can do many school assignments with a minimum of effort.

*Susan already can do well many of the things her less gifted age mates are just learning to do.

*Susan is comfortable when talking with adults and older children, but somewhat shy and reticent in group work with her peers.

*Susan wants to be like other children, and wants to get along with others, but also feels a need to remain independent.

*Susan is small in size for her age, and appears even smaller when grouped with older children in school.

*Susan's academic achievement in basic subject areas is approximately three years advanced from her grade placement on the basis of age.

*Susan has a large fund of general information, which she can express readily through language.

*Susan has a variety of interests, with many things she enjoys and does well outside school.
*Susan is an avid independent reader.
*Susan is developing a strong and mature sense of humor.
*Susan frequently prefers to work on her own rather than to participate in group activities, and she can occupy herself productively for a long time.

Home and School Background

It is not unusual for the home and school background of gifted and talented children to involve very complex relationships, and Susan's case is very typical.

When Susan's parents, and especially her mother, became aware of their daughter's ability, there was a very natural concern for her school experiences. Susan's mother concluded rather early in the first year of public school that, despite a generally supportive attitude, the school was not prepared to offer substantial special educational services for very young children. It has not been uncommon for schools to make very little special educational provision for the gifted in the primary grades. Of course, it is important that a child's early school experiences should be stimulating and closely geared to the child's interests and abilities, since these years may establish the child's attitudes about self, school, and learning. Susan completed kindergarten, apparently with no major problems resulting, although her parents' concerns were not satisfied nor were their doubts resolved about the school's response to her needs.

Home-school problems continued to increase during the next school year. The parents were concerned that the first grade teacher, although a pleasant, responsive person and a serious educator, did not have sufficient time or resources to attend adequately to Susan's special needs. The parents reported increasing signs of boredom and, through discussion at home, indications of dislike for school. Susan reported some problems at home that she did not mention in school, such as being unable to find interesting books in the library and being directed only to overly simple materials for young children. Continued consultation between the parents and the school led to Susan's transfer at mid-year into a room of first and second graders.

This change did not solve the problems for Susan, her parents, and her teachers, either, and there is evidence of continued worsening of the communication and relationships between home and school. Susan's mother reported that the child was uncomfortable in the class because of considerable emphases on competition against time requirements and among pupils. She was also frightened, her mother reported, by a classroom discipline system that emphasized "marks" that were given to offenders. Apparently Susan did not completely understand the operation of the discipline system, was too shy to inquire, and experienced considerable fear about incurring the dreaded "marks."

Susan's teacher, on the other hand, described her as a very capable child, who did extremely good work, but was shy and withdrawing from participation in group activities. She reported that Susan was persistent, attentive, a slow but meticulous worker, with considerable verbal facility. She described her classroom as a "rather loosely structured environment," with many learning centers and individualized activities. She believed that Susan received too much pressure from her parents, and that some of Susan's "difficulties" were primarily reflections of her mother's concerns.

Unfortunately, there was no systematic way for the home and the school to effect some clarification of these problems, whether real or imagined by parents or teachers. On the one hand, there does seem to be evidence supporting the teacher's concern about the nature and degree of pressures from the parents. It is also quite possible that some of Susan's reluctance to talk much about her attitudes and feelings about school may have been related to her perception and interpretation of her parents' concerns. On the other hand, given the lack of instruction which was carefully selected on the basis of Susan's abilities and achievements, it is also clear that there was substantial justification for the parents' concern. The teachers did not seem to be able to adjust the curriculum, the pace, or the processes of thinking according to Susan's actual needs. Evidence for this, at the very end of the school year, is provided by the teacher's summary evaluation report. The teacher reported that Susan (who was already able to work effectively at the fifth or sixth grade level) was "ready" to proceed into the third grade reading program.

After many hours of discussions during the following summer, Susan's parents decided that another school in the community might be better able to respond to Susan's unique learning characteristics and talents. Several conferences were held with school authorities, including the principals of both schools, and approval was obtained for the transfer. The new school, as we described earlier, is an open-space building in which several teachers are studying the special needs of gifted and talented students, and in which a special pilot program has just been initiated. The transfer has made it necessary for Susan to be driven to and from school by her parents, and her teachers see and talk with her mother very frequently. There is still some concern about the pressures that are placed upon Susan at home, but the teachers are planning to make special instructional provisions to help Susan work at an appropriate level while remaining, as nearly as possible, with other children nearly her own age.

Shortly after the beginning of the new school year, a special conference was held involving the three teachers who work in the section of the school in which Susan has been placed, an elementary counselor, a school psychologist, a university specialist in the area of education of the gifted and talented, and the school principal. The purpose of this conference was to review in detail all relevant information concerning Susan's abilities, achievement, interests, and background at home and in school, and to attempt to define initial steps that should be taken to provide a suitable instructional program for her.

Before proceeding to an examination of how instructional plans are developed for gifted and talented students like Susan, let us review the important facts concerning her home and school background:

> *Susan's parents, themselves well-educated and concerned about her education, recognized her ability early and expressed concern for her school program.
> *Very few special programs or services were available for Susan during the first two years in school, which encouraged the parents' misgivings and may also have contributed to Susan's feelings about school.
> *There were problems in communication between home and school which were increased by the parents' and teachers' concerns and defenses.
> *The strategy of accelerating Susan, by moving her from one grade to another in the same school year (analogous to what is commonly called "grade skipping") was attempted but did not solve the problem.
> *Susan's transfer to another school was carefully reviewed and discussed with school authorities, and approved on the basis of specific program opportunities at the new school.
> *Susan's program of study in the new school has been the focus of the attention, not just of a single teacher, but of a team of professional staff members (including teachers and specialists who have specialized training in education of the gifted and talented), utilizing data from a variety of sources.

Short- and Long-Term Educational Planning

Now we have arrived at the point where we ask, "What can and should be happening to provide Susan with the best possible education?"

To begin, we shall look briefly at some of the possible courses of action that might be considered. Kaplan (1974) has prepared an excellent handbook, which provides a great deal of valuable information about the development of educational programs for the gifted and talented, and Gallagher (1975) also includes a very thorough examination of alternative program arrangements and teaching strategies.

First, what kinds of program arrangements might be considered for educating gifted and talented children? For many years, educators have answered this question by referring to the need for "enrichment" programs. But it is very difficult to determine exactly what kind of program is implied by such statements. As Gallagher (1975) has noted: "It is discouraging to find that many teachers still believe that the primary program adjustment for gifted students is to give them longer and more extensive assignments of the same sort they would give to the average student." Piling more of the same work upon students may occupy more of their time, but it does not provide an adequate, nor even an acceptable, approach to teaching gifted and talented students.

Instead, it may be wise for us, following Kaplan's (1974) approach, to view enrichment as a goal, not a program: our purpose, through many different programs or approaches, will be to improve, or enrich, the quality of the educational experience for the child. This suggests that there are many alternative models or prototypes from which school programs may be developed. Kaplan groups these into three categories: (1) programs involving grouping of students; (2) programs involving acceleration of students; and (3) programs involving guidance or counseling of students. These three groups with illustrative program alternatives for each, are summarized in Table 5.1.

But knowing that there are really many kinds of program prototypes still does not really help us solve our problem. These prototypes are only administrative arrangements, and they are not inherently "good," "bad," "right," or "wrong" in any particular case. This is true partly because the value of any of the prototypes depends upon how it is actually implemented. No program prototype will be successful if it is carelessly planned and casually implemented by untrained or uncaring personnel. Any of the program prototypes must be utilized in a way that does more than just heap busy work on students. Gallagher argues that any adequate program must involve changes in program content, intellectual skills, and learning environments. The content of the program must be selected on the basis of the students' interests and previous achievements, freely extending above and beyond traditional grade-level content expectations. There must be ample provision for students to use complex intellectual skills, such as creative thinking, problem-solving, critical thinking and decision-making, not merely recognition and recall. The learning envi-

TABLE 5.1

Classification of Program Prototypes (from Kaplan 1974)

ENRICHMENT

ENRICHMENT is . . .
experiences which replace, supplement, or extend learnings as
the basis for each type of prototype. Enrichment is the reason
for the development or adoption of any prototype.

GROUPING	ACCELERATION	GUIDANCE
Provisions which facilitate the student's access to learning opportunities	Activities which promote learning beyond regularly prescribed curriculum	Experiences which promote understanding of the self and others and explore opportunities for careers
—Cluster grouping within the regular class	—Early entrance or preschool classes	—Individual conferences
—Special regular classes	—Double grade promotion	—Group meetings
—Part-time groups before, during, after school or Saturdays	—Advanced placement classes	—Career and vocational counseling
—Seminars	—Ungraded classes	—Educational counseling
—Minicourses	—Multi-age classes	—Community programs and sponsorship
—Team teaching	—Tutoring	—Scholarship societies
—Alternative schools	—Correspondence courses	—Study groups
—Resource room or demonstration classroom	—Extra classes for extra credit	—Special education classes
—Itinerant or resource teacher	—Credit by examination	—Tutoring
—Field trip and cultural events	—Independent study	
—Special summer	—Continuous progress curriculum	
	—Year-round school	
	—Flexible scheduling	
	—Block or back to back classes	

ronment must be conducive to active discovery, inquiry, and self-directed learning, not merely passive listening and responding.

Kaplan (1974) referred to "the learner's triangle" to emphasize that educational planning for the gifted must take into account what is to be learned (content), how the gifted child learns (processes), and the unique personal characteristics of the gifted. The "learner's triangle" is illustrated in Figure 5.1.

Kaplan (1974) emphasized that taking these factors into account, as well as the available resources of the school, teachers, and community, leads to what is called, technically, differentiation of the curriculum for gifted and talented students. Such differentiation involves approaches to the curriculum (with emphases on questioning, discovery, and problem-solving), attack on the curriculum (using teaching methods that emphasize independent research and complex skills), departure from the curriculum (emphasizing interrelationships of subjects and applications of knowledge), and the results of the curricular experience (stressing communicating what is learned, projects and applications, documenting solutions, changing attitudes, and finding new problems).

Renzulli (1977) has provided an excellent model, called the Enrichment Triad Model, for describing how these concerns might actually be implemented in school programs. The model is presented in Figure 5.2.

Type I Enrichment, which can easily be part of the regular classroom program (and which can be beneficial for many students, not only the gifted), is "general exploratory activity." Type I activities provide students with opportunities to pursue their own curiosities and interests, in a wide range of topics. These activities commonly involve topics or areas that are *not* part of the basic curriculum. They represent opportunities for the students to select freely from among many interest areas, using interest centers, stations, field trips, speakers, etc., as resources.

Type II Enrichment, which can also benefit many students in the regular classroom, involves "group training activities." These activities provided organized, planned opportunities for students to nurture critical and creative thinking abilities, problem-solving skills, and skills of inquiry or methods of research. There are many published curriculum resources available in which systematic provision has been made for the development of these thinking processes.

Type III Enrichment, which is uniquely suited to the needs and characteristics of gifted students, provides opportunities for individual and small group investigations of real problems." In participating in Type III Enrichment, the student is not merely a consumer of other peo-

FIGURE 5.1

The Learner's triangle (from Kaplan 1974)

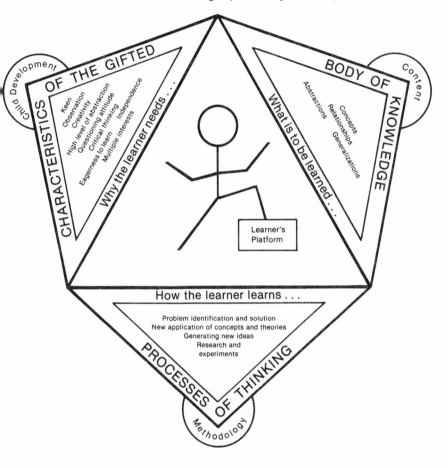

ples' ideas and information, but becomes actively involved in *producing* ideas or solutions for problems.

Although Type III Enrichment is particularly important for gifted and talented students, Types I and II should not be overlooked. They provide the foundation of interests, topics, and methodological skills, that enable the student to conduct Type III projects effectively.

The Enrichment Triad Model has been a major contribution in

FIGURE 5.2

The Enrichment triad model (from Renzulli 1977)

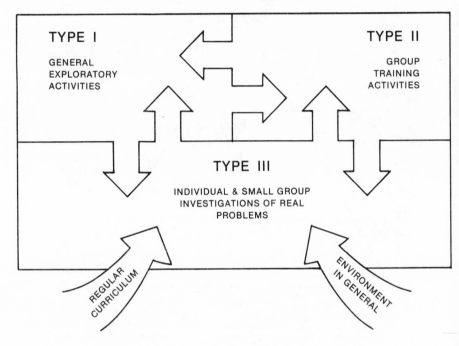

gifted education, since it has guided the development of practical procedures for enrichment, and provided a useful alternative to providing the student with additional assignments that may merely become "more of the same." This model has helped us prevent the concept of "enrichment" from becoming mere busywork for able student.

In order to examine specifically how a differentiated instructional program might be developed in Susan's case, let us first review what we know about her present condition and background.

Short-Term Planning

We should begin by considering some of the things we already know about Susan. Think about the information you already have about her current condition and her background. What do you know about Susan that may bear on how we should intervene immediately to plan an effective instructional program for her?

Your knowledge of Susan's *shyness* in school, for example, may have struck you as potentially important in planning instruction for her. We would need to plan learning activities for Susan that will neither encourage her to withdraw into a completely private "shell," nor force her to function constantly in large groups in which she feels anxious and uncomfortable. While Susan undoubtedly needs some independent work, at her own present achievement level which may be more advanced than many of her age mates, she clearly should also have some opportunities for work with other children, perhaps initially with small groups. Further, the group experiences should be in areas that will be interesting and not very threatening, so Susan can experience success in working with other children. Look again at her current condition and background. What areas do you see in which some work with small groups of children might be challenging and enjoyable for Susan?

You may have identified some of the same things that were reviewed in the staff conference about Susan at her new school. Her interests in reading, humor, and creating her own stories were particularly noted. These were discussed, with several alternative strategies being created: (1) participate in creative dramatics activities, with other children having similar interests, involving writing and presenting their own brief plays or sketches; (2) participating in a group to develop and illustrate short stories to be read to younger children at the school; (3) developing small-group research projects involving library research and sharing on such topics as types of humor, famous humorists, etc.

In developing an individually prescribed program for Susan, and other children of similar abilities and characteristics, we illustrate how the learner's triangle must be considered. It would not be adequate to give Susan extra work of the same kinds that other children are doing, for that would probably lead very quickly to boredom. The content of her instructional program must be varied. In addition, however, we should also plan instructional activities that involve many thinking processes, so Susan is not merely being asked to memorize and recall factual information. Finally, her individual personal characteristics (shyness, sense of humor, independence, etc.) must also be taken into account.

By identifying other students who share Susan's interests, such as in original stories and humor, a grouping approach can be developed. Although the flexibility of the open-space school undoubtedly facilitates the use of flexible grouping procedures, similar efforts could probably also be utilized successfully even in a traditional self-contained classroom, with some extra effort by the teachers.

Other approaches might be considerably less effective for Susan. If we attended only to her advanced achievement scores, for example, radical grade-skipping might have been suggested by someone. Almost certainly, however, placement of Susan in a group of fifth- and sixth-grade youngsters would have been a most unsatisfactory solution. Her small stature would have made her very distinctly different, and might have led to significant problems in relating to other pupils. In addition, most authorities now agree that mere grade-skipping is an ineffective strategy for most gifted students. The work in the new group may be challenging because it may initially be strange, but, in the long run, grade-skipping may reduce to the same strategy as piling on more of the same work at a faster rate.

The previous efforts that were made in moving Susan through grades one and two in one year were attempts at acceleration that did not prove to be very successful, for a variety of reasons. The research literature suggests that acceleration is frequently an effective strategy when the child is initially an older child in the lower grade level, and when the acceleration is supported by appropriate transition experiences (such as a summer program between second and fourth grades); this is quite different, of course, from arbitrarily moving a child from one grade to another.

If we attended primarily to Susan's previous achievement and her small size relative to other children her age, we might have recommended placing her in a group of age peers, but completely assigning her individual work at her own level. Aside from being difficult for a teacher to manage, this approach would risk encouraging Susan to withdraw completely from all instructional contact with other children; it would more than likely result in increasing personal problems for Susan in accepting her own abilities and in relating to other children.

Let us summarize our observations concerning short-term plans for Susan's case from the standpoint of the three changes Gallagher (1975) proposed as necessary in special educational programming for the gifted: content, intellectual skills, and learning environment.

Content

Susan will profit from an educational program in which the content is adjusted to take into account her present level of achievement. Analysis of her individual achievement tests indicated that she can already work effectively with basic arithmetic and reading skills. Her teachers should search for (and develop) learning centers or individualized programs that involve new topics, new approaches, or opportunities for guided discovery and inquiry. They should *not* expect her to spend more than a minimum of time and effort practicing basic computational skills and number facts that she already knows. Some group work can be arranged for her in the present school, since there are several other students who will also benefit from similar content modifications.

Intellectual Skills

Susan's previous teachers provided few opportunities for her to learn to use and develop complex intellectual skills. In her new school, however, many curriculum resources are available to assist children in working on interesting individual and group activities designed to foster creative thinking (see, for example, Torrance 1972; Davis 1973; Renzulli 1974) and problem-solving (e.g., Covington, Crutchfield, Olton, and Davies 1972). Teachers have also developed learning centers and activity cards for students, in which the students have systematic opportunities to think up many possible ideas (fluency), to think of different kinds of solutions to problems (flexibility), and to think of unique and unusual ideas (originality). Such activities will provide Susan with opportunities to utilize more complex thinking processes, and not to be engaged only in memorization, recall, and recognition activities.

Learning Environment

The organization and structure of Susan's school allows readily for flexible, multi-age grouping of students, and it facilitates the simultaneous implementation of a wide variety of individual and group activities. There are also regular opportunities for teachers, teacher aides, school psychologists, counselors, and other specialists to confer about individual cases. There are several teachers in the school who have special graduate training for work with gifted and talented students. These factors should make it possible for a learning environment to be created and maintained that will foster Susan's personal and intellectual growth. In addition, it should be possible to assist Susan in learning how to manage and direct her own learning without encouraging her to withdraw into isolation from other children. Such self-directed learning may be an especially important aspect of the learning environment for gifted and talented students (Treffinger 1975).

Although gifted students may have *potential* for independence, it is often necessary for them to have assistance in learning how to direct their learning effectively. Self-direction involves learning how to establish one's own goals and objectives, learning how to locate resources and materials, planning and conducting a project, preparing a product or report, and sharing one's learning with appropriate audiences. *Type III Enrichment* projects provide opportunities for students to practice and demonstrate these skills; however, the teacher should also recognize the need to establish a classroom setting in which these skills can be learned. Practical guidelines for creating such an environment have been presented by Feldhusen and Kolloff (1978), Kaplan, Madsen, and Gould (1976), and Treffinger and Barton (1979).

It is also important that the learning environment for Susan should include planful, regular opportunities for her to work with other children of similar interests and abilities. Although schools often hesitate to create special full-time programs for gifted students, it is widely recognized that the gifted and talented require for optimum personal educational growth regular, challenging opportunities to interact, and work with peers of similar talents (Gallagher, 1975).

Long-Range Planning

What does the future hold for a child like Susan? How can her parents and teachers help her to continue to grow personally, socially, and intellectually? How can she best be guided to translate her exceptional talent into a satisfying and productive adult life?

We have not always understood the effects of development on superior talent, and some misunderstandings, such as "early ripe, early rot," seem to be persistent. Evidence has been obtained from longitudinal studies in which the same group of gifted children was followed from childhood into adulthood that clearly dismisses such notions (Terman and Oden 1951). On the whole, their findings indicated that, rather than deteriorating with age, the gifted children extended their superiority in comparison with other people into the mid-adult years.

As the Terman and Oden group reached mid-adulthood (early and late thirties), far fewer women than men displayed records of outstanding achievements, and only a small minority of the women had actively pursued careers. This illustrates a problem that has been particularly important for gifted girls: social stereotypes and traditional role definitions may have operated to create pressures against full realization of their talents. It is very difficult for a girl to recognize and develop superior abilities in the face of such pressures toward conformity and suppression of talent. Given today's emphasis on the status of women in our culture, it seems quite possible that today's gifted and talented girls may be growing up in an environment that will be better prepared to nurture their talents and later to encourage and accept their contributions. Stereotypes which may once have resulted in directing gifted females away from pursuing significant careers in some areas (sciences, mathematics, engineering, and business, for example) seem to be breaking down. Today more teachers, parents, and counselors recognize that talented women are able to pursue any area that is consonant with their interests and abilities.

What specifically needs to be done, at home and in school, for a child like Susan? Some of the directions that have already been identified will continue to be important throughout her school years. Susan's teachers must follow her progress closely, and work together to identify areas of study that will be challenging and rewarding for her. Without doubt, there should be a continued emphasis on a blend of individual projects and group experiences. Her interest in reading can be sustained by helping her locate appropriate books as her interests change and mature. Continued work to help Susan develop skills of directing and evaluating her own work, and to employ creative thinking, problem-solving, and independent inquiry should be maintained.

It will also be important in the future for schools to provide Susan with programs that give her an opportunity, for at least part of each school day, to participate in projects and learning activities with other gifted children. If Susan's family remains in their present location, programs will continue to be available, since there is legislation that includes special educational programs for gifted children. Many states now have such legislation, or at least provisions for encouraging the development of special programs, and new programs are being developed in all parts of the country. If they plan to move to a new area, it would certainly be advisable for Susan's parents to investigate the nature and extent of special services that will be available for her.

Personally and socially, Susan's parents and teachers will also have to work together to insure her development and adjustment. Susan may always be small in stature, for example, and she can be helped to understand that as a description rather than a limitation; she can learn to accept herself as she is, rather than to feel inferior. This may be even more important during adolescence, when so many other physical changes will occur. Children in junior high schools vary widely in physical size and maturity, and Susan will have to be able to continue learning, personal contacts, and social relationships with other children despite such differences.

In summary, long-term plans for gifted girls like Susan, and for many other gifted and talented children, should be concerned with:

*fostering the skills of self-directed learning and problem-solving;
*encouraging the use of complex thinking skills, including creative thinking, critical thinking and decision-making, and communicating plans and solutions;
*learning to work effectively in groups as well as independently;
*learning to accept oneself and one's talents and limitations, and to accept others who are less talented;
*providing an environment for learning that is rich in resources, going outside the school as necessary; and
*encouraging positive attitudes toward careers and adult experiences that will build upon one's talents.

TEACHING THE GIFTED AND TALENTED: A CHALLENGE

As you consider a case like Susan's and think about millions of other gifted and talented children in our country, it is easy to see that there are great challenges. Such children are capable of learning basic material quickly and easily, and then proceeding significantly beyond such learning into more advanced problems. Thus, they require teaching that is not preoccupied with giving information. The classroom must be an arena for research, inquiry, and projects involving real products and applications.

Gifted and talented children also learn readily how to make choices and to evaluate information and evidence, how to think of unusual and imaginative ideas and use them in solving problems. They are curious, confident in their own ideas, independent, and persistent in their many interests. These characteristics create many significant demands for their teachers, who must be able to direct students' work in many different areas, stimulate new questions and problems, and offer support and guidance for students' independent inquiry. At the same time, the teacher must be skillful at helping children work together, helping them achieve socialization without sacrificing their independence and creativity. The teacher must be able to create an environment in which the student can pursue topics that are highly advanced—frequently beyond the personal competence of the teacher. This demands that the teacher relinquish the role of "expert" and assume the role of "facilitator," recognizing his or her own limitations, and helping the student locate other people and resources who can work effectively with the child on a particular subject or problem.

Despite these demands (or perhaps, because of them) it is also very exciting and rewarding to work with gifted and talented children. Many teachers have reported that their experiences with gifted students have helped them become interested in new learning themselves, and also caused them to try new approaches to teaching that have proved to be enjoyable and stimulating.

For further study

BOOKS

Davis, G. A. *Psychology of Problem Solving: Theory and Practice.* New York: Basic Books, 1973. An excellent introduction to creative thinking and problem-solving processes, with extensive descriptions of programs for classroom applications.

Gowan, J. C., Khatena, J., and Torrance, E. P. *Educating the Ablest.* Itasca, Ill.: Peacock, 1979; 2nd ed. An anthology, including important readings from major sources on all aspects of education of the gifted and talented.

Hauck, B. B., and Freehill, M. F. *The Gifted—Case Studies.* Dubuque: Ia.: Brown, 1972. Careful presentations of ten case studies of gifted children, illustrating many aspects of their behavior and development.

Torrance, E. P. *Gifted Children in the Classroom.* New York: Macmillan, 1965. A brief paperback which provides the reader with valuable ideas, especially in relation to creative talent.

Torrance, E. P., and Myers, R. E. *Creative Learning and Teaching.* New York: Dodd, Mead, 1970. A fascinating book that will be especially valuable for any teacher who is concerned with encouraging creative thinking and imagination through classroom instruction.

ORGANIZATIONS AND JOURNALS

Creative Education Foundation, State University College, Chase Hall, 1300 Elmwood Avenue, Buffalo, N.Y. 14222. Publishers of the *Journal of Creative Behavior* and many other materials to advance the development of creativ-

148   HUMANISTIC TEACHING

ity in education. The Creative Education Foundation also sponsors an annual Creative Problem Solving Institute in Buffalo, and several smaller regional institutes throughout the country.

Leadership Training Institutes, National/State Leadership Training, Institute on the Gifted and Talented, 316 West Second Street, Suite P4-C, Los Angeles, Cal. 90012. Publishers of a *Bulletin* of particular interest to educators, the Leadership Training Institute is a federally supported program to provide leadership training and technical services throughout the country.

The Association for the Gifted (TAG), Council for Exceptional Children, 1920 Association Drive, Reston, Va. 22091. TAG is a Division of the Council of Exceptional Children. It sponsors national and regional conferences on education of the gifted and talented and publishes an informative newsletter. The CEC publication *Exceptional Children* also carries articles on education of the gifted and talented.

National Association for Gifted Children (NAGC), Route 5, Box 630A, Hot Springs, Ark. 71901. NAGC is a nationwide organization for parents, teachers, administrators, and researchers in the area of gifted education. Sponsors annual meetings, professional publications, and publishes the *Gifted Child Quarterly.*

FILMS AND FILMSTRIPS

No Reason to Stay, Films, Inc., 1144 Wilmette Avenue, Wilmette, Ill. 60091.

More than a Glance, Ventura County, Superintendent of Schools, Audiovisual Department, 535 East Main Street, Ventura, Cal. 93001.

RAFE: Developing Giftedness in the Educationally Disadvantaged, University of Southern California, University Park, Cinema Department, Los Angeles, Cal. 90008.

Understanding the Gifted, Churchill Films, 662 N. Robertson Blvd., Los Angeles, Cal. 90069.

Who is the Gifted Child? National State Leadership Training Institute, 316 West Second Street, Los Angeles, Cal. 90012.

Why Man Creates, Pyramid Films, Box 1048, Santa Monica, Cal. 90406.

LAWRENCE J. TURTON

Lawrence J. Turton's professional career has been devoted to speech communication, from his undergraduate studies through his graduate work at the University of Kansas, to his present position as associate professor of Speech Pathology, Indiana University of Pennsylvania. He holds certification of clinical competence in speech from the American Speech and Hearing Association. He combined academic studies with direct clinical work and was the Associate Director for Training and Education at the Institute for the Study of Mental Retardation and Related Disabilities at the University of Michigan. He has taught at the University of Kansas, Bowling Green, the University of Michigan and the University of Nebraska—Lincoln.

This chapter concentrates to a considerable degree on the early development of John Mervin: The first year gave no cause for concern. And then the common vacillation begins between waiting for him to "outgrow" his lack of speech and the feeling that something must be done. As one follows the course of events, one cannot help think of how less likely it would have been for John to get help had he been born to parents with few resources.

6

Preschool Language Disabilities

LAWRENCE J. TURTON

In MANY RESPECTS, a chapter on communication problems in a text dealing with exceptional students should be considered redundant and superfluous. Except for the gifted child, communication problems are an inherent aspect of the majority of handicapping conditions which result in a child being placed in a special education classroom. Understanding the nature of these problems and the range of treatment procedures should be a core competency for every staff person working with handicapped children. Whether one is dealing with spoken language, alternative forms such as sign language, or the applied graphic forms of reading and writing, communication and language are central to any classroom.

Language is an extremely complex, dynamic human response system. It interacts directly with the speaker's cognitive, perceptual, sensory, and physiological systems. One of its important functions is to serve as the basic form for the transmission of knowledge, concepts, emotional affect, and social nuances. Its primary mode of expression is oral (spoken), and the principal context is the social interaction between speaker and listener(s). The oral mode of language usage is subsumed under the concept of speech—the sensorimotor processes used to modify the stream of air leaving the lungs into phonated, resonated, articulated sound patterns.

The range of potential disorders in the sphere of communication is correspondingly wide. Typically speech and hearing professionals and educators deal with childhood disorders, disruptions of the processes during adulthood, or combinations thereof. Psychiatrists and other professionals treating psychic and interpersonal problems will be concerned with inefficient or ineffective communication patterns. The actual num-

151

ber of children with different speech and language disorders is virtually impossible to obtain because sampling procedures for incidence studies have not been standardized.

In this chapter, we will focus upon only one child, a boy called John Mervin, who manifested problems with the acquisition of the language system of our culture during his preschool years. He continues to show the effects of his linguistic problem in the form of academic difficulties with reading, spelling, and mathematics. However, the preschool years will be emphasized because they constitute the period during which the vast majority of youngsters learn to speak using the oral mode adopted over the centuries by human cultures.

A PRESCHOOLER WITH A LANGUAGE DISORDER

This section of the chapter dealing with the case history of John Mervin will be organized along two dimensions: (1) the chronological history of the boy from birth to entry into a public school program, and (2) the objectives and procedures of the clinical process. Focusing upon these two factors will help to illustrate what happens to a child and the child's family when the youngster is diagnosed as language handicapped. The intervention procedures described in the case history could be considered "traditional" in speech and language pathology wherein the focus is upon individual cases and not an entire classroom as is common in education.

The two dimensions do intertwine rather easily because there is an inherent relationship between the identification, assessment, and treatment of a problem and the youngster's developmental history. John Mervin's case history will be divided into the following stages: (1) early history and identification of the problem; (2) initial referral, evaluation, and treatment mode; (3) second referral and evaluation; (4) the first year of clinical intervention; (5) the home program: parent training; (6) the second year of clinical intervention; (7) analysis of changes in John's oral language system; and (8) the school years. Item (7) is obviously not a stage in the lad's case history. It is included in this section as a summary of his progress in language therapy and to demonstrate the type of information that can be extracted from a language sample in terms of semantics and syntax. The final stage describing the school years is only an overview in that a detailed discussion of his academic disabilities is not pertinent to the main theme of this chapter.

Early History and Identification of the Problem

John Mervin is the oldest of the three children in his family. The second child is an adopted daughter and the third child is the natural daughter of the parents. In terms of social characteristics, the parents are both college graduates; the father is in a middle-management position, and the family income allows them to live in an upper-middle class suburb with other professional and executive families.

The lad was born in September 1962, approximately three years after his parents' marriage. Mr. and Mrs. Mervin had planned to delay the birth of a child for at least two years; however, gynecological problems forced an additional time lag. John was conceived after medical intervention resolved the problems. Consequently, he started out life as a "high-risk infant" in that his mother's condition made conception and a successful pregnancy low-probability events. Shortly after his birth, Mrs. Mervin was told that she would probably never conceive another child.

During the first twelve months of his life, John showed all indications of being normal. He weighed seven pounds, six ounces at birth, grew rapidly during the first year, and met every developmental milestone for social and motor growth specified in the infant care books provided by his pediatrician. In particular, he nursed well, slept through the night by eight weeks of age, and made the transition to baby foods with ease. He enjoyed motor exploration and play, giving the appearance of being "all boy."

During the age period of twelve to eighteen months, Mr. and Mrs. Mervin experienced their first concerns about him. Unlike the children of their friends and relatives, John was not using any words and stopped vocalizing except for cries of hunger and discomfort. Due to pressure from the grandparents, they had initiated toilet training during this period of time. On the advice of their pediatrician, they terminated this attempt and relaxed about his vocal development because the doctor also counseled them that it is not unusual for infants to reduce their vocal behavior prior to the first word. Furthermore, he pointed out that males are generally slower than females in the development of speech.

At two years of age, John could pedal a small tricycle but not vocalize or talk. He responded well to his mother's directions and would use gestures or physical manipulation to communicate his needs. His motor and play skills continued to match those of his peers and the normative tables of development. Socially, he matched his cousins and, in fact, tended to be a leader during family gatherings. A significant change occurred in the family structure when he was twenty-eight months of age; his adopted sister joined him in the family changing his status from only child to older sibling.

At this point in time, his parents became concerned that he might be a deaf or hard-of-hearing child or that he was displaying a negative reaction to the adoption procedures and his new sister. A visit to the pediatrician allayed their fears. The physician assured the parents that their son was not psychologically deviant due to the adoption nor was his hearing abnormal. He suggested that John would "outgrow" his lack of speech by three years of age.

The parents were not convinced, however, that John would truly outgrow his problem. The availability of cousins and neighborhood children his own age for comparative purposes, his use of gestures, and the significant discrepancies between his social and motor skills and his use of speech led them to believe that he had a problem. Consequently, they contacted a rehabilitation center in a nearby metropolitan area to request a comprehensive evaluation of their son.

Initial Referral, Evaluation, and Treatment Mode

When he was thirty-four months of age, John and his parents were introduced to the world of clinical evaluations and diagnostic procedures. Because they requested a comprehensive evaluation, they were first required to obtain birth records, a medical history from the pediatrician, and to complete a pre-evaluation questionnaire. The questionnaire was especially overwhelming in that it asked for responses to detailed questions on John's developmental history, paternal history and family, and maternal history and family.

Upon receipt of this background information, the center scheduled an evaluation date, indicating that John would be seen by a neurologist, a psychologist, and a speech and language pathologist, while the parents were being interviewed by a social worker. Like most parents, they were apprehensive about the evaluations and concerned that they were to be interviewed by a social worker, a discipline they associated with welfare cases and marital problems. However, they realized that without the evaluation their percepts of and relationship with their son would go unchanged.

At the end of the evaluation day, Mr. and Mrs. Mervin were told that the staff would require one week to assemble their testing information into a final diagnostic statement and treatment plan for John. One week later, they met with the neurologist and speech pathologist who interpreted the testing results to them. Their son was handicapped; he had a language disability of unknown origin commonly referred to as "childhood aphasia." He would not "outgrow" the problem but, instead, would continue to manifest it for the next several years. The neurological examination was essentially negative; but, the lack of language suggested specific brain damage.

The social worker, based on her interviews with the parents, felt that their expectations were too high for their son and that they might start to treat their children differently because of John's handicaps. They faced the risk of loving their daughter more than John as a result of her more normal behavior. The speech pathologist confirmed the diagnosis of the neurologist but considered John too young for formal treatment.

The recommendations were then specified for them:

1. Place John in a nursery school setting so that he was not in the home all the time with Mrs. Mervin. The nursery school placement would provide a social relationship with other children his age to facilitate language development while permitting Mrs. Mervin to observe other youngsters so that she could get a better perspective on child development.

2. The parents needed to develop a better relationship with their son. Their middle-class standards were too high for him; they expected too much perfection. The social worker did not feel that they needed counseling but they did need to reevaluate their percepts of John.

Initially, the findings of the rehabilitation center had little impact upon them. Visits to the nursery schools and visits to bookstores to find readings on "mild brain damage" occupied their time. Two weeks later, during a family discussion about the evaluation, the problems suddenly hit them. Their son was not normal; he had a "defective" brain. They were not "normal" parents; their expectancies were too high, too perfect. They did not "love" their son like they thought they did. Two additional concerns were introduced into their thinking. Who was responsible for the brain damage—Mrs. Mervin because she was a "high risk" bearer of children or was there some unknown genetic defect in one of their families? More importantly for them, was their relationship as strong as they had always thought it to be?

John was placed in a normal nursery school shortly before his third birthday. Being only three years of age and lacking speech, he had difficulty adjusting to his peers who tended to be at least three to six months older and, of course, much more verbal. He initially cried when left at the door by his mother, played by himself, and took his mid-session nap in a corner away from the other children. To Mrs. Mervin, he appeared to be socially withdrawn and immature because he did not display the confidence and "leadership" manifested in play with his cousins and neighborhood friends. However, by the end of the second month, these negative behaviors disappeared and he was again social, assertive, and confident.

By the age of three years, John was using his first words. They were difficult to understand; but, they were consistent sound patterns used to address the members of his family, to ask for things, and to name his friends and favorite toys. Following the lead of the nursery school program, Mrs. Mervin started to read every afternoon to John and his eighteen-month-old sister. During these sessions, John demonstrated that he could recognize the characters and events in the books. At her direction, John could find similar objects in the home or use gestures to indicate that he knew the story in his favorite books. In the same month, Mrs. Mervin was informed by her physician that she had conceived another child and would have a child in the late spring.

John's initial spurt of using speech quickly reached a plateau. The nursery school placement facilitated his growth in the cognitive domain, in the social areas, and in motor skills. He continued to learn new words but they were poorly articulated and were never combined into phrases. Mr. and Mrs. Mervin began to question the advice of the pediatrician. The feelings of guilt and doubt continued to be a factor in their family interactions. In the early spring, Mrs. Mervin called the pediatrician to express these feelings and also their anger at his expectancies for John to "outgrow" the language problem. The physician recommended that they schedule an evaluation at the hearing and speech department of the university medical center in their metropolitan area. A letter of referral was prepared by the physician and the Mervins were contacted for an evaluation; however, problems with the pregnancy forced a delay in the visit because Mrs. Mervin was required to remain at home. A little before his fourth birthday (two months after his new sister was born) John received his second language evaluation.

The Second Referral and Evaluation

The pre-evaluation activities of the medical center's program were essentially the same as those of the rehabilitation center. Once again, the parents obtained birth and medical history reports including those from the rehabilitation center. A second questionnaire was completed by them covering the same issues as the one from the rehabilitation center. The only major difference that they could perceive was that a speech and language pathologist would interview them as well as test their son. Their major concern was that they would experience one more evaluation of their son without any specific form of intervention.

The first part of the evaluation was conducted by the speech clinician in order to establish the assessment questions by exploring the parents' concerns over John's communication patterns. Through the examination of the information in the pre-evaluation questionnaire completed by the parents, the referral letter, and the report of the rehabilitation center, the evaluator was able to enter into the parent interview with some knowledge of their experiences with John. The important findings from the interview were (1) the Mervins continued to permit John to communicate with gestures, (2) they had a relatively good knowledge base of his strengths and weaknesses, and (3) they were particularly interested in enrolling him in a formal language treatment program.

The evaluation of the boy's organic integrity consisted of procedures used to assess the functional level of his anatomy and physiology relevant to speech and language. One assumption made by an examiner during a language assessment is that the communication problem is a consequence of sensory, motor, or anatomical deficits. In order to validate or reject this assumption, the examiner assessed John's hearing, examined the mouth for structural deficits of the palatal and dental areas, and observed muscular activity of the oral region. The findings in this area were negative; thus, the assumption of an organic basis was partially rejected.

Total rejection of the organic causation assumption was not possible in John's case because the neurological report from the rehabilitation center classified him as brain-damaged. The diagnosis of brain damage was very difficult to reconcile with other factors in his history. John demonstrated normal development in all areas except language. He had a negative history in terms of seizures, "Strauss Syndrome" characteristics, paralysis, or other manifestations of neurological insult. The reasoning behind the diagnosis is unavoidably circular: children who are brain-damaged often have language problems; therefore, children with language problems are brain-damaged. However, the statement was made by a neurologist and, once presented to the parents, was difficult to remove from their percepts of their son.

Following the assessment of organic variables, John's phonological patterns were tested using spontaneous word production and imitation procedures. Spontaneous production testing involved the use of a picture-naming task, with each picture selected to evoke production of one consonant and/or vowel sound of the English language in specified word positions—the beginning, middle, or final portion of the word. This procedure is essentially a screening device to determine which sounds should be assessed in greater detail (Winitz 1975).

On the spontaneous task, John produced only random examples of consonant and vowel sounds. None of these productions was correct in terms of the word presented to him. Consequently, the examiner reverted to the imitation mode of testing wherein a model stimulus was presented to John and he was expected to repeat all or some of the model. Isolated sounds and words were used as the imitative stimuli. Because he was unable to imitate any of the stimuli, the examiner described the results as "evidence of a severe delay in articulation development."

Next, the examiner moved to an assessment of John's language system in terms of semantics and syntax. However, because John did not produce any intelligible words, emphasis was placed upon screening for comprehension of vocabulary, spoken utterances, and parental percepts using a formal interview procedure. The *Peabody Picture Vocabulary Test* (PPVT), a vocabulary-based intelligence screening test, was used to estimate his intellectual development. On this test, John obtained a mental age score of 4 years 1 month at the chronological age of 3 years 10 months. This result confirmed the psychological testing conducted at the rehabilitation center in the previous year. It also suggested that comprehension of vocabulary was within normal limits for his chronological age. Testing for comprehension of simple commands, objects, and object attributes (color, size, shape, and number) indicated that John was again within normal limits except for number concepts.

Because John could not produce speech, the examiner administered the *Mecham Verbal Language Development Scale* to the parents. This scale is an interview procedure modeled after the *Vineland Social Maturity Scale*. In this type of instrument, the parents' responses indicate that the skills specified in the scale are not present, are in the developmental process, or are within the child's skill repertoire. The total points accrued through the interview procedure are compared to normative tables and a "language age" is assigned to the child. John's language development was assessed at the 2 year 2 month level, a 20 month lag behind his chronological age and 25 months behind the mental age score obtained on the *PPVT.*

The assessment of John's language development provided professional confirmation of the parents' observations of his strengths and weaknesses. His overall development was marked by strengths in the social, motor, and cognitive spheres with a significant delay in language acquisition. He lacked the ability to imitate verbal stimuli, a skill considered necessary for language training by a number of specialists; but, he manifested comprehension skills within normal limits. That is, he demonstrated the presence of a language system which permitted him to discern the meaning of the utterances (semantics) of others and to act upon his interpretations of the meanings.

Although he did not imitate the verbal stimuli of the utterances correctly, he did indicate by his attempts that he again understood the task and was at a "pre-imitation" level. The gestural language reported by the parents (but not observed during the evaluation) was rudimentary evidence that he also understood that he had to express his meanings to others; he had acquired a response mode which he could use as an alternative to oral language.

Using this information acquired during the evaluation, the examiner concluded the evaluation with the following statements:

    1. John manifested only an expressive language delay marked by a severe delay in articulation and an inability to produce syntactical patterns.

    2. John should be placed in a preschool language development group wherein his normal motor and cognitive skills could be utilized within the social context of peer relationships to facilitate language acquisition.

    3. As part of the language program, Mrs. Mervin should be included in a parent education program.

    4. The parents should no longer just respond to gestural language but should initiate the procedure of stimulating the use of the correct oral language forms to express what John was demonstrating with his hands and body.

    5. The prognosis for oral language acquisition was good. That is, his strengths indicated that he had a high probability of acquiring normal expressive language with formal treatment.

The First Year of Clinical Intervention

When John was four years old, he and Mrs. Mervin entered the preschool language development program of the university medical center. The program was designed for non-retarded, non-emotionally disturbed preschool children who were classified as language delayed. The language development program had two major components: the treatment program for the children which met for two hours, three times a week, and the parent education group which met concurrently with the program for children.

The program for the children was modeled after a normal nursery school in that significant emphasis was placed upon the acquisition of developmental skills within a social context. Given the needs of the students, cognitive and linguistic variables received the greatest stress, rendering the program pre-academic and not just socialization. The general sequence of the teaching format followed the pattern of cognitive skills being taught first, imitation and comprehension being treated simultaneously, and expressive language tasks being attended to last. The format was, of course, modified for each child. Individual treatment sessions were frequently scheduled during the group time to teach specific forms or structures needed by each child.

The parent program consisted of one day of discussion with a different topic each week, one day of demonstration of procedures for interacting with the children, and one day observing the children's group. Initially, the discussion topics were set by the staff; but, by mid-term, the mothers were determining the agenda. The discussions were supplemented by demonstration video tapes produced by the staff utilizing a role-playing approach in which one member of the team would assume the role of the child, another the parent. The tapes were used to illustrate situations of reading to children, using normal household activities (such as washing the dishes) as language stimulation periods, or handling negative situations. During the second term of the group, the mothers were video-taped interacting with their children in similar situations and the staff critiqued these tapes with the mothers on an individual basis. In addition, the mothers eventually took turns working with the children's group in place of the observations.

The total composition of the group included the author of this chapter, two graduate students in speech pathology, a consultant social worker, and eight sets of mothers and boys. Because John was superior to the other children in the cognitive and motor aspects of development, he quickly assumed a leadership role in the children's group. During cognitively oriented activities, he was used as a model for the other children or as the "instructor", *i.e.,* he was asked to present tasks to the other children or to demonstrate to another child the procedures for the task. Unlike his nursery school placement where his language problem gave him lower status relative to the others, he was clearly the superior youngster in the language group. His strengths also permitted the staff to attend to his expressive language needs very early in the program rather than the emphasis on cognition and comprehension required by the other children.

By the fourth week of the group, John was consistently imitating single-word stimuli presented to him by the staff. Essentially, the use of edible and social reinforcers shaped the "pre-imitation" skills noted during the evaluation and increased his imitation skills to a 100 percent level. His imitative productions were marked by misarticulations but he did demonstrate that this instructional skill was now a part of his learning repertoire.

At the end of the first term, John was imitating the names of subjects (nouns), their attributes (adjectives), and events (verbs). He also started to use the phrase "this is mine" whenever he worked with another child. Interestingly, this phrase was articulated correctly in contrast to the misarticulations in his imitative responses and his few attempts at spontaneous word productions.

During the parent group sessions, Mrs. Mervin freely expressed both parents' concerns about John, their reactions to being told that he was handicapped, and their problems with him. More than any other mother in the group, she represented both parents, particularly their feelings about being treated differently just because their son was labeled language-handicapped. That is, without that event in his history, the likelihood that a professional would have questioned their standards, their family structure, or their love for their son was extremely low. She taught the professionals working with the group that the entire family was "labelled," not just the child.

Within the context of group dynamics, she was the informal leader of the discussions. Mrs. Mervin could be described as a quiet, reserved, almost shy, person in that she spoke only when she had something significant to say or whenever she felt that something was better said by a mother than by a professional. She had particularly negative reactions to discussions that focused upon comparisons of the language-delayed child to the normal child because she felt that they knew their son was different and they needed help in changing him, not additional confirmation of the differences.

The second session of the group therapy (January to May) was a period of significant improvement for John in terms of language development. He expanded his vocabulary to include nouns, verbs, adjectives, adverbs, and prepositions. These words, however, were combined into two- to three-word utterances with inconsistency in terms of word order. For example, "boy play" was just as probable as "play boy" in the same context, making it difficult for the staff to determine the semantic intent of his productions. He could imitate five- to six-word phrases and sentences with relatively clear articulation. However, his articulation skills continued to affect the intelligibility of his spontaneous productions.

Socially, two variables appeared to affect his interactions with other people. John started to show signs of becoming frustrated with the other members of the group. The staff postulated that he now realized the discrepancies between his motor and play skills as compared to those of his peers and no longer received any gratification from being the leader. Consequently, he started to manifest isolated play behaviors and withdrew from group interactions.

More importantly, the use of syntactic structures contained positive and negative features for him. While he was enthusiastically rewarded with edibles and social praise for the use of his phrase utterances, a natural "punisher" was present at the same time in that the staff and others had a difficult time understanding him. Given his misarticulations, a natural delay occurred while others attempted to "decode" his utterances. Once this was accomplished, they had to unravel the ambiguities in his phrases in order to respond appropriately. In the example used earlier, combining *play* and *boy* in either order could mean that (1) he was describing himself, (2) he was describing someone else, or (3) he wished to play alone or with someone else. Quite often, the listeners would respond as if one of the three interpretations were correct, only to find that another option was intended at that time. After several attempts to communicate orally, John would revert to his gestural language to insure that his listener received the message.

His solitary play allowed the staff the opportunity to structure the environment to the degree that they could discern the meanings of his statements with greater probability. By the end of the term, he was actually receiving individual therapy in a group treatment room. During snack times, reading periods, and routine activities (*e.g.,* taking attendance), John would rejoin the group but would interact only when necessary. He was not "socially withdrawn" or "negative"; he simply recognized the discrepancy between himself and the other boys and dealt with it as well as he could.

The Home Program: Parent Training

Given this set of conditions and the skills which Mrs. Mervin had demonstrated in the parent education program, a decision was made in June, 1967, to shift the treatment emphasis from the clinical setting to the home environment. The mother would become the principal agent of change for John using naturally occurring family activities as the bases of language modification procedures. The intent of the program was not to make the mother into a therapist but to teach her ways of facilitating language acquisition through modeling, expansion, and imitation. Furthermore, the home program would provide John with a break from the schedule of nursery schools and clinics.

At the same time, another decision was made that had an adverse effect upon the parents and the boy. Based upon his level of language acquisition, the local school system rejected John for kindergarten placement. Despite the evidence of John's cognitive, motor, and social normalcy, the school system ruled (1) that his language problems were an effective barrier to full participation in the school program, and (2) that they could not offer language therapy because their clinicians already had too many children to serve. The second reason resulted from the fact that the state department of education did not reimburse the district for services to any child below six years of age. The parents finally accepted the decision, rationalizing that an additional year of maturity would be good for John.

The home program contained the following components:

1. A data-collection procedure was established wherein Mrs. Mervin would record all of John's responses ten minutes each morning and ten minutes each evening. Natural parent-child interactions such as mealtimes and bed times were selected for the recording periods.

2. Mrs. Mervin met with the author once a week for two hours to review the data records and to receive suggestions for facilitating language in a number of different settings.

3. Mrs. Mervin continued the reading time each day, particularly to enhance communication between John and the older of his two sisters.

4. Each parent selected periods of the day (or week) when they would relate with John either around a task or in play to utilize the suggestions given to them.

The strategies presented to the mother (to be used by both parents) were based upon the literature on child development prevalent at that point in time and upon a knowledge of the family situation. (That is, academia mitigated by common sense!) Knowing that the parents were already accustomed to verbalizing his gestural language for him, the logical advice was to have them modify this procedure to the next level, expanding his utterances for him. The target behavior was growth in the use of syntactic structures because he had already demonstrated an adequate cognitive system in other settings and testing situations.

The specific procedure for expansion suggested to the parents varied according to the type of utterance produced by John and the context. Thus, the daily records kept by the mother were an invaluable source of information. From a research perspective, the daily records would be of questionable value because there was no direct evidence of the mother's reliability as an observer-recorder. However, because the mother had received some training in this task during the parent groups, and because the records showed internal consistency from session to session, they were deemed to be more than acceptable for the purposes of the home program. The records did not reflect the articulation problem in that the mother was instructed to "correct" them when she wrote out his utterances.

Table 6.1 reflects the mean number of occurrence of utterances of varying length during the home program. The records were divided into six five-day segments to simplify the data. As can be noted in the table, John's use of the two-word utterance length was relatively stable with a slight increase in the number of occurrences between segment 1 and segment 6. The most significant growth was in the occurrence of utterances of three words or longer. The table does not reflect use of single word utterances because they were of little value as a sign of growth except in terms of their lexical category.

The information in Table 6.1 actually serves two functions. First, it can be construed to represent the mother's percepts of the growth of John's language during the home program period. Secondly, the early recording sessions are an indicator of the changes in his oral language from September (when he first entered the language group using only a few words) to June. His rapid growth in less than one year is best attributed to the fact that he entered the group with relatively good language comprehension skills and the group served as a catalyst for the use of expressive language. Similar growth would probably be unlikely in a child who lacked comprehension as well as production of language.

Quantitative measures such as those reported in Table 6.1 are not as illuminating as descriptors of qualitative aspects of language, *i.e.,* the use of language rules, lexical categories, and semantic intent. The home program was based upon these qualitative aspects because they constitute the form and substance of the interaction between a speaker and listener. Table 6.2 lists a selected sample of utterances produced by John during the first recording day. These samples reflect the type of information used as the basis for the weekly clinician-mother sessions. The possible purposes of each response (*i.e.,* linguistic) type were discussed with the mother and the suggestions for parental intervention were then made.

The suggestions provided to the parents were grouped according to three questions:

1. What influence does the context in which the utterance was produced affect their understanding or response?

2. Can they logically respond to his utterances without first giving

TABLE 6.1

Mean Number of Occurrence of Various Utterance Lengths per Five-Day Segments during Daily Recording Periods

Segments*	Number of Utterances				
	Two Words	Three Words	Four Words	Five Words	Six or more words
1 (10)	2.30	4.90	4.6	2.60	2.50
2 (9)	2.67	6.88	4.33	1.67	1.11
3 (9)	2.67	7.11	5.78	2.00	1.22
4 (7)	2.29	5.71	4.29	3.57	4.14
5 (7)	2.75	8.00	6.57	4.29	2.71
6 (7)	3.14	5.00	7.71	4.29	6.00

*Numbers in parentheses represent the number of recording sessions per segment

TABLE 6.2

Examples of Utterances and Linguistic Types Produced by John during First Recording Session

Utterance	Linguistic Type
1. To match	Infinitive phrase
2. You keep	Simple declarative
3. In here too	Prepositional phrase
4. Right back up	Locative, particle construction
5. Go downstairs get	Possible Imperative or Progressive Possible Infinitive (get)
6. Hurt my hand	Simple declarative; possession
7. Wake ring bell	Possible declarative, possible cause-effect
8. Ask Tim's come	Possible conditional (if Tim), possible progressive form (is coming), Imperative
9. Where put that?	Wh- question form
10. Where is the little girl?	Wh- question form

John an alternative form of the response as a model to insure that they understood the utterance?

3. Should the response need modification, what is the appropriate form of the modification?

There were certain responses which were extremely difficult to interpret and were only discussed in the broad context of the three questions but could not serve as a base for specific guidance. Sample utterance 1 ("to match") in Table 6.2 was such a response. The setting for that response was housecleaning. However, neither the mother's memory nor the set of utterances provided a clue as to its meaning. In such circumstances, the parents were counseled to probe with additional questions.

Utterance 2 was much more fruitful in terms of serving as a basis for suggestions. On the surface, it appears to indicate a declarative form of sentence ("You keep"). An interrogative form was initially ruled out because the mother placed a question mark after every such utterance in the transcripts. However, in the context of housecleaning, the response could have been a yes/no interrogative following the pattern of "You keep it in here, don't you?" Thus, the first topic of discussion was the role of intonation in deciphering John's response. The alternative interpretation offered by the mother was that he was telling her to keep a toy and not to throw it out. In this case, the sentence form was basically an imperative.

Item 7 ("Wake ring bell") provided an interesting situation relative to the confusion between the utterance form and his misarticulations. Accepting it in its present form, the utterance suggested that he was referring to an alarm clock. If, however, the mother did understand as a [k] what should have been a [t], the more likely form was "wait ring bell." In light of the fact that the mother was subsequently engaged in a telephone conversation, the latter interpretation seemed more likely.

Using the new form as a basis of discussion, the utterance suggested the following pieces of information:

1. He was again using the imperative form "wait." He appeared to be capable of using the imperative with (utterance 2) and without the personal pronoun "you" (utterance 7).

2. "Wait" may have indicated overgeneralization of the term from its basic notion of temporarily ceasing activity or delaying activity to a later point in time to the notion of complete cessation, *i.e.,* "stop" ("wait ring bell" = "stop, the phone is ringing").

3. "Ring bell" indicated difficulty with the basic concepts of the two words. "Bell" became a substitute for telephone and ring was used in place of the more appropriate predicate form of "is ringing." Obviously, the utterance also illustrated his difficulties with word order described earlier.

During the sessions, the analysis and interpretation of the utterances was conducted in an open discussion and not in a tutorial fashion. That is, the mother was free to provide interpretations different from those of the clinician or even the one she followed at the time the utterance was produced. In this way, Mrs. Mervin soon learned that the response of the parents could be better determined by them as they learned to use different techniques, resulting in less dependence on the clinician.

In terms of their responses, the parents soon learned the following techniques:

1. They learned to provide a response by modeling an utterance form when they realized that John was having difficulty producing an utterance.

2. They learned to model when the response was inappropriate because of word order, word choice, or some other factor.

3. They learned to expand his responses in a natural fashion. For example, for utterance 2, a logical response for the mother could have been, "Yes, I'll keep your toys."

4. They learned to probe for more information by asking questions of him. Possible responses to "Wake ring bell" could have been "Is this an alarm clock?" or "Do you want me to set the alarm on your clock?" To the form, "Wait ring bell", the simple question "Is the telephone ringing?" would have sufficed.

By the third week of the summer program, his mother was encouraged to require John to repeat the correct utterance forms after the parents. This decision was precipitated by two factors: (1) it provided a quick check on the accuracy of their understanding in that he was not likely to repeat a form that was not consistent with his meaning, and (2) it enabled them to take advantage of his imitative skills. For the last three weeks, his mother also recorded the number of repetitions and self-corrections (a new phenomenon for John) during the ten-minute sessions.

After five weeks, the home program was terminated for summer vacation. His parents were using the teaching strategies on a consistent basis in a variety of situations; and more importantly, the family needed a break from the routine of language services and meeting with professionals.

The Second Year of Treatment

Prior to the second year of therapy, John's articulation (phonological) skills were assessed using a spontaneous test (Hejna 1958) and imitative procedures (Sound Production Tasks, Elbert, Shelton, and Ardnt 1967; Shelton, Elbert, and Ardnt 1967). The former test samples the child's ability to produce consonant sounds correctly in a word initial, word medial, and word final position in response to a picture stimulus. The Sound Production Tasks (SPT) are more complex in design in that the subject is asked to imitate the test sound correctly in isolation, in nonsense syllables, word combinations, and sentences. The critical feature of the test is adapted from the McDonald Deep-Test of Articulation (1964) in that the test sound (*e.g., k*) is assessed in the context of other sounds (*e.g.,* vowel -*k-s* as in bo*ok*sale). Imitative testing is quicker than spontaneous testing and is considered by some authors (Turton 1973; Winitz 1975) to be a good indicator of the child's articulation skills.

The analysis of the spontaneous testing indicated that John had difficulty with every consonant sound except *h, t,* and *v.* Furthermore, the *t* sound or its voiced counterpart *d* served as the substitute for virtually every other sound, except where the consonant was omitted or produced correctly. Using a phonetic feature analysis (Turton 1973) wherein the tester is able to determine the phoneme that appears to be the focal point of the child's misarticulations, the phoneme *k* was selected as the initial sound to receive treatment.

In John's speech, the *t* was substituted for the *k* in the word initial position only. He was able to produce the *k* in isolation and in word final positions. He also used the *t* as a substitute for five other sounds. The voiced counterpart of *t,* the *d* phoneme, was used as the substitute for the voiced counterparts of the sounds for which the *t* acted as a substitute. The rationale for selecting the *k* was that modification of this substitution pattern would be relatively easy and the change could be used as a model for changes in other substitution patterns.

In terms of his language system, pronominalization (the use of pronouns) and noun modifiers (articles and adjectives) were selected as the therapy targets. The choice of these forms was dictated by two factors:

1. John's local school system used the pronoun substitution problem of *me* for *I* as one indicator of his rejection from kindergarten.

2. John's overall cognitive performance was not reflected in his language. The rationale was that correct use of pronouns and modifiers would not only make him sound better but that he could then use additional sentence types to express more semantic categories.

The individual therapy given to John was supplemented by a three-month placement in the preschool program in the local art museum and an additional six months of nursery school placement. The supplemental placements interacted with a new aspect of the home program to create an additional problem for him. Mr. and Mrs. Mervin were attempting to teach him to correct himself whenever he used an inappropriate pronoun (or omitted it). This pressure, in addition to his realization that he was older than the other preschool students, fostered a negative attitude on his part. He started to refuse to correct himself and refused to go to the preschool program.

For a period of time, the parents ceased their efforts to teach him self-correction. A psychological evaluation of his intellectual functioning and school readiness was conducted in November of 1967. The results and summary statement of the psychologist clearly indicated that he was ready for school. This evidence was sent to the local districts with a request for written confirmation that he would be accepted for kindergarten in September 1968. After this document was received, it was read to John followed by a discussion of the importance of his "talking." Once he had received assurance that he would go to a "real" school, his rebellious behavior disappeared and self-correction again became a part of his repertoire.

By the end of the first semester of individual work, John was using *I* and *you* correctly, the *k* sound, a wider variety of sentence forms, and he corrected himself when cued by an adult. During the second semester, he-she, has-have, and the *g, f, s, l,* and *r* sounds were incorporated into his treatment program. The final summary of his language therapy at the medical center was stated as follows:

> By the end of the semester, John was using the *k, g, l, a, have,* and *you* consistently. The *f* and initial *s* were also being used by him the majority of time. Although John could use the *r, l, she* and *he* most consistently during therapy, there was relatively no carryover outside the clinic or at home.

At this point, John was released from all forms of treatment and programs for the summer. Prior to this termination, he started to manifest mild disfluencies in his speech. The clinicians and the parents interpreted this as a sign that he had had enough in terms of assistance, modification, and special attention. By mid-June these disfluencies disappeared.

Thus, his contact with the clinical program of the medical center ended. In twenty-two months, he had gone from a nonverbal child to a youngster who could use sentences up to twelve words in length, could ask questions of his environment, and could verbally, not gesturally, communicate with that environment. His parents had acquired a number of strategies to assist him and he had learned the important strategy of correcting himself.

Analysis of Changes in John's Oral Language System*

The analysis of John's language growth will be restricted to semantics and syntax, the focal point of his clinical treatment. Although articulation therapy was provided to him in the second year of treatment, it did not receive major emphasis until he went to school. The data base for this analysis was the records of language utterances maintained by the mother during the home program and through the Thanksgiving break of the second year of treatment.

As noted earlier, John produced his first true words at thirty-nine months of age and his first phrases approximately one year later after having joined the language group. In general, his oral language could be described as being two years delayed relative to the norms for first words and phrases. However, statements such as this are inadequate when assessing the level of language functioning of a child or designing a treatment program. This analysis will indicate to the reader how John changed over the period of December 1965 to November 1967 in terms of certain measures of language development and relative to selected indices of natural language acquisition.

A total of 41 recording sessions were conducted by the mother yielding a total of 1,192 utterances for an average of 29.07 utterances per session. Although the original intent was to have the recording sessions last only ten minutes, in actuality, they varied in length of time. The situations varied from housecleaning, riding in the family car, mealtimes, play periods, and family conversations. The mother's persistence in maintaining these records is but one sign of her interest in John's progress.

The first measure of language change, selected Developmental Sentence Scores, is presented in Table 6.4 (only days in which more than 46 responses were recorded are included). The Developmental Sentence Scoring (DSS) system was devised by Laura Lee (1974) as a method of weighting a child's responses by the variables of developmental order, sentence comprehensiveness, and morpheme usage. It is based on 50 responses collected and analyzed according to rules established by Lee. The data in Table 6.3 do not conform to all of Lee's procedures in that the mother was probably affected by a number of stimuli during the recording periods. However, the summary in Table 6.3 basically substantiate the growth in terms of sentence length noted in Table 6.1 and suggest that his productions improved in complexity, *i.e.,* sentence transformations and morphemic forms.

*The author wishes to express appreciation to Stuart Schaefer and Shelley Traeger for their assistance with the language analysis reported herein.

TABLE 6.3

Summary of Selected Developmental Sentence Scores Derived from Language Samples Maintained by John's Mother

Date	Situation	Developmental Sentence Scores
June 16	Riding in the car	1.58
June 24	Reading a newspaper	1.87
June 28	Lunch time	3.02
July 1	Playing outside	1.73
July 3	Dinner time	2.14
July 4	Shooting fireworks	3.31
July 6	Painting	3.78
July 7	Dinner time	4.78
October 26	Conversation	5.48
October 30	Playing in the house	5.13
November 1	Playing in the house	5.79
November 7	Conversation	4.36
November 16	Conversation	7.57

TABLE 6.4

Comparison of John's Use of 14 Grammatical Morphemes to the Normal Developmental Sequence

Morpheme	Order of Acquisition*	Frequency of Usage	Rank Order† in John's Language
Present progressive	1	5	13.5
On	2.5	31	5
In	2.5	58	3
Plural	4	84	2
Past irregular	5	33	4
Possessive	6	158	1
Uncontractible copula	7	14	10
Articles	8	23	7
Past regular	9	5	13.5
Third-person singular regular	10	20	8
Third-person singular irregular	11	9	12
Uncontractible auxiliary	12	26	6
Contractible copula	13	10	11
Contractible auxiliary	14	19	9

*Taken from Dale (1976) according to Brown (1973).
†Rank order based on language records maintained in June and July 1967.

The development of morphemes is one indicator of language growth. Morphemes reflect changes in semantic usage, type of transformations, and the expansion of lexical categories. Dale (1976) has derived a table of the acquisition of 14 morphemes from the work of Brown (1973). Table 6.4 provides a display of the usage of these 14 morphemes in the early language samples taken by John's mother during the home program. The analysis was restricted to these samples because they represented the first set of data available on John's language. The table does not reflect his actual sequence of development for these morphemes but his usage of them approximately six months after the appearance of his first words.

Several interesting pieces of information can be gleaned from a comparison of Tables 6.2, 6.3, and 6.4. The first two tables provide support to the concept that John's use of sentences improved in terms of length and complexity. Because the rankings in Table 6.4 were derived only from phrases and utterances, they would further amplify the findings relative to his growth (or lack of it) in sentence forms. For example, the rankings indicate that four of his five most frequently used forms are not directly related to sentence types. Possession, plurality, and use of prepositions do not require significant changes in sentence form to be used. At the same time, the six lowest frequencies all involve verb forms that directly affect sentence patterns and forms. The use of auxiliary form is particularly important and has been used by a number of researchers studying handicapped populations.

The data from Table 6.4 would appear to reflect an increase in sentence length without an appreciable growth in sentence complexity. He simply became better at using the forms that were firmly established. There is another perspective, however, that must be used when evaluating the data. John did not learn to use language in his natural environment. He acquired it in the context of a treatment program wherein the stimuli were controlled by adults. The model of therapy followed the pivot–open phrase construction popular in syntax research in the mid-1960s.

From a positive aspect, Table 6.4 illustrates that John was certainly approximating the developmental sequence suggested by Brown's work (1973). During the six-month interval, John managed to acquire the morphemes used early and frequently by children acquiring language in a natural environment. His progress certainly tends to support the contention of Ingram (1974) and others that language handicapped children maintain the general sequence of natural language learning.

In terms of syntactic patterns, John's language contained the following forms by November 1967:

1. Noun phrases used as subjects and objects of sentences and objects of prepositional phrases.

2. Predicate phrases incorporating auxiliary plus main verb (but only infrequently, the progressive form), predicate plus infinitive complement ("I want to go there"), and modal forms *do, will.*

3. Sentence types of declarative, imperative, yes/no questions, wh-questions, negative, passive, and conjoined forms.

4. Transformations required for the sentence types, pronominization (use of pronouns), variations of the verbs, and phrase deletions.

5. Attribute modifiers for nouns (color, size, shape, number) and adverb modifiers of time and place.

These changes represent only the major highlights of the changes in speech skills. Essentially, they indicated again that John was capable of transmitting his cognitive-perceptual knowledge of the world into culturally-accepted language utterances.

The final area of change to be discussed is semantics. The morphemic and syntactic changes represented the growth in the acquisition of elements of language and his ability to structure them in a meaningful way. As with the morphemic analysis, only the records during the home program are used because they represent the earliest data on John's language growth.

An inspection of the home records indicated that John's early use of language was predominated by four of the seven cases postulated by Fillmore (1968): the agentive, the dative, the locative, and the objective. That is, his language suggested that he could communicate who was responsible for a course of action (agentive), who was affected or possessed something as suggested by the verb of the sentence (dative), where something occurred (locative), and who (or what) was acted upon by the action represented in the verb (objective). He initially had more problems with the instrumental, experiencer, and factitive forms of cases.

Translated into the sentence patterns and semantic relations, his language during the home program was dominated by verb plus object, subject-verb-object, verb-locative, subject-verb, and subject-verb-locative forms. The lowest occurring forms were rejection, denial, demonstrative plus predicate and notice forms. However, as with the morphemic usage presented in Table 6.4, John demonstrated the use of all of the forms of case grammar and semantic-syntactic relationships described by the research in language acquisition surveyed for this analysis. He varied the frequency of usage for these forms and did not necessarily demonstrate that he followed the developmental sequence they found in normal children.

His growth in grammatical and semantic forms, in morphemes, in sentence length, and complexity did support two of the original conclusions of people who evaluated him. First, his cognitive performance indicated that he had a sufficient grasp of his environment to serve as a basis for oral language acquisition. Secondly, his deficiencies were principally in the expressive component of language and treatment should have been effective in producing a change in this aspect of language. The fact that his language growth deviated from the normal sequence cannot be fully explained except, as suggested, that therapy was not properly scheduled according to the normal developmental sequence. A second possibility is that the difference in growth pattern is but one more reflection of the basis of his language disorder. The critical issue is that he did learn to talk, to use oral language.

The School Years

The kindergarten year was relatively uneventful for John. Given the nature of most kindergarten programs, it was an extension of his experiences in the nursery school, the language development group, and the art museum program. He received language and articulation therapy from the school's speech clinician and, by the end of the year, was functioning within normal limits on language tests but continued to experience articulation problems. A residue of his language problem was evident whenever he attempted to verbalize fine nuances of tense, modification, or an event. For example, statements involving "before-after" or "past . . . present" relationships continued to be troublesome for him.

The first semester of the first grade exposed him to the beginnings of reading, writing, and spelling in the form of pre-academic exercises. Because many of these tasks were not dissimilar to those he experienced during language and articulation therapy, he was able to maintain a performance record equal to or above his classmates. However, the second half of the year was disastrous for him. He was now expected to read aloud, to write words from verbal directions rather than copy, and to do simple computations. The last task was easily modified for him by the addition of dots or slashes above each term in the addition equations which enabled him to use rational counting to determine the answer to each problem. However, during a testing situation, where these aids were not available, and during simple subtraction tasks introduced at the end of the year, he was unable to perform. His only success during the year was in articulation where he attained normal performance levels and his speech services were terminated.

At the beginning of second grade, John was tested by the school psychologist to determine the nature of his academic problems. His success in language growth were reflected in his normal performance scores on the auditory subtests of the *Illinois Test of Psycholinguistic Abilities* (ITPA) and auditory discrimination testing. The visual subtests scores on the ITPA were, overall, slightly below age level but still within normal limits. On the *Wechsler Intelligence Scale for Children* he obtained an IQ of 107, placing him in his normal range for his age level. Thus, the testing did not indicate any specific reasons for his academic problems. The parents were told that he had a learning disability which was probably another manifestation of his developmental language problems. A tutor was assigned to John as a supplement to the classroom instruction offered by the teacher.

For the next two years, John received the tutoring/classroom instruction arrangement for reading, writing, and arithmetic. At the end of that period of time, a decision was made by the school staff that his writing skills *per se* were acceptable but that he would need continued assistance in reading, mathematics, and spelling. When John entered the fourth grade, the school initiated the resource room concept wherein John and other youngsters with similar problems formed a small class for the special programs but continued with their age peers for all other educational programs. According to Mrs. Mervin, John never experienced any social punishment from his peers because of this arrangement and, therefore, adapted quickly to it.

John is now, at age 13, in the seventh grade but continues in a combination resource room/regular classroom program. His grade average is in the C+ range with grades in reading-based subjects depressing his overall average. Achievement tests administered at the beginning of the seventh grade placed him at the fifth grade level for reading and fourth grade, seventh month in mathematics. Despite these problems, science is one of his favorite subjects and he consistently is in the B range for assignments and tests.

Since the age of 12, he has had a newspaper route and has a number of regular lawn-mowing and snow-shoveling customers. He does not participate in any team sports but prefers playing with his friends in the neighborhood on an informal basis. Mrs. Mervin reports that he is socially mature and is handling the early puberty and adolescence years without problems.

As a final family note, the academic problems are not restricted to John. Both of his sisters are also in a resource room/classroom combination for problems in reading, spelling, and mathematics. Obviously, this has been a disappointment for the parents. However, John's success over the years has made them conscious of the fact that progress is slow and that academic problems need not hinder the social development of their children. Furthermore, because one girl is adopted and the other is their natural child, they have learned to forget their concerns over "genetic faults" or other elusive causes. The inherent strength of the family relationships has served them well over the years.

SUMMARY

This chapter was designed to provide a case history of a youngster who experienced language learning problems during childhood and the impact of this condition on him and his family. In many respects, his history is not typical of all preschool children who are categorized as language delayed (or disordered). This is because he manifested primarily an expressive language problem, tested within the normal range on intelligence tests, and, above all else, was supported by a strong family led by two interested, warm parents.

His history was used because of these strengths and because his pattern of language growth illustrated important points regarding the use of natural language acquisition information and clinical processes. The academic problems he has manifested over the years are not unique to him. Other youngsters who manifest problems in acquiring spoken language evidence difficulties in learning to use the applied forms of reading, writing, spelling, and mathematics. John was fortunate in that he was in a school district which recognized his problems early and offered the necessary services. And again, the family support was critical to his success by providing encouragement, support, and a viable learning environment.

GERALDINE T. SCHOLL

Geraldine Scholl has professional experience in the vision field at many levels. In addition to advanced degrees she is a certified teacher of visually handicapped and emotionally disturbed and has taught in public and institutional settings, and has served as Chairman of the Special Education Program at the University of Michigan where she is now Professor. She has trained teachers and advanced students and has also been on the staff of the Bureau of Education for the Handicapped in Washington, D.C. Her publications include both research and material for teachers.

But there is a second special reason for the quiet depth of this chapter: it is her investment in persons of all ages with vision problems. One of her former students volunteered to "do his own case." What better way to understand the human side of this handicap than from firsthand experience? The frank and lucid observations of Rubin himself are in sharp contrast to the cant and jargon so prevalent in special education. He says it—but as he *knows* it. Dr. Scholl has known him over an extended period of time, and she parallels his account with her own observations, the human approach which is the theme of this book. Rubin lets the reader recognize the self-concept problems which develop and is most helpful in sympathetically indicating what family means to a handicapped individual. As Dr. Scholl says, Rubin's stamina and drive are unusual. Also there have been changes in the programs for the blind since Rubin's time, as the author indicates.

7

Vision Problems

GERALDINE T. SCHOLL

Visual impairments are a common human experience. Most are mild to moderate impairments and can be remediated through medication, surgery, or corrective lenses. About 1 in 500 pupils have visual impairments that require corrective lenses. These pupils usually manage in the regular school program with such modifications as sitting near the front of the classroom and with reminders about wearing their glasses.

Severe visual impairments, that is, those which interfere with normal functioning and performance in activities of daily living, are found in about 1.7 million persons, roughly 0.8 percent of the population; approximately 65 percent are 65 years of age or older. Slightly over 450,000 have little or no usable vision and are frequently labeled *blind*. Children with severe vision problems constitute one of the low-incidence groups in special education. Of the 3.7 million handicapped school age children who received special education services during 1976–77 only about 1 percent was visually impaired.

This chapter focuses on the significance of a severe visual impairment in the life, education, and subsequent functioning of one individual.

INTRODUCING RUBIN WALKER

The person selected as the case for this chapter was known to the author when he was in school. Rubin wrote much of the material included in this chapter and presents a handicapped adult's reflection on his past experiences in school, family, peer, and community relationships. He is a real person who speaks for and of himself:

179

I was born in a medium-sized midwestern city on October 6, 1934. I was the fourth child. At the time I was born, my father was 48 and my mother was 45 years of age. My siblings included a brother who was 23, a sister who was 21, and a sister who was 16 at the time of my birth. Of my siblings, all completed high school and my brother attended college for one year. My father died in 1963 of a coronary. At the time of his death he was retired. My mother died in 1967 of nephritis. She had been a housewife during all the years of her marriage. All of my siblings are still living. I live at the present time with my unmarried brother in the family home; both my sisters are married with grown children. One resides in the same state and has three children; the other lives in another section of the country with her two children.

Rubin may be considered atypical in that he was born into a family of adults. Children who have siblings as old as Rubin's are often overprotected and are exposed to multiple parental figures. During his early life Rubin's nieces and nephews were his siblings. He describes some early memories:

I was very close to my mother, in fact she was really one of the people who inspired me the most into doing what I have done. My dad was great also, but he reacted in a different way. If I wanted to try new things, or do things on my own, he'd say, "Why?" My mother would say, "Well, I can't be his playmate, teacher, and body guard all the time. He's got to have an education and learn to do things and go places by himself." Fortunately, my mother always won out!

When I was six years old my youngest sister married and moved away from home. My other sister had moved away from home before I was born. In fact I didn't really realize that she was my sister for a long while, as a little child. I thought she just came to visit on week-ends. She always got a kick out of that in later years, when I told her. She worked in a department store and my brother-in-law worked in industry. Then he bought a business of his own and they moved out of state. My brother always lived at home. He worked with my father in the family business. I remember my brother mostly from his cars. He used to take me for rides in his black 1937 Plymouth. I could always tell when he was coming home from the sound of the motor. I can still tell what different models of cars sound like by their motors.

Thus, Rubin introduces himself and his family. The remainder of the chapter will summarize his life experiences as a person with a severe vision problem. Ways in which he is similar to and different from others with vision problems will be discussed.

TERMINOLOGY

Historically, children with visual problems were labeled *blind* if their best corrected vision in the better eye was 20/200 or less, that is, able to see at 20 feet what the normal person can see at 200 feet; or if the widest angle of their visual field was no greater than 20 degrees, even though visual acuity in that narrow field may be better than 20/200. This is the legal definition of blindness and is relevant for the delivery of services within the social system but is of little practical use to the educator. Only about one-third of the children classified as legally blind have no vision.

The wide variation in how well visually handicapped children use their vision has caused educators to rely on observation and experience rather than on measured visual acuity in determining whether visual or tactile methods and materials will be employed. In order to describe more accurately the educational implications of a severe visual impairment the following terms are used: *blind:* those who must learn through sensory modalities other than vision; *low vision:* those who can see when objects or materials are held close to their eyes and who may or may not need to use tactual materials in the educational process; and *visually limited:* those who have some limitations in visual functioning but who will ordinarily learn through the visual mode. These three groups will be referred to as *visually handicapped* in this chapter.

VARIABLES RELATED TO A VISUAL IMPAIRMENT

Among the total population of the visually handicapped those born with defective vision account for approximately 10 percent; however, among the school age population, more than three-fourths are born with defective vision or acquire it soon after birth. Congenital defects, that is, those present at birth, are not necessarily hereditary and may result from prenatal factors, such as rubella and other infectious illnesses during pregnancy, trauma to the fetus, and inadequate diet in the mother.

Rubin has congenital cataracts but the condition was not discovered until he was about six months of age. His early memories are related to his eye condition. He writes:

> When I was a small child, one of my most vivid memories was when my parents and brother took me to the hospital. I can remember being carried from the house to the car and then from the car to the hospital. The car was a

1934 Plymouth. I also remember fighting the doctors as they were trying to give me ether. There was a nurse in attendance who was referred to as Aunt Maude. She was very understanding and tried to explain things to me. I was about 3 years old at that time. My mother told me later that I had two operations before this, but I don't remember anything about them.

Congenital cataracts are usually surgically removed in early childhood as Rubin describes, and the person is fitted with corrective lenses. These usually will not be of sufficient strength to give normal vision, however; Rubin's best corrected vision is 20/200 in both eyes which classifies him as legally blind. Some indication of the degree of vision he had as a child may be deduced from the following:

When I was three years old, I can remember being driven out the main street and noticing some orange lights. I called them moons because the shape reminded me of what I thought the moon looks like.

In the school-age population, retrolental fibroplasia is still the leading cause of blindness, although it decreased dramatically when the administration of oxygen to premature infants was more rigidly controlled during the late 1950s. Cataracts, optic nerve atrophy, and albinism are the next most numerous eye affections causing blindness.

In the school-age population, there are more males than females with visual impairments; however, in the total population, there are more females, due in part to the longer life expectancy for females.

EDUCATION

Early Childhood

The birth of a visually handicapped infant into a family can be a traumatic experience. Frequently parents have had no prior experience with the blind or blindness. Even where adequate resources are available within the community, medical personnel who first identify the child often do not make referrals. One of the most challenging problems and area of greatest need is an effective identification and referral system for the preschool age population. Any child-find program must involve medical personnel in order to reach parents when they first learn their child has a visual impairment (Faye 1970).

At the appropriate age, regular nursery school experiences can stimulate social, emotional and educational development. The preschool years are the ideal time for handicapped children to attend programs with normal children since emphasis on the acquisition of academic-type skills is at a minimum and most activities can easily include visually handicapped children.

In general, the physical growth and development of children with visual impairments proceeds in the normal sequence but sometimes at a slower rate. For example, physical coordination may be retarded because the absence of vision reduces opportunities to learn through imitation.

A visual impairment does have an impact on cognitive development. The anecdote where Rubin described how he thought the street lights were moons illustrates one of the problems. The sense of touch is the blind child's only access to the world of objects. Limited vision provides imperfect visual access to objects. Objects which are too small or too large cannot be perceived accurately by touch. Thus the child must often rely on descriptions for information. Someone in Rubin's family talked to him about the moon; he interpreted and related the description to his own experience, namely, the street lights. To facilitate cognitive development parents and teachers must provide many concrete experiences. Verbal description to substitute for the real experience with an object tends to promote verbalism, the excessive use of words without supporting comprehension. The use of vision, no matter how limited, and of other sources of sensory input should be developed. For example, activities such as Rubin's identification of different models of cars by the sounds of their motors improve auditory discrimination. The visually handicapped child needs help in attaching meaning to the object world and whatever is done during the early years to maximize visual functioning and the use of other senses will lay a good foundation for later school learning.

The visual impairment itself does not directly affect either social or emotional growth and development. Environmental factors are much more significant. The attitudes and adjustment of the parents to the child with a disability are critical. In this regard Rubin observes about his parents:

> My mother, I feel, was not overprotective, but more supportive; that is, if I wanted to do something, she'd say, "Well, go ahead, if you think you can

do it." My brother was the same way. My dad, on the other hand, had the fear that something might happen to me. I remember well an incident that occurred later in my life but which illustrates the point. I told Dad I wanted to go to Denver to a convention. He said, "Who's going to go with you?" I listed individuals but that didn't satisfy him. Then I said, "Well, you know, Dad, we never travel alone." Then his comment was "Who in the hell is going with you?" My answer then was "God." He didn't say any more. Anytime I wanted to do that again, I just did it. I could anyway, whether he wanted me to or not, because I was old enough.

Sometime during the preschool years, children with a visual impairment may recognize that they are different. Usually this realization comes gradually. Rubin describes this dawning reality:

I guess I thought something was different about me when I had to go to the hospital so many times when I was a little kid. I remember one time when I was about 4, one of the neighborhood kids called me "cross-eyed." I didn't know what that meant so I asked my mother, and she said not to worry about it. She really didn't tell me anything about my sight. I guess maybe she didn't want to tell me. I knew I was really different when I didn't go to the neighborhood school, but rather to a special school.

Parents often experience difficulty in coming to grips with the reality of their child's impairment. Their acceptance of limitations, however, is essential to the subsequent adjustment of the child.

Types of Educational Settings

Visually handicapped children are educated today in a variety of settings: a special school which may or may not be part of the regular school system; a residential school; a special class in a regular school; or a regular class with or without special assistance. Rubin is somewhat unusual for his age group in that his school experiences included three different settings.

The first school Rubin attended was a small segregated class in a special education demonstration school operated by a teachers' college. He describes this school:

In September 1940, when I was almost six years old, I remember being taken to a school in the next town where I was introduced to the principal. He seemed to be a very kind man and I felt comfortable being with him. He took me into the rest room one time and I thought he was taking me to a hospital because I saw white bathroom fixtures. I cried but he assured me that I was not going to the hospital. Then I was alright.

This anecdote also illustrates the traumatic effects that some visually handicapped children share with other handicapped children whose conditions require numerous and often extended stays in the hospital.

This school was a small day and residential facility enrolling children representing the broad range of special education categories. The children in attendance had no educational experiences with normal children and the school was designed to meet the needs of the handicapped. Such schools are now rare partly because the current trend is on mainstreaming in a regular school setting where maximum contact with normal children can be provided. Rubin attended the special school for a relatively short period of time. The school records showed that his attendance record was good and that he adjusted well to the school situation. After one and a half years, the school recommended that he be sent to the residential school since the program for blind children was being discontinued.

Rubin describes his next school experience:

I stayed at this first school for around a year and a half, then I was transferred to the state residential school for the blind. The reason for this was that the program at the other school was not appropriate for my needs. I participated in as many activities as possible, such as rhythm band and chorus. I did learn the alphabet and numbers but really wasn't benefitting from the program. So in the fall of 1941 I was taken to the school for the blind for a visit. In fact, I was taken up there twice to see the school. Then a man who was called a social worker came down and talked to me and my folks about the school. On March 23, 1942, I entered the school. I can remember the first three days rather vividly. I was put in a classroom with other kids, similar to the one where I went before. On the third day I remember my mother going home, I thought the world had come to an end. She said she'd be there to see me and wasn't. My sister had evidently talked her into going home. My sister thought it would do me good to be on my own. I look back on that experience as being good now, but it wasn't very good then because I was a child of 7.

Residential schools are often criticized because they remove the child from the home environment. From his adult vantage point, Rubin reflects on this aspect:

My early experience at the school for the blind was very valuable to me in later life, because I learned to get along on my own: I didn't need mama and daddy. I was able to master the idea of independence, and skills in dealing with people in situations, and I learned to take buses and other forms of transportation on my own. I can remember one time being stranded in the bus station after having missed a bus. This was when I was small. At first I cried and then I learned that you ask the man, and he'll tell you. He'll get an answer and help you. When I got home that particular time, I was met by my folks. They were worried because I was late. I learned a lot from that experience.

Many visually handicapped children can and do profit from a residential school experience. It helps them learn independence which often cannot be taught within an over-protective home setting. Later, Rubin will talk about a disadvantage of his residential school experience, namely, removal from the community, and how he compensated for that.

When he entered the school for the blind, Rubin was placed in an ungraded class for the remainder of the school year after which he entered the first grade in the fall of 1942. He repeated the second grade although his grades were not significantly low; the retention was considered advisable for other reasons. In the elementary grades, he received average and above average grades in academic subjects, and below average grades in handwork and physical education. From the seventh through the tenth grade, he maintained a B average, and did receive As in history and civics courses.

During his school years there is a record of one achievement test: The Stanford. His overall score was 5.3 and his grade placement at the time was 5.6. The school records include two tests of intelligence. The Hayes-Binet was administered when he was 10-4 and reported an IQ of 92.6. When he was 13-2, the Wechsler-Bellevue Test Form I was administered; his verbal IQ was 90 on the six subscales pro-rated.

When Rubin was in school, the routine administration of achievement tests was uncommon. Today greater use is made of such measures. Both the Metropolitan and the Stanford Achievement Tests are available in braille and large type.

Tests of intelligence for visually handicapped pupils today are the successors of those administered to Rubin. The most commonly used are the Perkins-Binet which is based on the 1960 edition of the Stanford-Binet, and the Wechsler Intelligence Tests. Both are individual tests and should be administered by a qualified psychologist. In addition to tests of achievement and intelligence, a wide variety of measures is now available for assessing various aspects of growth and development.

Rubin's last school experience was in a regular public high school. He describes his experiences thus:

I first got the idea that I'd like to try what I considered a normal high school setting when I was in tenth grade. I asked my mother to call the principal of the school in my home town. He was glad to have an interview with me so on the 14th day of February of 1953 I went in and talked to him. The principal was pretty frank. He wanted to know if I thought I could handle the work and I told him what I was able to do. At that time I could use the typewriter to type pages, I took notes in braille and was able to navigate around places without any assistance. The principal seemed to think I was sincere, and was willing to give me a chance. When I went back to the school for the blind, I told them what I wanted to do. Some encouraged me; some wished that I'd stay there. That summer I decided I wanted to really try this, to see if I could do it. I took an English composition course where we had to read plays, and I had to type themes. I managed to pass with a C. They told me that this would be equivalent to a B in many other high schools. I was told that I was graded just like any other student, and that's the way I wanted it. I didn't want anything handed to me. I started in the fall and took courses just like anybody else. I participated in regular activities just like any other student. I was on the Student Council representing my homeroom. I went on the Washington trip. This was quite an interesting thing. My dad kind of poo-pooed that idea at first. He said, "Who's going to take care of you?" Well, we worked that one out. My brother and mother couldn't have been more delighted that I would want to participate with the other kids. I went to New York on the train with my class, saw the same things they did, and met relatives I'd never seen before.

Education in a public school setting is by no means a new concept in the education of the visually handicapped. Indeed, it was suggested as early as 1810 in Europe and 1866 in the United States. Day school programs may be of the following types: the special class, the resource room, teacher counselor, and teacher consultant. Each has a different pattern for mainstreaming or integration with regular classes. It should also be noted that combinations of these major types of services may also be used.

In the *special class* model the child is enrolled in a classroom with a teacher trained to work with the visually handicapped. The extent of integration varies according to school policy and the educational needs of the child. Special classes range on a continuum from almost complete segregation from the remainder of the school's curricular and non-curricular activities to total integration wherein the child uses the special class only for his homeroom.

In the *resource room* model, the special teacher functions as an on-call consultant to regular teachers; works with the visually handicapped children during their free periods; makes certain that materials and specialized equipment are available when needed; provides instruction in the special needs areas discussed later in this chapter; and in general functions as a resource to child, parents, and regular teachers.

In the *teacher consultant* plan, the teacher carries out functions similar to the resource room teacher but serves more than one school. In the *teacher counselor* plan, the teacher provides indirect service to parents and regular teachers as they work directly with the child. Teacher counselors may also work directly with the child on a regular basis. This plan is most appropriate for those pupils who are ready for full-time integration or mainstreaming.

The decision of educational placement should be a joint one. An educational placement and planning committee should include educators from general and special education, school and community diagnostic personnel who have knowledge of the child's strengths and weaknesses, the parents, and the person himself where appropriate. A continuum of services including a residential placement should be available to meet specialized needs as identified through this team approach.

Objectives of Educational Programs

The major goal of education for pupils with visual impairments is the same as for all pupils, namely, to provide them with opportunities to become self-sufficient, contributing members of society. As with other handicapped groups, the extent to which this goal is achieved varies and the variability may be attributed to personal characteristics and to cultural and social factors which may place barriers in the path of the person attempting to become a self-supporting, contributing citizen. Throughout their lives, visually handicapped persons are usually required to demonstrate more than average ability in order to attain the ultimate goal of being self-supporting, contributing citizens. This discrimination will continue until all handicapped persons are recognized for what they *can* do and are permitted to demonstrate their abilities as guaranteed to them under Section 504 of the Vocational Rehabilitation Act of 1973.

Presently there is little agreement about the most effective methods of educating visually handicapped pupils. In general, it appears that children with visual impairments learn to read by the same methods as those employed with "normal" children and that no one method will work with all. Many educational problems are the same: some visually handicapped children have trouble with school learning tasks; some are behavior problems; some have emotional and/or learning problems. Rubin says:

> My problems in school were the same as for all the other kids. I just had to find different solutions for some of them.

Modifications are necessary for certain school activities. Rubin talks about these:

> For some subjects like biology, I had verbal descriptions rather than viewing diagrams. If I were asked to describe something on a test, I would give the oral description to the person who gave me the exam. They had student teachers at that time who would administer the tests or the instructor might even do it himself. I took most of my tests orally, or sometimes I would type them. I had book assignments read to me either by my parents or kids that were in the class with me. They had to read the assignment anyway, and they were delighted to do it. I offered to pay them but not one person accepted.

Other test-taking procedures include: recording the test on tape; transcribing into braille; permitting the student to write his answers during class in braille and reading them to the instructor or typing them later; typing answers in class; or dictating answers on tape. These illustrate minor modifications that can be used to accommodate pupils with a visual impairment. Other suggestions for program modification may be found in Scholl (1968).

After acquiring the basic tools for learning: typing and braille reading and writing or efficient use of low vision aids to use regular print, visually handicapped children can usually participate in most school subjects. For arithmetic, the abacus provides an aid for rapid calculation. Technological aids such as tactile and auditory displays for calculators assist visually handicapped pupils to compete with sighted peers in computational skills. Models and raised diagrams, including maps, are available for social studies activities. In a science such as biology, physics, or chemistry, a sighted partner or aide can be assigned for laboratory work.

Public Law 94–142 now assures visually handicapped pupils access to two subject areas for which they have great need: physical education and vocational education. Rubin had no such opportunities and says:

They wouldn't let me take physical education at the high school. I did when I attended the school for the blind. I bowled there and took physical education all the way through school. I took shop, chair caning, and salesmanship at the school for the blind too but didn't take any vocational subjects at the high school because they wouldn't let me do that either. They only wanted me to take academic subjects.

The guiding principle for curriculum planning should be to permit the visually handicapped pupil to try out his skills in all regular subject areas and expect as much as is reasonable given the visual limitation.

The "Special" in Education for the Visually Handicapped

The preceding section described briefly how visually handicapped pupils may participate in the regular school program. There are other learning experiences that should be included in their curriculum and training in these areas is provided by qualified professionals. These include daily living skills, orientation and mobility, auditory and tactile substitutes for written communication, and training in maximizing residual vision.

Daily Living Skills

In a society where a high premium is placed on appearance and appearing "normal," social skills including dressing, make-up, hair styling, and other aspects of personal appearance must be emphasized. Lacking access to a mirror and being unable to learn through visual imitation places the child at a distinct disadvantage. Learning to dress oneself presents problems for the young child. Rubin says:

> I can remember as a child having trouble buttoning my shirts. This was evidently true with a lot of kids. Tying my shoes: I was darn near ten when I finally mastered that! I remember I was at a cub scout meeting when I finally succeeded. The leader was kidding me and teasing me, but I think she was really trying to motivate me, but I didn't see that at the time. I remember when I finally mastered it, the whole cub troop clapped. Tying neck ties was also a problem. Now I just use the clip ones, because they look a lot better, and when they wear out, I just throw them away, or when someone tells me it looks bad, I get a new one.

One of the social disadvantages of a visual impairment is the lack of access to nonverbal communication. Without vision, the person does not receive feedback on the impression being made on others. Rubin says:

> Since I can't see people's faces, I have to look for other ways of knowing what they are thinking about me or whether they understand me. I listen for voice inflection as my big indicator. Sometimes, especially in my business contacts, I ask people whether they understand something because I can't see the questions on their faces. Sometimes I can tell such things from their voices or hesitations in talking.

Mannerisms that call attention to the person as being "different" should also be eliminated. These include rocking, poking the eyes, head shaking or rolling, shaking the hands high in the air, and other stereotypic behavior. When asked about such mannerisms, Rubin replied:

> I've been told that blind people do have some mannerisms like sticking their fingers in their eyes, holding their heads down, and improper posture. I know I have some! I don't stick my fingers in my eyes but I do hold my head down and I could look at people when I talk with them more than I do. I walk with an odd gait, especially when I'm thinking of something else. They do probably make people hesitant to talk to me when they first see me but I don't think they have kept me from getting a job or anything like that.

The remedy for most of these mannerisms is prevention: keep the young child busy, active, and sufficiently motivated so that the child does not have time to engage in self-stimulation activities, thus acquiring a set of behavior patterns that are difficult to eliminate.

Instruction in daily living skills should also include formal sex education. Children with visual impairments frequently need models and more detailed explanations to learn about anatomical differences. What children with vision learn naturally in the home, movies, television, and other visual media, visually handicapped children must be taught. Sex education begins in the home with the preschool child. It is interesting that Rubin's parents apparently realized his need for instruction in a natural setting during his preschool years but he later had to learn the facts of life on his own:

> When I was a little kid, my mom and dad dressed and undressed in front of me if I were in the same room. So I guess I learned about differences be-

tween boys and girls naturally that way. I did have instruction at the school for the blind in the seventh grade in physiology but they didn't really go into it. Some kids used the exploratory method behind one of the old buildings— at least that is what I was told. I think kids should have been told more than I was at school.

This anecdote also illustrates that boys and girls with visual impairments will find out about each other in spite of the staff! If Rubin were in school today, he would probably have included in his curriculum from kindergarten through high school instruction in sex education and family living.

Orientation and Mobility

One major restriction of a severe visual impairment is on the ability to move freely and easily in the environment. Formal instruction in orientation and mobility is now an integral part of the curriculum. The use of the white cane is taught in a prescribed way, known as the long cane technique or cane travel. Rubin's degree of vision is such that he can travel independently. He carries a cane, however, and here is his story:

> I use the cane as an identifier to motorists, so they know that I do have a visual problem, and that I would appreciate it if they would kind of cool it with their wheels.

Instead of the cane, some visually handicapped adults use a dog guide. Dogs are not recommended for school-age pupils, however, partly because they lack the maturity and judgment to use one effectively. Not all blind persons can use a dog successfully and one with as much vision as Rubin probably would not be accepted for a dog guide training program. Here are Rubin's thoughts on the matter:

> People sometimes ask me why I don't have a dog, and I say I don't because, first of all, I'm not fond of them and I just don't like to be bothered with them. Then I say, kind of humorously, besides they can't have as much fun as I do at conventions.

Almost all persons with a severe visual impairment will be accompanied at times by a sighted guide. The guide should let the person take his or her elbow. This naturally places the visually handicapped person a half step behind the guide and gives some warning of turns, steps, or obstacles. It is also helpful if the guide tells the person whether such changes in terrain as steps and escalators are going up or down.

Technological developments in electronic mobility aids are advancing rapidly, and many visually handicapped persons now use such devices for increasing their ability to get around.

Auditory and Tactile Substitutions for Written Communication

Access to the printed word is a major restriction on the person with a visual impairment. About one-fourth of the visually handicapped pupils do not have sufficient vision to use print and other visual media in their instructional programs even with maximum magnification.

Braille is probably the oldest and most widely used tactile reading aid. It is a shorthand system of embossed dots based on a six-dot cell. Various combinations of these dots indicate different letters of the alphabet and the contractions or shortened forms of words.

One major advantage to braille is its usefulness for writing. Braille is written on a braillewriter, a machine about the size of a portable typewriter. Braille writing on this machine is usually introduced in the first grade. Later, the pupil learns to use a slate and stylus for writing. This device can be carried in a pocket or purse; writing is accomplished by pressing the stylus into the paper which is placed between two pieces of metal hinged at the left side. Writing progresses from right to left so that when the paper is removed and turned over, the raised dots may be felt by the finger.

Rubin learned braille, but if he were in school today, he probably would be introduced to large type and/or the use of a low-vision aid with regular print. He did find braille useful, however:

> I used braille all the way through the school for the blind, and in high school I took notes in braille, too. In fact, I used braille all the way through college. It wasn't really until 1963 that I began to use large type. I don't use braille now, however, not even for keeping my own records.

Two electronic reading aids have been introduced. The Optacon translates the printed letter into a tactile image; the Kurzweil machine translates the printed word into audible speech. Both devices are slow but give instant access to the printed word.

Auditory access to the printed page has been in the past primarily through the talking book. These are records similar to phonograph records played at a reduced speed. Through the Library of Congress the federal government subsidizes the production and distribution of talking books. Tapes and more recently tape cassettes give another auditory access to the printed word.

Rubin made extensive use of auditory aids throughout his schooling:

> I used tapes in high school and college. I had materials to be read put on tapes. That was easier than having someone read to me, especially when I wanted to listen to it again. I could play back the tape, whereas I sometimes didn't want to ask a reader to re-read a certain passage.

Maximizing Residual Vision

When Rubin entered school, he was discouraged from using vision for any purposes. This practice reflected the philosophy of that time, namely, that school programs should focus on "saving" or "conserving" sight. Subsequent research has showed that wise use of vision can help the child function more effectively in a visual world. Consequently today's pupils with visual impairments participate in programs designed to increase their visual efficiency. From an early age they are encouraged and trained to use their vision to maximum efficiency. In addition, those with any amount of vision are evaluated for using an appropriate low-vision aid. Such aids include magnification systems that project enlarged materials on a television screen or individually fitted aids. Technology is continually providing new and better equipment; educators should be alert to these developments that will enable pupils with very restricted vision to make use of it to the greatest degree possible.

Future Directions

Rubin's look back into his educational experiences was related in the preceding sections to current practices in the education of children with vision problems. What of the future? Can trends that are now under way be identified and projected into the future in order to gain some sense of what kind of educational programs will be available to children with vision problems? This section will speculate on a few of these trends.

Cooperative arrangements between medical and/or optometric personnel and educators will ultimately result in better educational and supportive help to parents as soon as they learn their child has a visual impairment. With increasing recognition of early childhood programs as part of the public school system, medical and paramedical personnel will turn to educators as a resource for their very young as well as their school-age patients. In response, more school districts will employ personnel who may not necessarily be trained as teachers to perform the accepted role of "teacher" but rather as parent educators, early childhood specialists, and consultants to nursery school teachers so that at the appropriate age children with visual impairments can attend regular school well qualified and ready to work side by side with their sighted peers.

At the other end of the school-age continuum, more secondary programs will emphasize adequate preparation for future vocations and avocations. Again this will be undertaken primarily in the regular school setting with the help of consultants who are qualified in both special and vocational education. This cooperative effort is essential if the current restricted range of vocational choices is to be expanded and if persons with vision problems are to be provided with job training in a greater variety of occupations. Career and vocational education programs will include the most needful groups, namely, the handicapped.

Increasing numbers of children with vision problems will be enrolled in regular schools. The predictions and dreams of early educators of the blind will be realized. In the nineteenth century, Johann Wilhelm Klein, founder of a school for blind children in Vienna, predicted that some day blind children would be educated side by side with the sighted. Later, in 1866, Samuel Gridley Howe, the founder of what is now the Perkins School for the Blind, the first residential school in the United States, foretold the ultimate demise of the residential school. However, instead of the demise of the residential school, it is more likely that it will become an integral part in the continuum of services available to children with vision problems, their parents, and regular school personnel as cooperative arrangements increase between residential and day school programs. Through in-service education programs regular teachers will become accepting not only of pupils with visual impairments but of all handicapped children and with the assistance of qualified consultants will be able to modify the school curriculum, teaching methods, and materials so that such children can be profitably educated with normal children. As a result, all children will have experiences with those who differ from them, and as adults, they will be more accepting of the handicapped as fellow workers and citizens.

Technology will greatly expand the horizons for people with all degrees of visual impairment, thus reducing the disabling effects of their impairment. Braille will remain an important tool for access to the printed word, but to supplement braille, other aural and tactile direct print-reading aids will be used extensively. Instruction in these will be as much a part of the curriculum as braille and typing skills are currently. Low-vision aids will improve so that more people with limited vision will be able to use regular print effectively. Technology will have a beneficial effect on mobility instruction, and instruction in the use of ultrasonic and other technological mobility aids will be part of the curriculum. Such aids will supplement those currently used—the long cane, the dog guide, and the human guide. Technology should foster greater integration of visually handicapped people into society at all levels.

Unless the current trend is reversed through advances in medical science, the school population of the visually handicapped will include increasing numbers of children with multiple disabilities. The education of such children will require an interdisciplinary approach as well as a cooperative effort on the part of educators from different areas. These children will need creative and concerned teachers to help plan effective educational programs for them.

In general, the future looks brighter for children with visual impairments, thanks to advances in technology and to legislative and judicial actions that are working toward assuring equal educational opportunities for all.

ADULT ADJUSTMENT

Post-Secondary School Experiences

Teachers often view graduation from high school as the end of the pupil's life. This, of course, is not true: every graduate must enter the adult world. This means college or university, a vocational training program, an apprenticeship program, or direct entry into the world of labor. Graduates with vision problems usually require additional training to become employable. Rubin writes:

> I graduated from high school in 1955 and entered college that fall. I was sponsored the first semester by the vocational rehabilitation agency. I was given the battery of tests to see what my prospects were. The psychologist

pointed out that I might make it with difficulty, so I had to live with that fact. I was determined to make it. The first semester didn't look like I was. I had an E in English. I think the reason was I spelled a lot of words phonetically and that's not always good. However, I find that other people do that, too. I couldn't read what I wrote. As I got into college and took more English and speech courses, I saw how things fell together in an introduction, body, and conclusion type of setting. Then I began to do better. The rehabilitation agency came along at the end of that semester and said, well, you're really not cutting it. So a job was offered to me selling candy at the post office. I wasn't madly interested in that. I was determined to stick it out in college. Maybe I should not have, but I don't feel sorry that I did because I did finally get through with the help of a lot of good people. It wasn't a one-man effort by any means. My major was sociology with minors in speech and music. It took me five years to finish because I took reduced loads every semester. While in college, I attended concerts, football games, dances, and other things students did. I didn't let anything hinder me.

Several aspects of Rubin's experience related above should be discussed. Most persons with handicaps are eligible for services from their state rehabilitation agency. These agencies usually require a psychological and vocational assessment. A brief summary of results for Rubin's are as follow: on the Wechsler-Bellevue Form II he had a verbal IQ of 115; vocational interest tests showed a strong interest in business and personal-social fields. The psychologist questioned his ability to attend college. Because of his determination, the agency agreed to sponsor him the first year. When his progress seemed questionable, Rubin had to find other resources, mainly from local service clubs and from his family. It is to his credit that he did finish college in spite of the odds. He is probably atypical in that he did not give up.

The agency counselor's recommendation after the first year is interesting, too, in the light of the restricted vocational range of occupations available to persons with vision problems. Operating a stand in a federal building is a typical occupation for the blind. Others include chair caning, piano tuning, and door-to-door selling. Studies of the occupations of employed visually handicapped persons indicate that the range for them is approximately one-half the range of their parents' occupations.

Rubin's problems in spelling are quite typical. It will be recalled that braille is a system of contractions so that one sign or letter may mean an entire word. For example, the letter *e* is the word *every* when it is standing alone. Braille-reading children should be introduced to the typewriter in the early elementary grades so that they will do most of their spelling and writing activities on the typewriter where each word must be spelled out letter by letter. This practice helps alleviate some of the spelling problems that are attributed to the use of braille.

Developing typing skills is essential. If Rubin were attending school today, he probably would begin using the typewriter in the second or third grade. Typing does present some problems, too. As Rubin stated, he was not able to read what he had written in order to correct his mistakes. A special device attached to an Optacon now assists the person in correcting typing errors. There are other problems he did not mention. He cannot see whether the ribbon of the typewriter is working. In order to compensate for this disability, blind students use carbon paper for a second copy so that even if the ribbon is not working properly, the carbon copy will be readable. Another difficulty arises when the fingers are on the wrong keys. To illustrate, when Rubin was typing materials for this chapter, one paragraph began: "As far as ,u re;atopmajo7 qorj ,y aoarera qas cpmcermed." Translated, this was: "As far as my relationship with my sisters was concerned." An analysis of what he wrote shows that his right hand was positioned over the wrong keys and at one point his left hand was moved over.

Special summer programs sponsored by many agencies, schools, or colleges provide students intensive instruction in a variety of specialized techniques that will be useful to them in college. These include typing, braille speed reading, Optacon reading, orientation and mobility, using tapes and tape cassettes, and other aids to study. These programs have helped many students find college life more satisfying and successful.

Students who do not wish to attend college or who do not have the abilities to do so may receive additional vocational training in some occupation.

Entering the Employment Market

Like other handicapped persons, Rubin encountered more problems than his sighted peers when he looked for employment:

> I graduated from college in 1961 and went job hunting. I wanted to get into corrections. I always had been interested in penal institutions—ever since I was a kid. I used to listen to murder mysteries on the radio, and for some unknown reason was concerned with how these people were treated. My college work substantiated the fact that I did care about people. I had the privilege of touring several prisons while I was in high school and college

and so I decided to look for a job in corrections. I went to talk to people in several places. At that time they said that the hazards behind the walls might be too much and there were insurance factors, at least in their minds, that precluded them from giving me any opportunity. They didn't feel I should go into it. It was then recommended that I go into the insurance business. I talked with a blind man who also went to the school for the blind, and he was in that business. I found out how he operated, that is, keeping his records in braille and having people read the materials to him. It seemed like a good deal and I went to see an insurance agent I knew and he said he would give me a chance. He did and that is what I'm still doing today. I like it.

Employers are reluctant to give handicapped people a chance. The excuse is often that their workmen's compensation insurance regulations do not permit the employment of handicapped. Many handicapped persons are forced to try a variety of work settings before someone will finally give them an opportunity to prove themselves. Continuing problems are made more acute during an era of high unemployment, and the handicapped are among the first to be out of jobs.

Much is being done to assure equal educational opportunities for all within the public school system. Much less is being done to insure equal employment opportunities for the handicapped after they leave school. Attitudinal changes are necessary so employers will accept the handicapped as potential employees. Professionals in the field of rehabilitation need to expand potential placements and to seek out more jobs that the handicapped can perform as well and perhaps even better than the nonhandicapped. The narrow range of occupations currently available must be expanded so that the handicapped too can select from a wide variety the one that best meets their interests and abilities.

Integration into Society

Throughout this chapter selected references have been made regarding aspects of social development. Earlier Rubin described his family and early experiences. This section will focus on both the past and the present as they are related to his adult integration socially into society.

Rubin's first move into the community came when he returned from the residential school to his home community. He says:

When I transferred to the high school from the school for the blind, I knew that I was going to live in the community where I was from. I knew that I didn't know a lot of people. I made up my mind that I was going to compen-

sate for that by getting involved. I got active in things like the student council, choral groups, and so on. When I got into college, I wanted to get into a
fraternity. Everybody seemed to be in one and so I did too. Well, I went and
I never heard from them. A year later I got a dues notice! That was kind of
nice of them but in the interim a friend of mine invited me to a Young Re-
publican meeting and that was the beginning of that. I got involved, was accepted by the people, given tasks to do, just like anybody else. They didn't
say, "Well, you can't do it, because you can't see."

Rubin had sufficient determination to get himself involved in community activities, and today, as an adult, he remains active. He has served
on city commissions related to transportation and youth activities; he has
been president of the local Jaycees, the Y's Men's Club, and a local service club; he is active in his church by teaching Sunday school and has
served as president of one of the church groups. His interest in politics,
which began while he was in college, has continued, and he attends local,
state, and national conventions of his political party. Finally, he has
served on a state committee related to the education of handicapped children. His community activities and contributions certainly exceed those
of most citizens.

All Rubin's civic and social activities are with sighted persons. This
is not true with many handicapped who frequently join and are active in
groups where members share a similar impairment. Of this Rubin says:

I am in no groups that are specifically geared to the visually handicapped because I've felt that my work-a-day world was going to be with people with
all sorts of problems, not just visual. I feel that you've got to have a broader
perspective than what's going on in your own backyard. You have to understand, shall we say, the whole football field, rather than just the first half
of it.

Rubin never married. He says of marriage:

I've considered it, but I am not pushing it. I see so many of my friends and
they're normal regular people who have been in and out of marriage and I
want to make sure that if I get in it, I'm going to stay there.

One problem among visually handicapped persons is that of the tension that results from constantly facing the unknown. Rubin says:

I feel more relaxed now than I did years ago. I think as I work into things, I get more relaxed. Occasionally I'll become tense, then I have to just sit down, and just kind of step back and say "Hey, how are we going to handle this." I have a religious faith, plus the ability to communicate with people I felt could help get me through any problems I have.

Rubin has found his own way to resolve his problems. He has not resorted to alcohol or drugs or withdrawal but rather has met situations head on and pushed himself through.

He has encountered discrimination because of his visual impairment, as many others do. He says:

I think the rejection is based on ignorance rather than because of the blindness or visual impairment. In other words they don't understand the problem and don't know how to cope with it. For instance, I went up to apply for a job at a camp once. I wanted to go quite badly, because several of my friends worked there. It was a summer job. I could see their problem rejecting me. It was based on just not being familiar with how people like myself operate. I could have taken a sign and gone up there and picketed but I don't think that would have been a good thing at all. I think the thing to do is to get where you can prove yourself and people are going to respect you for that.

Happiness is a relative matter, and it is difficult to assess both one's general state of happiness and satisfaction with one's life. On these subjects Rubin says:

I would say in many ways I am just as happy as most of my friends. I have the same activities they have. I love children and I love people, but yet, I think it is the Lord's will that I don't have any wife and children and I just have to realize that. If it's going to come, it is going to come. I feel satisfied with my life, too. Of course, I feel as though I always want to upgrade it. I'd like to do more things, be a better person, learn more. I think you can never learn enough. I just feel I like to keep abreast of things, and I think this is true of anyone who is conscientious or tries to be.

At mid-life Rubin has made an adequate adjustment for himself as a person with a visual problem. Other persons might select a different pattern. He realizes that at some time in the future, he will be without his brother. He, however, plans to continue living in the household as he has done in the past. He is happy and content with his many activities and with his job. If success is measured in terms of annual income from a job, then Rubin may not be considered a geat success. On the other hand, if success is measured in terms of self-sufficiency, contributions to the community and contentment with one's state in life, then Rubin can be considered a success.

SOPHIE L. FRENCH

Sophie L. French conveys an appreciation of the nature and significance of hearing problems in a rare way. She began special education work at Columbia University with affiliation at Lexington School for the Deaf. She has academic certification from the conference of American Instructors of the Deaf. She has also studied programs for the deaf and consulted throughout the United States, in Scandinavia and New Zealand. In addition to teaching deaf children, Ms. French has had a long association with teacher training as a supervising teacher and instructor in all areas of education of the deaf, including language, speech, and school subjects. She served as coordinator in the Area of Deaf and Hard of Hearing. She is now Associate Professor Emeritus from Eastern Michigan University where she taught until 1973. She recognized the need for early intervention and intensified her work on the evaluation and training of deaf infants.

Ms. French knows first hand the parents' dilemma since she herself faced this situation with her son. In the 1950s she founded a Parent Counseling Clinic for Deaf Infants which worked with parents and children in all aspects of hearing limitations. At present she is consultant at the Oral Program for Hearing Impaired at Redford Union, serving Northwest Wayne County, Michigan.

The fact of controversy in special education techniques is evident in this chapter. To sign or not to sign is one such question. Sophie French points out these arguments along with the story of Charles, a child and family she has known well over an extended period of time.

8

Impaired Hearing

SOPHIE L. FRENCH

CHARLES, CHARLES! Here I am! Don't cry. I'm *here,* right here behind you." Charles, nine months old, had crawled to a closed door and while crying was banging on it with his little fist. He thought his mother was behind the door, and he wanted her. But his mother, unseen by Charles, had come in from another room and was now standing only six feet behind him. She called his name several times again, louder, then even louder still. But Charles paid no heed. Then quietly the mother went up and touched her son. Like a flash Charles turned, ceased his sobbing, and hugged her hard. Then she knew—he hadn't heard her! And at the same time she realized that a nagging fear about his hearing had been lurking just below the surface of her mind for some time. It was such an enormous fear that she had successfully suppressed it until now.

Charles was a beautiful baby, well formed, healthy, and alert. His parents were delighted with him. He was their first child and in most ways was developing normally and rapidly. There were, however, a few differences between him and other babies. He did not babble in his crib as constantly as they babbled and he did not imitate the cooing sounds mothers make to babies. He laughed and cried in normal fashion, but when he wanted attention, he would scream in a loud, high-pitched, irritating voice. He often was unhappy and restless when left alone, more so, his parents thought, than other babies his age. His parents had wondered at these things and discussed them, but they had had no explanation until now. Charles did not appear to be different in any other ways. But this recent episode might explain it all. Perhaps he did not hear.

If Charles did not hear normally, what would it mean? What is hearing? How do we hear? What can go wrong with hearing? If one doesn't hear, what happens? What can be done to help children who do not hear normally and who will help them? These were the questions Charles' parents asked themselves and these are the things that we must look into before we go back to see what happened to Charles and what happens to other children who cannot hear their parents' voices.

HEARING: WHAT IS IT?

Hearing is a sense that most of us take for granted. It begins to function as soon as we are born, and we use it continuously thereafter for a multitude of purposes. We use it for information, for pleasure, for warning signals, but above all else we use hearing for communication. We learn to understand speech and to use speech ourselves through hearing. During their first three years children all over the world are busy learning the language of their culture, and they do this through use of their ears.

Damage the hearing of an adult and what happens? Inevitably there is an interruption in the chain of communication that interferes with all social functioning. Severely hearing impaired people can no longer understand what is said to them, and they may become isolated and lonely. But damage the hearing of an infant and the results are devastating. A block is thrown in the path of the development of speech and language that affects the child's total functioning and thinking. If the hearing is only partially impaired, the child will partially develop language. If the child is extremely hearing impaired, he may never learn to talk in a normal way nor will the child be able to understand the speech of others adequately. The result can be a language deprivation of such severity that it will delay or prevent the child's educational progress to a degree rarely understood by those not acquainted with the problem. Educational achievement is dependent on language, on words and how they are put together to create meaning. We not only converse in language; we think in language; we read and write in language. Without a language of some sort a child can never reach his fullest intellectual potential. Without special education, therefore, the deaf child can become extremely handicapped. Charles is going to need a great deal of special assistance if indeed he does not hear as others do.

The case of Charles illustrates what can be done with a severely hearing handicapped child given the best of all conditions. His is a success story. Many are not. We shall look at the reasons why as we follow Charles and learn more about the significance of a hearing loss.

We hear and understand what we hear because of a combination of rather simple anatomical mechanisms and very complicated neurological systems. From the simplified diagram in Figure 8.1, we can see the ear has three basic parts: the outer ear, the middle ear, and the inner ear. Sound waves enter through the outer ear. They pass through the ear canal and hit the ear drum, causing the drum to vibrate. These vibrations are then transmitted to the three tiny bones of the middle ear—the malleus, incus, and stapes. These bones, the smallest in our body, are connected to one another in such a way that if one moves, all three move and pass vibrations on to the inner ear. In the inner ear these mechanical vibrations are converted into nerve impulses which are then conducted along the auditory nerve to the brain. Different nerve cells transmit different frequencies, with some cells transmitting low-pitched sounds and others high.

If the brain is normal and can receive these impulses, there will be a normal reaction to whatever electrical signals do reach the brain. If there is damage in the brain itself, there will be other problems. If Charles is not reacting to sound in a normal way, where does the problem lie? Is it in the outer, the middle, or the inner ear? Or could the difficulty lie in the brain itself?

CAUSES OF HEARING LOSS

Difficulties that cause hearing loss can occur anywhere in the hearing system. If the difficulty is in the outer ear, the listener experiences only a reduction in the loudness of what is heard. The sound is partially blocked and is less intense when it reaches the middle ear. Such a loss is referred to as a *conductive loss.*

Some of the causes for problems in this area are minor. The ear canal may be plugged by wax, by infection, or by some object that lodges there. More serious is a malformed auricle or a canal that is blocked by a fleshy bump. Occasionally the canal itself is completely closed or nonexistent. All of these conditions respond to medical treatment, although the congenital malformations that require surgical procedures usually cannot be dealt with until the child has passed the preschool years. As a result, there may be delay in language development because the child does not hear enough during the crucial developmental years.

More serious problems occur in the middle ear. The most frequent of these in young children is continuing infection that causes the middle ear to fill up with fluid, replacing the air that usually surrounds the ossicles, thus preventing proper movement of these bones. Although most of these cases respond well to medical treatment, not all do. If continuing in-

FIGURE 8.1

Anatomy of the ear

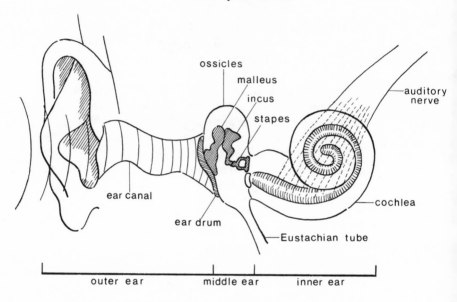

fection and resulting decrease in auditory stimulation persists, there can be damage to the auditory nerve.

Another middle ear problem, a congenital malformation of the ossicles, occurs occasionally. They may be missing or malformed so they do not function properly as transmitters of vibrations. Modern surgical techniques can, in some cases, remove or bypass the ossicles with extremely fine wires. However, again because surgery cannot take place until after the preschool years, the child may remain functionally hard of hearing during the normal language learning years. In some instances, nerve loss may accompany this condition. When conductive and nerve loss are both present, the term "mixed loss" is used.

The inner ear, however, is the area where the most serious impairments occur. No surgical or medical treatment has as yet been effective in correcting damage after it has occurred here. "Sensorineural losses," those resulting from cochlear damage, are permanent and usually far more severe than those that occur in the outer or middle ear. The losses can range from affecting only certain frequencies (the high frequency nerve receptors are the ones usually involved) to almost total hearing loss. The cochlea may be malformed, causing nerve damage so great that virtually no nerve impulses reach the brain. Inner ear difficulties almost always result in severe or profound hearing loss (see below, Varieties and Degrees of Hearing Loss).

Genetic Causes

Genetic or inherited deafness can be a dominant, recessive, or sex-linked trait. The best estimates of the percentage of deafness that is genetic in origin vary between 50 percent and 55 percent; the remainder is non-genetic in cause. According to Nance (1976), 84 percent of all genetic cases are the result of recessive genes, 14 percent dominant genes, and 2 percent sex-linked. Deaf adults tend to marry each other, and many will have deaf children. If two hearing parents carry recessive genes, they may have hearing-impaired children. The mother who carries a sex-linked gene may pass that on to her children.

Genetic causes of hearing loss may be found in all parts of the ear. In the outer ear they consist of the malformed auricle or blockage of the ear canal as described above. In the middle ear they result in either missing or malformed ossicles. In the inner ear they affect the development of the cochlea and the nerve receptor cells.

Adventitious Causes

Hearing impairments that are not genetic in origin are called adventitious and are most frequently acquired in two ways, either by disease of the mother during pregnancy or by a viral disease contracted by the child. Of all diseases, spinal meningitis has the most serious impact on hearing, but any of the childhood diseases such as measles, mumps, chickenpox can result in a permanent hearing loss. Rubella, or German measles, when contracted during the mother's pregnancy, causes not only hearing loss but other problems as well. There may be eye cataracts, a faulty heart condition, or learning disability. It is hoped that vaccine now has this virus under control. Hearing loss to a lesser extent can be caused by the administration to the child of certain myecin drugs and occasionally is the result of a severe blow to the head, sufficiently strong to damage the bony structure of both ears.

The cause of Charles' loss is unknown to us at this point, but we can say that he did not have any visible damage to either the outer ear or the ear canal. There was no known severe illness or administration of drugs to either mother or child.

VARIETIES AND DEGREES OF HEARING LOSS

Several factors are involved in describing a hearing loss and understanding the implications such loss will have. These factors will include the age at which the loss occurs (age of onset), the extent of the loss, and the nature of the loss. We have already noted that children are very busy learning their language during the first three years of life. Many of the key aspects of language are mastered before the child is eighteen months old. Age of onset of hearing loss, therefore, is of critical importance. Children are divided into the following two major classifications accordingly: (1) prelingually hearing impaired (the hearing loss either is present at birth or occurs before language has been established), and (2) postlingually hearing impaired (the hearing loss occurs after the establishment of speech and language). In this chapter we will be primarily concerned with the prelingually hearing impaired child. Charles is one of these.

The other factors cover the severity and nature of the loss. These two factors are inevitably intertwined. Sound, and therefore the ability to hear, must be measured along two dimensions. One is the intensity, the perceived loudness of a sound, and the other is the frequency, the perceived pitch of a sound. Intensity is measured in decibels, while frequency is measured in Herz or cycles per second. We are concerned with both in discussing hearing loss because damage is rarely consistent at all frequencies. Differing losses of intensity occur at different frequencies and have different effects on a person's ability to hear. One may experience merely a loss of loudness of sound at all frequency levels or experience increasing loss of loudness at higher frequency levels. The first situation may be largely remedied by use of sound amplification. Unfortunately this situation rarely exists. We are more often dealing with a distorted perception of sound due to hearing loss at high frequencies. This means that most hearing impaired children do not merely hear dulled speech; they hear distorted speech. The differences in their ability to hear will be very large. Although classifications are made, there is variation and overlapping within and between categories.

CLASSIFICATIONS

Professionals working in the field of hearing impairment may use as many as five or six classifications to denote the degree of hearing loss. Northern and Downs (1974) list five: (1) mild hearing loss (15–30 Db.); (2) moderate hearing loss (31–50 Db.); (3) severe hearing loss (51–80 Db.); (4) profound hearing loss (81–100 Db.); and (5) anacusis or total hearing loss. However, it may be simpler to think in terms of three major groups of children who will need special educational services. It is also the current trend to refer to all these children as hearing impaired. To clarify the difference between each group we shall use terminology that has long been in use. In all instances we are assuming bilateral (both ears) involvement.

1. *The Hard-of-Hearing*: This child hears most sounds but at a diminished level. The child experiences a loss of loudness and with use of amplification can perceive most speech sounds. Hearing can be this child's main avenue of learning.

2. *The Severely Hearing Impaired*: This child will hear some sounds, particularly those of low frequency. The child's hearing, however, even if augmented by use of a hearing aid, will not be adequate for language learning without some visual reinforcement.

3. *The Profoundly Deaf*: This child will have almost no hearing. The child reacts to sound only when it is so loud that it is difficult to determine whether the child is hearing sound or feeling vibrations. The child's language learning will have to be visual, through use of lip-reading, or perhaps fingerspelling and sign language.

Estimates of the number of children that fall into each category vary, and many of the hard-of-hearing may not be counted because they have identified themselves as belonging to the hearing world rather than the deaf world and therefore do not report their hearing loss in surveys. Schein and Delk (1974) give us the following figures: 3.2 percent of the total population have significant hearing impairments. However, only .08 percent of the total population are profoundly deaf; and .02 percent acquired the loss before the age of nineteen or during school years. Only .01 percent are prelingually deaf. According to statistics given in the *American Annals of the Deaf* (May 1976, p. 144), the total enrollment of schools and classes for the deaf as of October 1975 was 52,485. This figure does not include mainstreamed children. Fortunately the prelingual profoundly deaf group is the smallest in number. However, these children present the greatest educational challenge, and controversy over the best educational management for them is not yet resolved.

Whatever the loss and wherever it occurs, its impact will inevitably be affected by the child's home environment and the family's actions and reactions. The child's self-esteem and ability to adapt to his or her hearing loss will depend on how the child's family sees and interacts with the child. One set of parents may emphasize the fact of the loss, treating their child as deaf and unable to hear and talk. Another will emphasize the residual hearing and the amount the child can hear and treat the child accordingly. Thus two children, given equal losses in both intensity and frequency range, may turn out to be very different individuals. The one will be a person who hears inadequately, the other a deaf person who is not expected to be able to talk or understand the speech of others.

Into which category will Charles fall and how will his parents see and react to him?

CHARLES' STORY

The first step taken by Charles' parents after the dramatic episode at the closed door and the sudden emergence of their fear that Charles did not hear was to call their pediatrician. This doctor examined Charles to the best of his ability. He found him to be in excellent health and alert in every dimension that he could measure. While he was not able to determine whether Charles could hear, he did know that it was vital that Charles have further examinations for he knew the importance of early diagnosis and early intervention in the event there was a hearing loss. Fortunately he knew an audiologist skilled in working with infants and referred the family to him. This pediatrician was better informed than most and urged the family to make no delay. Charles was now ten months old. His parents immediately phoned the audiologist.

An audiologist is a person trained to evaluate hearing, to recommend rehabilitation procedures, and to make hearing aid selections. He or she will usually work in a hospital, speech clinic, or university setting. The audiologist's chief tool is the audiometer used to measure the loudness level necessary for the patient to respond at varying frequencies. The audiologist develops an audiogram, a graph of the patient's hearing. It is ideal when audiologists, who work with very young children, function in a team setting with a person experienced in child development as well as in the education of the hearing impaired (see Figure 8.2).

FIGURE 8.2

Three typical audiograms

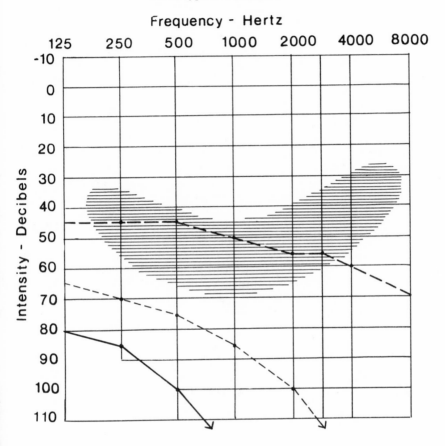

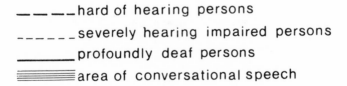
_ _ _ _ _ hard of hearing persons
_ _ _ _ _ severely hearing impaired persons
_____ profoundly deaf persons
≡≡≡≡≡ area of conversational speech

Charles and his parents together visited the audiologist. They sat with Charles in a chamber equipped with speakers through which sounds of all types could be transmitted. Sitting on his mother's lap, Charles paid no attention when music, voice, or any sound came through the speakers until it reached such an intensity that it almost hurt his parents' ears. At that loudness level he would look around with a questioning glance. What was that? Where did it come from? It was clear to both parents that Charles did not hear normally, and yet there was a point at which he consistently did respond when the sound was loud enough. Charles' audiogram can be seen on Figure 8.3. Later, when Charles was more able to tolerate them, ear phones would be used to deliver sound to his ears; the audiogram would be validated in this way.

The audiologist explained the meaning of the audiogram to Charles' parents. Charles did have a severe to profound hearing loss, but he still responded to some sounds. With training he would probably respond to sounds at lesser intensity because until now he had undoubtedly been ignoring them as meaningless. A hearing aid could not be prescribed until Charles had been examined by an otologist to check for any possible medical problems for which there might be cures. In the meantime the parents should sing and talk very close to Charles' ear in order to induce him to pay more attention to sound. The closeness to the ear was important, for sound decreases in intensity with the square of the distance. Thus, conversational speech is nine times louder spoken at the ear than it is three feet away. The parents departed determined to do as they had been instructed and also to see an otologist as soon as possible.

An otologist is a medical specialist who deals with the ear and frequently works closely with the audiologist. The otologist looks for the cause of the impairment, while the audiologist attempts to determine the extent of the loss. In some cases medical and surgical treatment is possible. If no medical treatment is needed or can be useful, the case is referred back to the audiologist for further evaluation and the selection of a hearing aid.

The parents returned from the otologist knowing that Charles' outer and middle ears were intact. He had a severe sensorineural loss, probably caused by a mild illness the mother had experience during the third month of pregnancy that may have been rubella. Charles was also examined by a neurologist and appeared to have no handicap other than the hearing loss. In fact in visual perception and motor skills he appeared to be an above average baby. Charles and his parents returned to the audiologist and the teacher of the hearing impaired to embark on an intensive training program that would emphasize auditory training (learning to listen) and speech and language development.

FIGURE 8.3

Charles' audiogram

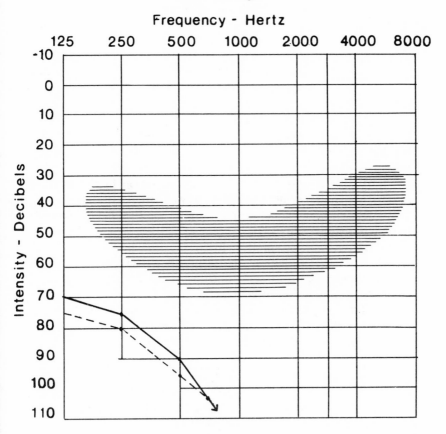

Frequency - Hertz

Intensity - Decibels

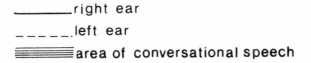

_____ right ear

_ _ _ _ _ left ear

≡≡≡≡≡ area of conversational speech

Many people confuse speech and language assuming the words are synonymous since normal children master both simultaneously. There is, however, a clear distinction. Speech is concerned with *how* we talk—voice quality, rhythm, pitch, intonation, phrasing, and articulation. Language refers to *what* we say—vocabulary (the words we use) and syntax (the code we use) to convey meaning. There are two aspects of language—expressive language for expressing ideas to others and receptive language for understanding or receiving the ideas of others. Expressive language can be spoken, written, signed, or even transmitted by Morse Code. Receptive language can be heard, read, received visually as in the case of sign language, and even felt as in the case of Braille. The syntax or grammatical rules cover word order, verb tense, use of transformations such as plurals, possessives, comparatives, etc. Recent research reveals that children are mastering the rules of grammar and making their own generalizations about them between the ages of one and two. By kindergarten age most children have mastered the majority of speech skills as well as most of the grammatical code. Vocabulary continues to grow most of our lives, but our speech patterns and the rules of our language are fixed when we are very young.

Hearing impaired children have severe problems in both speech and language. In speech these occur because they lack auditory feedback. They cannot monitor themselves and do not know when they have spoken correctly or incorrectly. In language they occur because so many of the vital aspects, the plural *s,* the possessive *s,* the prepositions, the transformations are all unaccented and therefore both inaudible and invisible. Intensive teaching at appropriate developmental ages is vital in both areas.

> Charles' parents were extraordinary in that both had studied language and had an unusual understanding of the potential effect of a hearing loss on the acquisition of both language and speech. Nevertheless even they were unprepared for the work that lay ahead and in retrospect have more than once said that they wondered if they would have undertaken the task had they known what was involved in terms of constant repetition all day long of the words and phrases that Charles was learning to use. However, embark on the program they did, and it was successful. Within weeks Charles was fitted with two very powerful hearing aids.

A hearing aid is a battery-powered instrument that picks up sound waves, amplifies them, and then delivers them directly into the ear canal. Modern hearing aids are very small and very powerful. They possess the potential to deliver as much sound as the ear can tolerate. Two types are illustrated in Figure 8.4. Hearing aids are manufactured by a variety of companies. They vary a great deal in power output, frequency response,

FIGURE 8.4

Three hearing aids

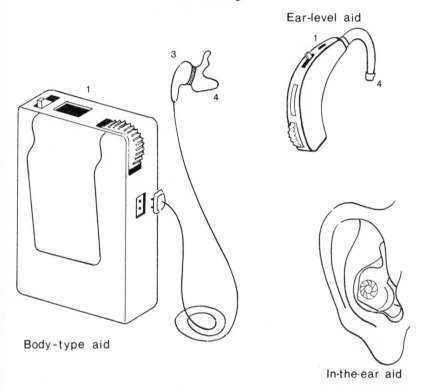

All hearing aids have three basic parts: (1) a microphone which picks up the sound and converts it into electrical energy; (2) an amplifier, battery-powered, which increases the loudness of the signal received; and (3) a receiver which converts the electrical energy back into sound. Individual ear molds (4), which are custom fitted for each person, deliver the amplified sound to the ear.

and quality. A hearing aid should never be purchased over the counter or from a visiting salesman. It should be prescribed by an audiologist after careful evaluation. A common misunderstanding is that hearing aids can restore a person's ability to hear to normal. This is never the case. Great benefits result from the proper use of hearing aids, but the hearing aid user will never hear normally. In most instances two hearing aids are used in order to stimulate both ears and to permit the location of sound source. It is interesting to note that the hearing aid was the direct result of the invention of the telephone by Dr. Alexander Graham Bell. Dr. Bell was a teacher of the deaf and was married to a hearing impaired woman, one of his former pupils. With the money he received from the Volta Prize, awarded to him in 1881 for his invention, he founded the Volta Bureau, Washington, D.C., which is devoted to the teaching of speech to the deaf.

When Charles acquired his own hearing aid, his aided audiogram looked like Figure 8.5. Compared with Figure 8.3, this audiogram shows that Charles can hear sounds at certain frequency ranges approximately 40 decibels better than before. Charles adjusted to his hearing aids very easily and soon was using them all his waking hours. With these he learned to pay attention to sounds, to locate them, and to identify them. Within a month he was responding to people who spoke close to him. He began to understand a few words and started to use them himself. His screaming stopped; his voice became pleasant; he began to babble syllables. His language development was far behind that of a normal baby his age, but he was beginning to follow the normal developmental pattern. At age two he had a vocabulary of fifty words and understood much more. At age three he was using brief sentences.

But this did not come easily. His parents set up a schedule so that one or the other of them were with him all his waking hours. They talked and talked and talked to him, using ten times the repetition one uses with a hearing child. This was necessary to compensate for the fact that he never heard the words perfectly and could not learn from over hearing conversation, the radio, or the television as does the normal child. He heard only what was clearly directed at him, clearly spoken, and he understood only those words that were meaningful. "Do you want to go *up,* Charles, *up, up, up*—Oh, you're *up*—Whee! You're way *up* high. And now let's go *down, down, down, down.*" With this Charles would be walking up or lifted up or climbing up and then coming down. Thus the words *up* and *down* were accented, the meanings made clear. And Charles would one day use them. So it was with all his early learning until he realized that speech and language were the tools with which he could manipulate his environment.

When Charles was first seen at the speech and hearing clinic his psycho-social adjustment was good in all but one respect. He tired of playing with objects very rapidly and at times expressed his frustration at not getting his messages across by using a high-pitched scream. He seemed to be saying, "Look at me and pay attention to me." But in general he was responsive, trusting, and happy. He was fortunate in that his parents became involved in his training immediately after discovering his hearing loss and

FIGURE 8.5

Charles' aided audiogram

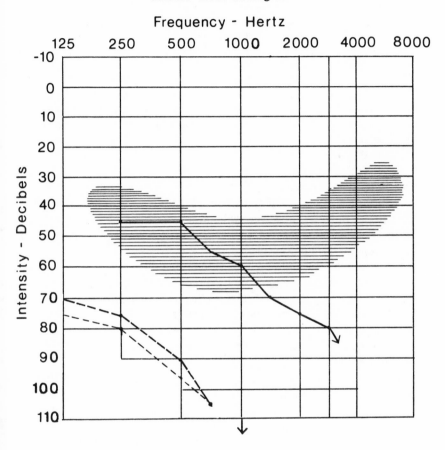

Frequency - Hertz

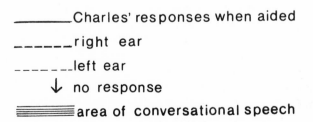

_____ Charles' responses when aided

_ _ _ _ _ _ right ear

_ _ _ _ _ _ left ear

↓ no response

≡≡≡ area of conversational speech

did not themselves go through a long period of waiting for diagnoses and treatment. They grieved, as all parents have to grieve when they learn that their child is impaired, but these parents were able to deal with this through constructive action and became a happily busy family. This reflected itself in Charles' happiness and self-confidence. At age three, after two years of work under the guidance of the audiologist and the teacher of the hearing impaired, Charles was a charming child, constantly smiling, beginning to talk, and expecting to be talked to.

When Charles was three and four, his parents experimented with a dual educational program. He spent three mornings a week in a regular nursery school, thus being exposed to the behavior and activities of normal children. The balance of his time he spent in a preschool class for hearing impaired children.

A preschool class for hearing impaired children will normally have five to six children in it: like all preschools one major purpose will be to develop social skills, learning to share, take turns, and play with others. The prime purpose, however, will be to accelerate all communication skills. The curriculum will place heavy emphasis on speech, speech reading, auditory training, and language.

A preschool should be housed in a quiet soundproofed room, carpeted, and draped. The purpose is to reduce any background noise that may interfere with the sounds that go through the hearing aid. There will be the usual toys, easels, books, sandtables, etc. But in addition there should be high-quality auditory trainers which will enable children to hear to the maximum. There should also be special equipment used for teaching speech and language. There should be mirrors in front of which children can sit and watch their own faces and lip positions as they attempt to imitate the words, syllables, and phrases the teacher is saying.

The teachers of such a class and all classes for the hearing impaired have received special training, usually a year or two beyond that of the regular teacher. They must know all aspects of language and curriculum development. They must know how to handle amplification equipment. They must be able to interpret the audiograms of each child so that they can estimate what aspects of sound the child can hear. They must know speech development and how both to teach speech and to correct speech errors. When hearing is inadequate for the purpose of learning speech, it will be supplemented by the use of touch and vision. The child will hear a sound or word as well as he or she is able, see on the teacher's lips how the sound is made, and watch himself or herself in the mirror as he or she attempts to say it. He may be saying *vye, vye* for *bye-bye.* The mirror can show the difference. (Try it and see.) Or he may be saying *mye-mye,* which looks just the same as *bye-bye*. In this instance, the teacher will let him feel the different vibrations on their faces. *M* vibrates on the nose while *b* does not.

The teachers always are developing language in all they do. The activity of cutting a pumpkin for Halloween, for example, will be not just for fun but to teach. The teacher's objective for one child may be to help him learn the words *eyes, nose,* and *mouth,* learn them so that the child can say them, understand them when they are spoken, and perhaps even to recognize printed forms. For another child it may be centered around learning the phrase "I cut out the mouth, nose, and eyes." At an older stage the activity could be used to teach the future tense. "We will cut out the eyes, nose, or mouth."

Charles responded well to this program and grew in independence as well as in language and cognitive skills. He was isolated from the children of his neighborhood, but he had companionship in both schools and thrived on it. When he left preschool, he could talk in short sentences; he knew his colors and numbers; he had a fairly large vocabulary, including verbs, nouns, adjectives, prepositions, etc. Although still language delayed, his word order was good. He could ask questions, use negatives, change his verb tenses and use some pronouns. Because his family had kept an illustrated daily journal for him since he was two and because the preschool used much print, his reading skills were above those of the average hearing child his age. He was confident, curious, and happy, and did not yet know that he was different or missing things other children had in terms of language or experience.

When Charles was five years old, another change had to be made. He had outgrown both the regular preschool and the special preschool class for the hearing impaired. The special classes for the deaf were attached to a public school in a town six miles away from his own school. Charles attended this for one year. He spent his mornings in kindergarten, where he learned to do what the others did. His teacher was a regular kindergarten teacher with no special skill, but she did make things as easy for Charles as possible. She would see that he sat near her so he could watch her face as she spoke. She learned to let him sit with his back to the light so he could see her features clearly. She was aware that he might misunderstand and was prepared to repeat things to him, speaking clearly, but at normal rate and loudness.

Charles spent afternoons with the special teacher who gave him continued speech and language lessons. His teacher kept close tabs on what went on in kindergarten and what would come up in the future. In this way she knew what particular vocabulary and language would be used and she could prepare him for it. At the end of the year he tested above average in readiness for first grade. His parents were now concerned that because he had always travelled to a different school Charles was an isolate in his own neighborhood. They therefore determined to follow another track.

When Charles turned six, he entered first grade in his local school, arriving at school 45 minutes before it opened to receive special help from a teacher consultant. He and the teacher consultant did their work early so that Charles need not miss much of the regular classwork. Without the teacher consultant help, Charles would have had a much more difficult time.

A teacher consultant (or itinerant teacher) travels from school to school serving the children who have sufficient speech and language to be mainstreamed. He or she keeps close contact with the classroom teachers and prepares pupils for materials that will be coming up in the class. The itinerant teacher will work on new vocabulary, new concepts, and new language, and ascertain that the pupil can understand what the regular teacher is talking about. The itinerant teacher also helps the regular teacher understand the difficulties a hearing impaired child will have such as: the child cannot understand what the teacher is saying if the teacher is talking while writing on the blackboard; the child will not hear the talking of children who are far away; the child cannot lip-read unless he or she sits close and is not facing the light. A teacher consultant will also work closely with the parents and will serve as ombudsman when difficulties arise.

Charles also received special help in speech from a speech therapist several days a week. However, most of the time Charles was a first grader among first graders learning what they learn and attempting to do what they do. At home his parents constantly reinforced what he was doing and also worked on all new material that came up. Charles' success is, of course, due not only to the fact that he had outstanding ability. The supportive help of teachers and parents was essential.

This educational pattern was continued for Charles during his second, third, and fourth grades of school. Academically he has done well and is in the top reading group of his class. His other academic skills—mathematics, spelling, science, even composition—have all kept pace. His speech is usually intelligible and pleasant. He understands others very well if he can see them talking. But he is still not quite a normal child in terms of social interaction with the other children. Why not?

Let us remember that a hearing impairment is a communication problem. Charles cannot understand everything either the teacher or the children say, so at times he makes errors. He uses a combination of lip-reading and hearing to understand. In any group situation he is at a disadvantage because he may not be able to identify who is speaking in time to lip-read the message. The older the children grow the more complicated their conversation becomes and the more they use idioms and slang. Charles may miss out on these.

While Charles was in first and second grades, his social situation was good. The children were interested in him and in his hearing aid. He had several close friends and was included in birthday parties. Third grade proved more difficult. Each third grader was beginning to explore his own world and found less time for Charles. They formed their own little groups and went off chatting and playing. Charles was often left out and several times came home crying. He did not know how to cope with being so alone and felt hurt.

Things improved during fourth grade. Charles matured and learned to make advances himself. Teachers and parents made an effort to see that he knew the rules of games, that he was taught the slang and colloquialisms of his peers. His participation in recess and gym activities increased and with this his self-esteem was largely restored. He still has no "group" of his own and spends much time alone with his parents, but he is more a part of the class group than the year before.

What is ahead for Charles? He will continue through sixth grade in his present school with his present class, receiving daily help from the itinerant teacher. His social situation should improve as his classmates grow in tolerance and understanding. Charles is never a behavior problem or an annoyance. He is a charming, alert, intellectually curious boy. Largely the problem is that he cannot understand all of the conversation that takes place around him. It is a little bit more difficult to talk to Charles. The fact that he must be watching you to get the total message takes a bit of patience and effort from others. Charles has the patience and makes the effort. Other children are often lacking in both.

Charles is remarkably realistic about his situation and undoubtedly will make his way successfully through junior and senior high schools. Since he is currently performing above average in his school work, it is expected that he will continue to do so. Success in high school may well be followed by university work and some sort of professional career.

To date Charles has been educated orally and lives and communicates entirely with hearing people. His parents, early in planning for him, looked into alternative educational tracks and chose this one for him. They, along with his teachers, gave him the training necessary for him to function in the hearing-talking world. His parents have seen to it that he is able to achieve in the "mainstream."

What were the alternative educational philosophies they looked into and what alternative educational tracks were available to Charles had he been unable to function successfully in the route chosen?

EDUCATIONAL APPROACHES

When Charles' parents began to investigate the educational opportunities open to their son, they soon learned that there are two fundamental communication systems in use today with the hearing impaired both in the United States and abroad—the *oral* and the *manual.* Oral communication makes use of the speech and hearing mechanisms, while the manual makes use of the hands and fingers. A real controversy has existed throughout the history of the education of the deaf as to which system of communication should be used in educating the child. Those who support the use of oral communication have as their objective the integration of the hearing impaired child into the hearing world. They believe that this can best be accomplished by teaching the child in an oral environment, using exclusively oral receptive and expressive language. There is no disagreement on the appropriateness of this approach for the hard-of-hearing or the less severely hearing impaired child. The disagreement centers around the most effective approach for the more severely hearing impaired and the prelingually profoundly deaf.

Those who support the use of manual communication believe that communication and the exchange of ideas which lead to expanded information are more important than the form of communication used. They therefore advocate use of whatever system is easiest for the child and emphasize the importance of visual communication for the profoundly deaf. They are less concerned with the ability of the child to communicate with hearing people than they are with his self-concept as a happy, productive hearing impaired individual who may or may not derive his social satisfactions from the hearing world. They believe that the child will learn language more readily and reach a higher achievement level if he grows up with a manual language. They also believe that he will be a less frustrated and better adjusted individual.

The Oral Approach

The oral approach emphasizes oral communication, setting as its prime objective teaching the child to speak and to understand spoken language through a combination of use of residual hearing and lip-reading. It involves testing the amount of residual hearing a child has, fitting the child with the appropriate hearing aid, teaching the child to use it, and stimulating the child to talk to express his or her ideas and get his or her wants satisfied. Obviously the more a child hears, the more successful this approach will be. Since most hearing impaired children are born to hearing parents (Schein and Delk 1974), this is usually the approach used first. This was the approach Charles' parents chose.

In recent years the emphasis in oral education has been on early identification and use of an intensive auditory approach. The hearing losses of young children can be accurately measured as young as six months. They can be fitted with hearing aids. Parents can be trained to surround them with sound and continuous repetitive speaking. It has been clearly demonstrated that the resiliency of young children is such that even the severely deaf can learn to make use of very small remnants of residual hearing and learn to develop speech and language in the natural way, through their ears. This requires parent education and close guidance, for the process is not easy and language input must be continuous.

The oral approach can still be successful, even in cases where early identification did not take place or when the loss of hearing is so severe that the use of hearing alone is not adequate for language learning. In these instances the hearing is reinforced through use of speechreading. Children slowly learn to understand what is said to them through watching the lips and face of the speaker. Amplification is used, both to improve speech quality and to add information to the messages being received, but primarily the child understands what is said through use of his or her eyes. There are many difficulties involved, not only because many of us use careless articulation, but because speech reading itself is an imperfect communication tool—50 percent to 60 percent of our speech sounds are invisible. Many speech sounds look alike. The words *pie, by,* and *my* appear to be formed in the same way if one is only watching the lips. So do the words *toe, dough,* and *no.* Speech reading also requires good lighting. It demands that the speaker and listener look at each other, thus keeping the eyes from performing other tasks. To understand the inadequacy of lip-reading all you need to do is to turn the sound off your television and sit and watch for five minutes, trying to understand. Nevertheless many children, including some profoundly deaf children, become extraordinarily successful lipreaders and have reached high language levels. When this has occurred, it has involved many years of special education at the hands of teachers skillful in a variety of techniques for developing speech and language as well as in teaching subject matter. Those who support the oral approach know that manual communication may be easier for the profoundly deaf child, but they believe that use of it will interfere with the mastery of speech and speechreading.

The Manual Approach

Manual communication has primarily been used to supplement or take the place of oral communication for the profoundly deaf. Recently the use of manual language has received much publicity through increased use of interpreters in public places. Frequently interpreters will translate the news for hearing impaired listeners. Signing was also used during the 1976 presidential campaign by several candidates. Historically there have been two main forms of manual communication: fingerspelling and sign language.

Fingerspelling uses a manual alphabet with specific finger positions that represent each letter of the alphabet. In the United States only one hand is used; in some countries both hands are involved. Fingerspelling parallels print. Words, phrases, and sentences can all be spelled out. Illustrations of the positions that represent letters are given in Figure 8.6.

Fingerspelling obviously presents a very clear message and can eliminate the ambiguities of lipreading. It is not as rapid a form of communication as speech, but it is precise and can be very useful in teaching new vocabulary and language structure. It is seldom used by itself in communication but either accompanies speech or is intermixed with signs when no sign exists for a word to be used. One long-established educational approach, the Rochester Method named after the Rochester School for the Deaf in Upstate New York, combined speaking and fingerspelling. High educational achievements have been attained by graduates of this school.

Sign Language is a linguistic system where standardized hand or arm gestures are used to convey the meaning of a word, concept, or idea. This visual language was developed in France at the end of the seventeenth century by a monk, Abbé Charles Mitchell de L'Epee, who devoted his life to teaching the deaf. The communication system slowly spread and was brought to the United States by Thomas Hopkins Gallaudet, the founder of the first free school for the deaf in America in 1817. With few changes and alterations this became AMSLAN, the American Sign Language. As traditionally used sign language does not follow English syntax. Word order is unimportant. Many grammatical constructions are completely omitted; among these are articles, prepositions, word endings that denote verb tense, noun transformations such as plurals and possessives, and comparatives. It is, however, a very rapid means of communication and is used widely among the adult deaf. An illustration of sign language is presented in Figure 8.7. Orally the question would be, "Where does your father work?" In sign language it becomes, "Where work your father?"

FIGURE 8.6

The American manual alphabet

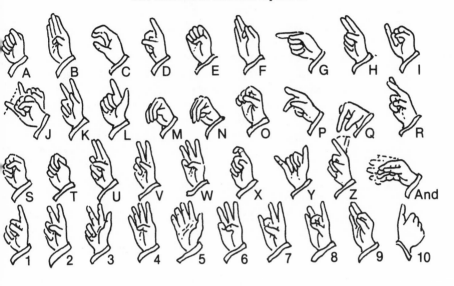

FIGURE 8.7

American sign language

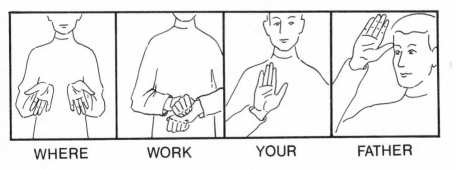

WHERE WORK YOUR FATHER

Source: adapted from C. J. Springer, *Talking with the Deaf,* 1961.

There have been several recent attempts to alter sign language and to make it follow the English pattern by using word order, word endings, and all parts of speech. These revisions are designed to improve the language and reading level of the deaf as well as for increasing the accuracy of communication. Several of these revisions are described in detail in *Gallaudet Today* 5(2)(1974–75). These adaptations are being made in the hope that those who use this communication will also be using correct English. Children using this, therefore, will have higher levels of reading and language. Other countries in Europe are carrying out similar revisions, adapting the traditional sign language to fit their own linguistic system.

Some schools are experimenting with using these new forms of sign language along with speech and the use of hearing aids. This approach is called total communication. It is described by Dr. Sidney Wolff (1973) as follows: "In this system all methods of communication are used and encouraged because all can contribute to the acquisition of a usable language system by the deaf child. In the past schools have used the oral system until the child is perhaps twelve and begun total communication in the middle and advanced schools. Some schools now, however, begin total communication when the child first enters school at age three or four" (pp. 116–17).

Those who strongly support this approach believe in early intervention services which will teach parent and child sign language along with oral communication. Dr. Wolff's recommendation is: "ideally the deaf child should have three things: a manual communication system together with maximum use of residual hearing at home, training in speech and speech reading at a clinic, and the opportunity to participate in an early childhood education program" (p. 115).

Total communication is a philosophy rather than a methodology. It is applauded by most manualists who strongly believe that children can learn both oral and manual communication simultaneously. In other words children would be bilingual. As we have seen, oralists cannot support the approach for most young children because they believe that the use of sign will interfere with learning oral skills. There is as yet no research that supports one side against the other.

Another interesting recent approach is cued speech, devised by Dr. Orrin Cornett (Cornett and Henegar 1971). In this instance finger positions close to the lips are used to signal which of several sounds that look alike are being used by the speaker. It must accompany speech and is an attempt to both accelerate the development of language through reduction of ambiguities and to improve the production of speech itself. It is assumed that as the child grows the cues can be dropped and the child can rely solely on speech and speech reading. This approach is being used experimentally in several schools for the deaf in the United States and Australia. It has not been widely accepted by the adult deaf themselves.

The failure to agree on an appropriate educational approach can create a real dilemma for parents who are faced with the responsibility of choosing which avenue of communication to use for their child. In many instances they have inadequate information on which to base their choice and they may also have limited avenues to choose between in their home community. As we have seen, most hearing impaired children have hearing parents. It is only natural, therefore, that most parents initially choose the oral approach; 85 percent of children in schools and classes for the deaf are currently being educated in this way.

Parents who live in a community where there is no provision for early intervention and training in oral communication skills can take advantage of the John Tracy Correspondence Course established by Mrs. Spencer Tracy in Los Angeles. This course is free for all who wish to participate. Whether the oral or manual approach or a combination is most appropriate depends on the individual child and the attitudes of the child's parents. Most children can learn effectively through a well-organized oral approach and should be enabled to do so. In the cases where this fails or is inappropriate, alternative systems should surely be available. Whatever the system may be, it should not be looked down upon as inferior else the child's own self-esteem becomes inevitably damaged. If manual or total communication is used, it is essential that parents and siblings also learn the system so that full conversation can take place in the home. This means that when in the presence of the deaf child all members of the family should converse with signs. The child can then learn from "over-seeing" conversations as the hearing child learns from "over-hearing." The child will also, of course, learn from conversations in which he or she is directly involved.

This will not be an easy task. Learning sign language may be easy for young deaf children, but it is difficult for most hearing persons. For adults to become skillful in both receptive and expressive sign language is a task as difficult as learning a foreign spoken language.

EDUCATIONAL PROGRAMMING

The educational programs available to hearing impaired children vary in setting as well as in philosophy. Parents again may have severe difficulties deciding which is appropriate for their child. The incidence of hearing impairment is sufficiently low so that most small communities do not offer adequate programs for the severely deaf. Charles' parents were fortunate in that they had good facilities nearby. However, in most states there are the following educational opportunities.

The current trend in special education is toward mainstreaming for many exceptional children. This is appropriate for the hard-of-hearing and some severely hearing impaired *if* early intervention has enabled the child to close the language gap, and if supportive services are available. Most professionals working in the field of the hearing impaired are very concerned about mainstreaming when a serious hearing impairment is present and a language delay exists. Particularly important is the ability to read and write on a level equal to that of the class. If the child has not reached this level, he or she may just sit in a classroom and never know what is going on. The child's situation is similar to that of a child who attends a class where all teaching takes place in a foreign language. Charles was mainstreamed only when he had mastered the skills needed for first grade and when it was clear that supportive services from the teacher consultant were available. He could communicate with both teachers and children.

The next most normal situation consists of special day classes in a regular school setting. There will be special rooms for the hearing impaired. Most will be equipped with high fidelity hearing equipment as well as many visual aids such as overhead projectors, film projectors, and a variety of teaching machines. The teacher-pupil ratio is five to six pupils to a teacher. This differs from state to state. Teacher aides are provided where there are very young children or in classes for the multi-handicapped. This situation is good when there are sufficient children of approximately the same age so that grouping becomes possible. It is no more advisable to have a wide range of age and ability in a class for the hearing impaired than it is in a class for the hearing. Such a setting also requires good supervision for consistency of teaching and support for the new, inexperienced teacher. If a local school system can support only one class for its hearing impaired children, it will do better to transport these children elsewhere. Most day class programs follow the oral approach and will integrate children for social purposes, moving to academic integration when the child is ready.

Large cities frequently have separate day schools for the deaf. Children are bused to these schools and stay there all day. Historically these schools have been oral in philosophy. However, since they will frequently have programs extending to children of high school age, manual communication may be used for academic and pre-vocational teaching. Such schools are often burdened with the fact that their successful pupils leave them for integrated programs and as a result they find that at the upper grade levels they are dealing primarily with children who do not have good communication skills.

Almost all states also have residential schools for children who come from rural areas where no day programs exist, or for the very profoundly deaf who are not succeeding in oral day programs. Although many of these have for years used the oral approach in their classrooms, American Sign Language is used after school. Some schools have used a combination of fingerspelling and sign language. Increasingly others are experimenting with Total Communication as described earlier.

Residential schools take students through the high school years and offer both academic and pre-vocational programs. They also offer counselling and guidance programs. Many people are prone to criticize the residential educational setting as unnatural and restrictive. On the other hand, many of the prelingually profoundly deaf have needed such a protective environment. Loneliness for the child may disappear when he goes there. After-school hours can be full of activity. Students may meet their future spouses at such a school and they may make friends that will stay with them throughout their lives (Bellefleur 1974). However, many of these schools are now down in enrollment as public day school programs expand. A very real question concerns the future use of all state residential schools which frequently have very large and excellent plants but which are not now fully utilized. It is presumed that residential schools will remain and are needed, but some change in objective and in personnel served may take place (Brill 1975). The graduates of these schools tend to find their social satisfactions in the deaf world although their work place may be in the hearing world.

In addition to these public-supported schools are many private schools, both day and residential. These schools are primarily oral in approach and have been generally successful. In some instances states will pay the tuition of a hearing impaired child to attend such a school if facilities are not available in his home community.

When a deaf young adult has graduated either from a day or residential program for the deaf, but is unable to function in a regular educational program, he still has some special educational facilities open to him on the post-secondary level. The oldest of these is Gallaudet College, a liberal arts program for the deaf in Washington, D.C. This was established in 1864 by the U.S. Congress to provide opportunity for higher education to those whose oral communication skills made attendance at regular post-secondary educational institutions impossible. The Simultaneous Method, the combination of sign, fingerspelling, and speech, that is similar to total communication, is used in all classes. In previous years most graduates of Gallaudet either became teachers of the deaf in residential schools or became librarians or clerical workers for the federal government.

Much interest in post-secondary education for the intelligent but prelingually profoundly deaf young adult followed the publication of the Babbidge Report in 1964, which clearly revealed the inadequacy of the existing educational institutions for meeting the needs of the hearing impaired population. Students who were graduating from public residential schools had at best the equivalent of an eighth grade education. Five-sixths of deaf adults were working in manual jobs as contrasted to only one-half the hearing population. A strong recommendation was made for the establishment of post-secondary programs with particular emphasis on technical and vocational education. A direct result of the study was the use of federal funds for this purpose, and many post-secondary programs have since been set up. The best known of these is the National Technical Institute for the Deaf which is affiliated with Rochester Institute of Technology in Rochester, New York. Here students are trained for the vocation of their choice provided they have the ability. Special classes are provided when needed to raise skill levels such as communication, language or reading. Interpreters and tutors assist students in participating in the regular RIT classes. Notetaking may be done by others.

During the past decade ancillary services have also been added to other technical schools and some community colleges that permit the non-oral deaf to participate in their programs. *A Guide to College-Career Programs for Deaf Students* (Rawlings *et al.* 1975) listed forty-three of these in 1975. Among these are computer programing, engineering, drafting, and in fact all technical and professional jobs that specifically do not require hearing. Graduates today of Gallaudet, NTID, and other postsecondary programs can be found in a range of occupations far wider than a decade ago.

THE HEARING IMPAIRED ADULT

It is difficult to describe clearly the achievements reached by the hearing impaired adult today. The hard-of-hearing and many of the severely deaf who have been successfully mainstreamed are not counted in statistics.

They have joined the hearing world, may be found in all walks of life, and do not consider themselves members of a special group of people. Charles will probably join this group.

We have with us, however, a community made up of profoundly deaf people who join together because they understand each other. The deaf world is not an unhappy world. It is not a ghetto into which people have been forced. Rather it is a world that people have chosen because of ease of communication. It is centered around skill in use of manual communication. There are clubs, athletic teams, churches, and much social life. Many deaf people marry each other and may or may not have hearing impaired children. Most will have friends and relatives in the hearing world and will find their jobs there. For fun and social support, however, they seek their own society.

The recent invention of Telecommunication for the Deaf (TTY) has increased the ability of this group to communicate with each other over distance. When two teleprinters are electrically connected with each other by a standard telephone wire, words typed on one teleprinter are converted to tone-code. This code travels the wire and is reconverted into word forms by the second teleprinter. No speaking is needed. Obviously this invention widens the deaf person's ability to communicate very much (Bellefleur 1976).

The rate of unemployment in this group is not high, but the rate of underemployment is. The median income earned by deaf families in the United States is only 84 percent of that earned by the average family. It is hoped that the expansions of post-secondary education will do much to improve this situation.

ADDITIONAL CASE HISTORIES

Not all hearing impaired children will be like Charles, and as their parents look at alternative philosophies of communication and alternative educational tracks, they will be influenced by different factors. Their child may have more or less hearing. There may be additional impairments. The home environment may have different factors at work that affect the developmental and the educational progress of the child. A brief look at some additional cases may be helpful in understanding the range of types of children that are included in the group designated as "hearing impaired" and the complexities that are involved in educational planning for them.

The Hard-of-Hearing Child

The hard-of-hearing child is one who experiences loss of loudness (see Figure 8.2). The child can hear voice, the rhythm and inflection of speech, and parts of words and phrases. As a result the child babbles as an infant and appears to be more normal than does the severely deaf child. But the hard-of-hearing child is frequently, therefore, not identified as early as was Charles. He or she has far more to build on, and amplification will be extremely useful.

This child will probably not hear all sounds even with a hearing aid. There will be particular difficulty with the voiceless consonants, such as *p, t, k, s.* The phrase "Happy Birthday" will sound like "a-ee-birday" because the *p* and *th* are inaudible. The child will also have difficulty hearing the small unaccented words of our language, such as articles, prepositions, and connectives. As a result the child will have both speech defects and language delay. The child's language may in fact resemble a pidgin English and at times may lapse into a jargon similar to what a two-year-old child uses when imitating adults on the telephone. Early language and speech therapy can be very effective indeed, and usually this child can attend regular school provided he or she is given adequate supportive help and is understood by his or her teachers.

One of the main difficulties the hard-of-hearing child experiences is that because the child speaks with rather normal voice quality and can communicate well in one-to-one conversations, people think the child can hear better than he does. The child may be labelled lazy, inattentive, or even mentally retarded when the real difficulty is that the child is not hearing all that is said. The child will always have difficulty in noisy situations since it will be hard for the child to separate background from foreground noise. A teacher's message may be drowned out. Since sound decreases rapidly with distance, the child must sit near the teacher. If the child is using lipreading to reinforce what he or she is hearing, the child must be able to see the teacher. Often, to alleviate some of these difficulties, the regular classroom teacher will wear a microphone that broadcasts what he or she is saying directly to a high fidelity hearing instrument that the child wears.

Straining to hear and to understand is tiring. The hard-of-hearing child may become tense and high strung from strain. The child will need special help in speech and language through most of the school years. Also the child and all who work and live with the child will benefit from counselling that helps them to understand the child's particular problems. The prognosis, however, is excellent provided rehabilitation begins while the child is young and consistent support is always present.

The Severely Hearing Impaired Child

A child with an audiogram similar to Charles' will usually be noticed as "different" about the time Charles was or shortly thereafter. To this child the phrase "Happy Birthday" may only sound like "a-ir-ay" since other sounds are beyond the child's hearing range. In many cases the problem may not be as quickly diagnosed as was Charles', or the audiological and otological examinations may take much longer. This may be due to parents' delaying action, to pediatricians' delaying referral, and to lack of facilities in the area in which the family lives so that travel and the time necessary for arranging the trip delays evaluation and the beginning of training.

In many instances the parents cannot carry out the intensive work that Charles' parents performed. Many parents are so overcome by grief that they are immobilized, or they go through periods of seeking for cures and causes. They may endure self-blame or blame each other. The total home environment may become tense and strained. There may be other siblings of close age in the family who have their own needs and who often show extreme sibling rivalry, sensing the concern over the child who cannot hear and resenting the time and worry this child is causing. These situations can all be handled, but they cause difficulties that were not present in Charles' case.

The result of all these factors may be a delay in the use of auditory stimulation and an extension of the language retardation. If the delay lasts until the child is two years of age, the child may rebel against the use of a hearing aid. The child is too busy running around and exploring the environment. The child's very lack of communication is causing increasing frustration. The child may develop tantrums, may learn that loud screaming is the way to get attention. The child has already almost missed the crucial language learning period without developing any useful receptive or oral language. As a result the child becomes difficult to live with and places a real burden on the family.

Such a child will not enter preschool at age three using some speech and language as Charles did. The child will need to learn social behavior and attention skills before much real language learning can take place. In this instance psychosocial problems have been added to an already existent hearing problem. This child will need intensive special teaching in a special classroom for many years. The thought that the child, at age six, can enter first grade and, with educational support from a teacher consultant, maintain normal educational growth is unrealistic. Given experienced teachers and a consistent education program the child may succeed in an oral-auditory program. However, if the child falls too far behind, his or her full potential will not be reached and the child may perform as if he or she were profoundly deaf.

The Profoundly Deaf Child

The profoundly deaf child is even deafer than Charles, and the child hears only enough to detect one or two changes in pitch and intensity. The child probably will not hear the phrase "Happy Birthday" at all or it will sound like "a-u-u." In some instances the child may only be able to detect the presence and absence of sound. Like Charles, the child will be identified while still very young, will experience all the difficulties that the severely deaf do and more, too. Amplification with the most powerful of hearing aids may assist the child in controlling the loudness and pitch of his or her voice, but it will not assist the child greatly in learning language. For that the child must rely on visual input. Some children become very skillful speech readers, but others do not and at some point in their educational career shift to some form of manual communication.

The profoundly deaf child may learn to talk adequately, to work, and to get around in the hearing world, but the child's speech will rarely be natural in quality. It probably will be flat, lacking in intonation and rhythm, and will draw attention to the child as "different." In many instances the child's lip-reading ability will not permit easy conversation with others. The child may, therefore, frequently seek out the companionship of other deaf people and will get social satisfactions from this group. If the child becomes dependent on manual communication, it is essential that the child's family also learn this. Otherwise parent and child will find themselves separated by an insurmountable communication barrier. It is very unfortunate when parents and children cannot talk things over. Profoundly deaf children usually cannot learn at the same rate as hearing children. The language delay is so large that it frequently causes three to four years delay in educational development. Gentile (1969) reports that deaf eight-year-olds read at the level of high first graders. This is a retardation of 1½ years. This reading retardation increases as the pupil progresses, so that by age twelve the child is four years retarded and at age sixteen, six to seven years behind. It has generally been assumed that profoundly prelingually deaf adults today seldom have achieved above a fourth-grade education.

The profoundly deaf child obviously needs special education, either in the special class or special school. If the child is to succeed in developing oral communication skills, the child needs extremely well-trained and skillful teachers. In most instances the child will use manual communication in adult life. This is the child who may benefit most from Total Communication.

Hearing Impaired with Additional Handicaps

Secondary impairments can accompany any type of hearing loss and include visual, physical, mental, and psychological problems of all types. These particularly occur when the cause of the impairment is rubella, prematurity, or birth trauma. Obviously the greater either the hearing impairment or the additional impairment the more serious the educational problem becomes. If the secondary impairment is overlaid on a profound hearing loss, the educational approach may be manual, more frequently sign language than fingerspelling. If the hearing loss is moderate to severe, an oral-auditory approach will be more successful. In all instances of multihandicap, careful diagnostic teaching is required. Helen Keller is today's best-known deaf blind individual. However, she always said that she thought her deafness was more a handicap than her blindness, for it prevented normal communication.

The Post-Lingually Hearing Impaired Child

The child in this group that is of most concern to educators is the child who suddenly experiences a severe cessation of the ability to hear. In most cases it will be a child who has had meningitis. The key difference between this child and others of parallel hearing ability is that the child will already have established language. The child will experience receptive language problems depending on the extent of his or her hearing disability, but the child will retain the ability to speak despite the fact that there may be changes in voice quality, rate of speech, and articulation skills. The child's greatest difficulty may be psychological, for the trauma that accompanies the sudden removal of sound from life is very great.

Rehabilitation efforts here will be two-fold, first to probe and find if any residual hearing remains. If it does, auditory training and use of amplification is immediately commenced to keep the residual hearing functioning. The second effort will be to develop speechreading skills. This will be an easier task than for the prelingually hearing impaired child because the skill can be attached to an already known language. If the child was old enough to have already learned to read and write, that child's communication problem will be much less than if not. If all goes well, this child can remain in the mainstream if given supportive help during the adjustment period and while developing lipreading skills.

The Child from the Home of Nonoral Deaf Parents

No presentation of varying cases of hearing loss would be complete without some mention of the special circumstances that accompany the hearing impaired child who grows up in a nontalking home. In some respects a deaf child born to deaf parents may be better off. The parents are not surprised that they have a child who does not hear normally. There may be no period of grief and adjustment in the home. Also this child will in most instances be exposed to and learn sign language very young, during the language learning years. Hence the child comes to school frequently better adjusted than does the child from a hearing home and also may come with a more developed concept of language even if it be manual. The child who is most handicapped by spending early years in the nonoral environment will be the child who is hard-of-hearing or severely hearing impaired. This child will not in most cases get an early exposure to sound and may never make the fullest use of whatever hearing potential exists. The child's parents may fail to understand either that the child does have residual hearing or that it is important. Furthermore, in many instances the parents cannot themselves expose him to oral speech. The child does not have, therefore, an equal opportunity to learn speech.

SUMMARY

Charles' case history, along with background material and the briefer presentation of alternative cases, has been presented in an effort to show that hearing impairment is one of the least understood and most complicated of all handicaps. Hearing people do not fully understand the ramifications of a profound loss because ears cannot be completely shut nor can all that has been learned through hearing be eradicated from the mind. Hearing loss is usually classified as a physical handicap, but the results of the physical damage to the hearing mechanism are primarily intellectual, social, psychological, and vocational in nature.

There is great need for increased public education concerning this impairment, both to improve the chances of the young deaf child to overcome the deficit and to improve the acceptance of the adult deaf by the hearing world. The prime need is for early detection, early intervention, early use of amplification, early parent education, and intensive effort spent toward enabling language development to take place during the formative years in the most natural way possible. For the child it is vital that parents and educators alike understand the differences among degrees of hearing loss, the significance of hearing loss, and the need for intensive special education. For the adult it is vital that particularly the working world understand that a deaf person who does not speak well may still be a person who thinks, feels, understands, and can perform in many areas as well as his or her hearing counterpart.

As always there is need for increased knowledge. There exists today too large a gap between the language and nonlanguage intelligence quotients of both deaf children and deaf adults. The question of how to reduce this gap in all instances has not been answered. There is an interaction effect between degree of hearing loss, intactness of other cognitive and perceptual areas, socioeconomic home environment, and parental support that calls for investigation of each case and individualized prescriptive programming for each child. This is a costly and difficult undertaking, but every hearing impaired child is surely entitled to it. The successes of many deaf adults and the contributions they have made to society make it clear that it is well worth it.

Most people who work with and for the hearing impaired are tireless and devoted. Their goal is that each and every hearing impaired child may be enabled to reach his full potential as it appears Charles will do. Most will do it through developing oral communication skills. But not all can and not all do. For these we need improved techniques for language development. It may be that we need to devise ways of determining at a younger age which child can learn orally, as did Charles, and which child cannot and therefore needs an alternative early intervention system (Downs 1974). It may be that we need to improve our alternative communication systems. We certainly can improve our educational techniques.

The children like Charles in our society, and those who also experience a severe hearing loss but may not be so fortunate in other ways, present us with an enormous challenge. Dr. Alexander Graham Bell wrote: "Of one thing I become more sure every day—that my interest in the deaf is to be a lifelong thing with me. I see so much to be done—and so few to do it. . . . I shall never leave this work" (Bruce 1973).

These words hold true today. Much has been accomplished since Bell's day, but there still is much to be done. The education of the deaf and hard-of-hearing is a fascinating, multi-dimensional, never-ending but greatly rewarding endeavor.

WILLIAM M. CRUICKSHANK and LAWRENCE J. LEWANDOWSKI

William Cruickshank's long and intensive career in special education has covered almost every facet of the field, and he is equally at home in many of the categories. His roles include extensive publication, research, administration, training, program development and parent involvement. He came to the University of Michigan in 1966 as Director of the multidisciplinary Institute for the Study of Mental Retardation and Related Disabilities after more than twenty years as Director of the Division of Special Education and Rehabilitation at Syracuse University. He holds professorships in four departments, and is Chairman of Special Education Programs as well. He is a consultant in the United States and many foreign countries. His erudition and scholarship are combined with his humanistic concern both for children and his many students who have become leaders. Parents found him demanding service for their children long before it was required by law. He knows many special youngsters as people and follows their careers.

Lawrence Lewandowski was a student of Cruickshank and brings to the work a keen analytical mind and a persistent search for new ways of looking at special education. His first-hand experiences with these children has sharpened his attention to their feelings and life destiny. At present Lewandowski is Psychologist and Supervisor of the Outpatient Diagnostic and Evaluation Services, Southgate Developmental Disabilities Center, Michigan Department of Mental Health.

9

Physical Handicaps

WILLIAM M. CRUICKSHANK AND LAWRENCE J. LEWANDOWSKI

THE CENTERVILLE TRANSPORT COMPANY bus pulled to a stop at the corner of Third and Central Streets, where three passengers waited to board it. A fourth, a young man, Terry Sloan who worked in a nearby bank, hastened toward it with his usual staggering gait, fists clenched, and jaw set. Just as he reached the bus, the driver who had seen Terry moving toward the bus stop, pulled away, remarking to a passenger seated behind him, "No drunks on this bus. Let 'em walk." "You're wrong," responded the passenger, "I know that man. He's an employee of the bank there on the corner and he has some sort of handicap—cerebral palsy, I think." "Well, he looks drunk to me," retorted the driver, "and I'm not going to take a chance."

While not all cerebral palsied adults are mistaken for those who have had one drink too many, those with mild spasticity, athetosis, ataxia sometimes are judged as such by those who have had little or no familiarity with the problem. The driver's behavior illustrates one of the problems physically handicapped people face in their daily lives, i.e., a lack of public information. Public employees need orientation to these problems, for not only do they unintentionally perform a disservice to the handicapped individual, they also place themselves as potential defendants in suits of discrimination and violation of the handicapped individual's civil rights. Other attitudes expressed toward the physically handicapped people are based on fear, guilt feelings, historical stereotypes, myths, and faulty information.

Cerebral palsy is but one of many different types of physical disabilities affecting children, youth, and adults. A child with cerebral palsy, actually Terry Sloan as a child, will be the focus of this chapter and the next.

The goals of this chapter are, first, to illustrate the scope and variation of physical handicaps in children and youth; and second, through the identification of a child, Terry, who is physically handicapped, to illustrate not only the problems related to that medical category, but also aspects of the individual's life, growth, and development, family and community living, wherein the disability plays a vital and often determining role.

THE PROBLEM AND CHARACTERISTICS

Who Are the Physically Handicapped?

Although there are numerous definitions of handicapping conditions, no one of them is fully satisfactory. The Office for the Handicapped in the U.S. Department of Health, Education and Welfare defines the problem in behaviorial terms in a manner concerned essentially with the individual's ability or lack of ability to function in his or her normal environment. The Social Security Administration defines the problem in terms of one's capacity to earn a living, while educators focus on ability to assimilate educational opportunities which lead to personal and social independence. The Office for the Handicapped recommends that a handicapped person is one who, "because of a physical or mental disability, is at a disadvantage in performing one or more major life activities." Such activities include self-care, socialization, education, employment, and movement.

There is a great variability among handicapped persons in their performance of the activities which are basic to modern living. Not only is the concept of individual difference between and among persons involved here, but also the degree and extent of the handicap itself. Two individuals of the same sex, age, intelligence, ethnic background, and social experience may have significant differences insofar as their interests and activity preferences are concerned. But even if these variables also were identical, their capacity to perform would be different if one, for example, were handicapped by a club foot and the other by lower extremity paraplegia. This stress on individual differences has been made in previous chapters, but it is accentuated again, for not only does this group illustrate the emotional and intellectual differences noted earlier, but also an extreme number of quite different problems related to the disease or illness.

Handicapping conditions are generally referred to medically as mild, moderate, or severe, depending upon the realities of functional limitation. This variability results in extremely complex problems with which families and school personnel must deal. Its impact on the life situation of the handicapped individual will be discussed in the following chapter, but it is introduced here because it is a pervading factor in all considerations of physical disability. While it is impossible to define physical disability as a single entity, this large group of children, youth, and adults is characterized by many different types of specific problems, some congenital and some adventitious; some resulting from accidents or injuries, others from illnesses and disease. Some physical handicaps still can be found in the columns of "cause unknown," although this number is reduced year by year as research provides new understanding of both cause and treatment.

Denhoff and Robinault (1960) categorize physical disabilities under several headings insofar as chronic disabilities in childhood are concerned. Their outline, here in expanded form, may be helpful in providing an understanding of the extent of this problem. Included, but not exhaustive of all physical disabilities, are the following:

I. Neurologic
   A. Syndromes of cerebral dysfunction
      1. Cerebral Palsy
      2. Mental Deficiency
      3. Epilepsy
      4. Hyperkinesis—behavior syndrome
   B. Sensory disorders, including vision, hearing, speech, perceptual and conceptual disorders, kinesthetic and tactile disorders. These are included here because each of the problems mentioned can be found in a given individual *in addition to* another physical disability. For example, a child with epilepsy may also be characterized by mental retardation, perceptual processing deficits, or possibly a visual disability.
   C. Miscellaneous
      1. Hydrocephaly
      2. Brain-tumor effects
      3. Progressive cerebral and lenticular degeneration (familial disease associated with cirrhosis of the liver)
      4. Cerebromacular degenerative diseases (skin discoloration, progressive)
      5. Other progressive neurological diseases
II. Orthopedic
   A. Residuals of trauma and accidents
      1. Sequelae of burns
      2. Spinal cord injuries
      3. Amputations

    B. Malformations
      1. Achondroplasia and chondrodysplasia (types of cartilage mal-
         formation, dystrophy)
      2. Foot deformities, dislocation of the hip
      3. Spina bifida (defect of spinal column through which spinal
         membranes protrude) and related congenital diseases
      4. Clidocranial dysostosis (absence or partial development of the
         clavicles and defective ossification of the skull)
III. Blood
    A. Leukemia
    B. Hemophilia
IV. Psychiatric
    A. Psychoses
    B. Neuroses
    C. Psychosomatic disorders

Five broad etiological factors which result in various forms of crippling: (1) congenital abnormalities, (2) infection, (3) metabolic disturbances, (4) traumatic conditions, and (5) unknown or miscellaneous
causes.

The term *congenital* refers to conditions which have their origins in
genetic, familial, or inherited determinants. The term has the same con-
notation as when it is used with blindness, deafness or other disabilities in
earlier chapters. There is a great variety of problems included in this category of the physically handicapped consisting of such disabilities as cerebral palsy, which has already been mentioned, Erb's palsy (a condition
resulting in paralysis of the muscles of the shoulder, arm, and hand),
spina bifida (paralysis due to lack of closure of portions of the bony elements in the spinal column), bone imperfections and hemophilia (congenital blood coagulation problem), congenital amputations, and a series of
postural deformities, such as wry neck, spinal defects, postural foot deformities, and many other similar conditions.

Physical disabilities due to *infection,* although still prevalent, are
unnecessary in civilized and developed countries. Included within this
group of problems are poliomyelitis (infantile paralysis), tuberculosis and
osteomyelitis (disease of the growing portion of the bone structure), ar-
thritis, myositis, and epiphysitis (inflammation in the ends of the long
bones).

Metabolic disturbances appear to be the cause of such progressive
problems as muscular dystrophy, congenital myasthenia, multiple sclerosis, myasthenia gravis. Muscular dystrophy often does not make itself
known until the child has learned to walk when numerous falls, unsteady

gait, and nonrhythmic stride become noticeable. Likewise multiple sclerosis is a disease of a degenerative nature, which has its onset in young adulthood. Loss of muscle power in myasthenia is often congenital, and the prognosis is poor if untreated. With treatment, mortality in myasthenia gravis decreased from 80 percent in 1934 to 15 percent in 1956 (Osserman & Shapiro 1956).

Traumatic factors which result in crippling conditions are more commonly understood. Fractures and burns constitute the two greatest etiological problems in this category.

While the categories mentioned in the preceding paragraphs illustrate numerous physical problems in children and adults, by no means are they a complete listing of all the types of problems which may result in physical disability or crippling. Each, however, is unique and each when found in a child of school age presents challenges in understanding and programming to the school personnel. Each demands total attention and the readjustment of many family attitudes and arrangements. In post-school years each will require a society which is responsive to individual human needs and opportunities commensurate to those needs which make a full life possible.

Emotional problems such as have been discussed earlier are also characteristic of many physically handicapped children and youth particularly those with chronic and traumatic problems. Psychotherapy is often warranted as an intervention technique to alleviate some of these problems.

Chronic medical problems of a long-term nature also must be considered in any discussion of crippling conditions. These are usually classified under the heading of chronic problems rather than crippling conditions, but often their impact is equally serious. Included in this problem area are many diseases such as rheumatic fever, congenital heart defect, tuberculosis, cystic fibrosis, nephritis, Bright's disease, colitis and ileitis, hepatitis, allergies of numerous kinds, and malnutrition. Epilepsy, on which books have been written and which deserves more than mere mention here, is usually included in this group of childhood and adult problems. Diabetes, in a sense as much a developmental problem as some others which have been mentioned earlier, is likewise considered a chronic medical problem. Cancer, including leukemia, is a leading cause of child death, accounting for almost 12 percent of all deaths between the ages of one and 14 years (Connor 1975).

This long list of chronic disabilities in childhood is not included here to impress or confuse the reader, but to indicate the complexity of this problem as it must be conceptualized by educators; psychologists; physicians; occupational, speech and physical therapists; and others who will work with the child in order to bring him or her to maximum capacity. As the individual grows into adulthood and maturity other types of problems serve to handicap him. Industrial and automotive accidents take their toll and produce handicapped persons. The numerous wars in which the United States has participated since 1918 have also produced a significant number of handicapped persons with long-term disabilities. Degenerative diseases play a significant role in adult disability.

Kakalik *et al.* (1973) reported 1,676,000 children and youth between the ages of birth and 21 years in 1970 categorized as being crippled or having other health problems. There are estimated to be 83.3 million children and youth between the ages of birth and 21 years in the United States, 9.5 million of whom are handicapped in some way. Fifty thousand additional persons of the same ages were categorized by Kakalik as multihandicapped. Mental retardation in some degree, as discussed earlier, accounts for the most frequent multiple conditions. These are just estimates, however, and are often based on less than adequate reporting systems. It is obvious that the incidence of handicapping conditions and physical disabilities in the United States in 1979 remains one of significant proportions.

While the authors do not wish to overwhelm the reader with endless facts and statistics, some additional data may be helpful in providing background to the central theme of this chapter. The President's Committee on Employment of the Handicapped stated in 1974 that the handicapped population in the U.S. compares unfavorably with the general population in terms of education, economic status, and employability. The incidence of intellectual retardation is higher in some categories of physical disability than in the nonhandicapped population. Thus, it is to be expected that the educational levels might be different. However, it is also obvious that many handicapped persons have not been expected to achieve, to be educated, or to be employed just because they were physically disabled, an archaic attitude which often serves to penalize the physically handicapped and to deprive them of their constitutional rights.

Developmental Disabilities

The term "developmental disability" has been in popular usage since about 1970. While from the point of view of the federal legislative definition this term includes categories of problems not included in this chapter, it does overlap with the usual definition of the physically handicapped. Child and adult problems such as mental retardation and autism are defined as developmental disabilities, but unless there is a multiple problem, these would not be included in a chapter on the physically hand-icapped. Developmental problems like cerebral palsy, epilepsy, dyslexia, autism, and similar or related problems do overlap with others in the broad category of the physically handicapped.

There is not universal agreement regarding the use of the term de-velopmental disabilities, and the human problems included within the scope of the term are not always mutually exclusive to other diagnostic categories. There is an arbitrary basis, perhaps political as well, for the grouping which has taken place with the definition of developmental dis-ability. Generally speaking, however, developmental disabilities have life-span implications, and they require long-term therapeutic, educa-tional, and vocational services for the individual. Hobbs (1974) pointed out that "mental retardation, cerebral palsy, epilepsy, and childhood schizophrenia are the four most common causes of adult disability origi-nating in childhood and together account for more than three-fourths of those receiving special social security benefits as adults." It is also of in-terest to note that three of these debilitating conditions (mental retarda-tion, cerebral palsy, and epilepsy) can and often do occur in the same individual.

The Demography of Physical Disability

Few studies are concerned with social factors relating to handi-capped children and youth. More adequate data of this nature are avail-able pertaining to adults than to children. Allan and Cinskes (1972) state:

> In general, the disabled are older, poorer, and less educated than the total adult population, but they are similar to the total population in their marriage and child-bearing rates. Women are more likely not to be working at all if disabled, and men are likely to work part time. Of the severely dis-abled who remained in the labor force, nearly five times as many as those in the total population were unemployed. The family income of the disabled was about half that of the nondisabled. Forty percent of the disabled family units with children have less health insurance and greater medical costs. A look at the short-term disabled reveals few differences between them and those disabled more than six months. The short-term disabled were some-what younger, less severely disabled, and more likely to be involved in reha-bilitation programs.

Individual Differences and Complexity

We stated earlier that the central theme of this chapter would focus on children and youth with cerebral palsy, as examples of the global problems of the physically handicapped. The term *physical handicap* covers dozens of specific clinical categories, almost any one of which could serve as the theme of this chapter. Cerebral palsy has been selected as the example around which the ideas of this chapter are clustered. While all children with physical handicaps present unique individual differences, those with cerebral palsy do so in the extreme. This is due in large measure to the fact that the problem is one of the central nervous system which, when damaged in some manner, affects the total organism in a variety of ways.

CEREBRAL PALSY AND COMPLEXITY

Cerebral palsy is a long-term, nonfatal, noncurable disease resulting from accident, injury, or illness at the prenatal, perinatal, or early postnatal periods. It is primarily physical; that is, it shows itself in defects of the nervous system which result in faulty muscle control and use. Secondarily, however, since the nervous system is involved, children with cerebral palsy are often characterized by a high incidence of lower mental ability, by perceptual processing disabilities potentially involving all the sensory modalities which in turn result in learning disabilities, and also often by other physical disabilities such as the loss of hearing or visual acuity (Cruickshank 1976). These secondary correlates of cerebral palsy are usually more significant than the primary neurological problem, since they have an important implication for all aspects of learning, social adjustment, and for vocational careers. Cerebral palsy is an excellent example of a multiply handicapping condition.

The problem, however, is more complex even than what thus far had been described. This is due to the great variability within any group of cerebral palsied children. For example, there are several different subtypes of cerebral palsy, the most frequent of which are spastic, athetoid, ataxia, and rigid. Each has its own characteristics and limitations. Various types of damage will result in various types of limitations for the individual. Thus, cerebral palsy may evidence itself in a condition of hemiplegia (one-half of the body), paraplegia (usually the lower extremities of the body, but less frequently the upper extremities only), monoplegia (one arm or one leg), or quadriplegia (all extremities and usually the trunk, speech mechanisms, and facial characteristics as well). These terms apply to other disability categories, for example, poliomyelitis or paraplegia as in the case of serious water, skiing, or automobile accidents.

In addition to variability with regard to the location of the neuro-muscular problem, the perceptual disabilities mentioned earlier also may vary between and among children. For example, a child may be characterized by visual perceptual problems, but have normal auditory and tactile (haptic) perception. A second child may have an auditory perceptual problem, but be unaffected insofar as other modalities are concerned. A third child may be characterized by both auditory and visual perceptual problems. The combinations may be even more varied. When the variable of different intelligence levels is inserted into the picture, the issue of complexity becomes even more obvious.

Individual Differences

In a community cerebral palsy treatment center one of the groups of children includes several boys and girls. Variability within the group will be obvious to the reader. In addition, the authors suggest that the reader keep a number of things in mind as the next few pages are read and considered. First, one should note the range of physical and intellectual problems encountered in this small group of children with cerebral palsy. Second, the implications of the degrees of severity of the children's problems should be considered. Third, the reader should note and be cognizant of the different parental attitudes—attitudes which will have a significant impact on the total life experiences of the child. Finally, one should consider the different responses to these children which will be required of both treatment and educational systems.

Paul is seven years of age. His parents are middle-class people; the father is an accountant, and the mother maintains the home for the family, which consists of an older sister, aged eleven, and a brother who is nine years old—both of more than average mental ability. In comparison to other children with cerebral palsy, Paul is fortunate. He has a mild right spastic hemiplegia. He attends the treatment center primarily because he comes from an isolated rural area of the county, and lack of transportation has prevented his attending the public school. Paul could function perfectly well in a regular elementary classroom, for his disability is not great and his intelligence is normal. He is a well-adjusted child emotionally. His parents have always treated him as an equal to the other two children in the family, and they have expected him to assume his responsibilities in the home. His physical condition was noted by the parents and by their pediatrician at almost the same time, so that when he was not yet one year old the necessary physical therapy, parent education, and home training was begun. As a seven-year-old boy, Paul has few characteristics which separate him from his peers. Perceptually, there are no problems, and he learns with ease. When he is ready for junior high school, he will enter a public school, since the transportation problem will be solved. In the meantime, Paul's mother is forming a Cub Scout group of local rural boys, and in other ways is providing social experiences for Paul with boys of his own age. His social adjustment appears to be good.

> Mother's comment: At first, Paul's father and I devoted our every waking minute to him. We carried him around on the proverbial pillow. Then a friend of ours who lives on the next farm told us that we were making ourselves a slave to our own son, and that we would do better for him if we left the treatment of Paul to those who knew more about it than we did and devoted our time to giving him the most wholesome childhood we could. So here we go into the Cub Scouts, 4-H, when he's older, church activities, and we do everything we can to look on him as a normal boy. His father has a pony for him, and he is learning to ride. He swims a bit. Our hope is that he'll be a happy, well-liked boy at every age. We also have faith in the people who are trained to help kids like Paul.

Doug is eight. His father is president of the Rotary Club; his mother is active in many social groups in the community. The Wabash Country Club is an important hub for the family activities. There are no brothers or sisters. Doug has a moderate spastic hemiplegia which, in contrast to Paul, is more severe. This is because his intelligence level, measured as accurately as possible on the Wechsler Intelligence Scale for Children, shows a verbal IQ of 78, a performance quotient of 64, and a total IQ of 71. Perceptually, Doug does not have any unusual problems. Treatment of him did not begin until he was three years of age, for the parents had been traveling much of his young life, and although he had been with them, assisted by a maid, the parents were not in any one place long enough to provide him with consistent treatment. They had also been advised that the delay of a few years would not hurt him any. The fact of the matter is that although he is of an educable level, Doug functions at a much more immature level, and is far below the readiness level for any type of work with reading or number concepts. His writing skills are exceedingly poor. If the parents could accept the problem, Doug would profit from continued and supportive psychotherapy. This will probably never happen.

Mother's comment: Of course, we have given Douglas every possible advantage. We have really spared nothing. We had a private duty nurse for him until he was three, but after that it seemed that a good maid could probably do what was needed. I am sorry it has been so difficult for me to get here to visit with you, but I am overworked with engagements, you know.

Father's comment: I don't know why this had to happen to us. I could have given that boy every advantage in life—a business, a social career, even politics, if he'd wanted it. I'm well known around, you know. But he'll hardly make it, I guess. I'm really disappointed in Doug.

Terry is eleven. He is a left spastic hemiplegic of a very severe degree. His problem has been known since he was an infant, and the parents sought treatment for him at the time he was eighteen months, but they moved to another community five months later, and treatment stopped for quite a while. Terry's problems are serious. His physical condition is complicated by a low mental ability (IQ presumed to be about 60) and by visual perceptual problems, auditory perceptual problems, and resulting speech and communication problems. Terry's father is a milkman; his mother works in a neighborhood bar. There are four other children, one older and two younger than Terry. As an eleven-year-old boy, he compares favorably with Paul, who is four years his junior. Terry has poor skills in almost all aspects of his performance. He is in the treatment center for the first time, his parents having only this year moved into the community. He has been in six other schools or clinics for short periods of time since he was five years old. There are no data on him regarding his infant and early childhood development.

Father's comment: You might say I'm dumb. I don't know why Terry's like he is. He isn't like other kids. I guess his Mom didn't follow what the doc said before he was born. If'n she had, he'd probably be OK. But she didn't, so we'll make the best of it. I don't know what'll become of him though; he ain't got much of a future, that's for sure, but you know? I sort of love the kid even the way he is. What d'ya think'll come of Terry?

Jeff is nine. He is diagnosed as a quadriplegic athetoid type of cerebral palsy. His arms and legs are all seriously involved. He has unintelligible speech. His chewing and swallowing abilities are poor. He cannot suck from a straw. He must be fully cared for in all aspects of his physical needs. Like many athetoid children, his mental ability is estimated to be quite good. He cannot respond accurately to any intelligence test, but the qualitative evaluation of Jeff would indicate that he is capable of functioning at the normal or above normal levels. Jeff's parents are professional people; the father is a physician, and the mother was formerly an X-ray technician. There are no other children, the parents being unwilling to risk having another handicapped child. The mother had had two miscarriages before Jeff was born, a factor which often characterizes the family history where cerebral palsy is reported.

> Father's comment: There is no question about it. My wife and I were shocked when we realized that Jeff was cerebral palsied. I've given advice to a hundred patients' families about cerebral palsy, but when it hits home, it is a different thing. At first we couldn't accept it. We read everything. I consulted my colleagues here and elsewhere. I joined the American Academy for Cerebral Palsy to learn more. We gradually came to learn that Jeff's future is poor. If we can get him to any level of self-assistance, we'll be lucky. I guess the reality of the thing really set in the day I took out an annuity for Jeff so that I can assure that at least during his life, whatever that may be, he will have decent care.
>
> Mother's comment: My husband and I really had to support one another as the reality of Jeff began to sink in. It took months, but we made it. We will give Jeff every possible assistance he can use. We don't intend to look inward because of Jeff. I doubt we'll ever have another child born to us, but we are thinking about adopting—perhaps even a handicapped child who has the capacity to achieve if we give him the opportunity.

Mary is also eight years old. She is, like Doug, a right spastic hemiplegic. She, however, is a brilliant and only child whose intelligence level is estimated to be a gifted range. However, in contrast to Doug, Mary shows many characteristics of perceptual disability in haptic as well as in auditory and visual modalities. These problems have a serious impact on her ability to utilize her intelligence. She fortunately has two parents who do all they can to carry out the training regimen which the treatment center advocates. As a result, the child has made gains which are obvious to both the center staff and the parents as well. Her prognosis is not as good as some of the other children in her treatment group at the center.

> Mother's comment: Yes, we've really tried all the fancy fads and fashions with Mary. I guess I've read more books than any doctor. We—her father and I—have finally gotten all the bits and pieces of information into what we think is a rational concept. This includes the physical therapy program, the perceptual motor training, the communication development program, and a dozen other things which have to fit into the overall plan for

her. We'll work it out. Fortunately, we've got the time to give to her without smothering her, for she's got to learn to make decisions independent of us some day. We'll make it, I'm sure, but it certainly changes your life. I could be the most bitter woman in Wabash, but I'm not about to let this thing get me down—get us down, for the whole family is involved.

Ron has a paraplegic ataxic subtype of cerebral palsy. His medical record notes his problem to be "severe." Intellectually, he is normal. Emotionally he is seen as hyperactive and is subject to severe emotional disturbances if he is crossed in any way. This happens frequently because, due to his stumbling and uncoordinated gait, he is constantly inhibited insofar as motor activity is concerned. His balance is very poor, and as a ten-year-old boy he requires adult assistance to move, except for crawling. He must wear a helmet at all times, for he "falls hard," as his record indicates. He has broken his nose twice, once when he was six and more recently just before his tenth birthday. Ron is not handicapped by perceptual or learning problems. He is seen to be progressing quite well in activities related to school achievement. Ron is one of a set of twins. His twin sister, Peggy, is similar to him intellectually, is developing emotionally, and as a result of her more normal social adjustment, is obviously the favored of the two children by both parents. This parental favoritism does not assist Ron, who is aware of the position he holds in the family. Although Ron's slower physical development was noted by his parents, they did not bring the matter to the attention of their physician until Ron was three. Before that they assumed his failure to walk was just a matter of "developmental lag," a term which Ron's aunt, a teacher, used in characterizing the boy. Cerebral palsy is not something which can be left to the course of unassisted development.

> Mother's comment: Poor Ron. One handicap is enough, but *two*— that's almost more than *I* can take. If it weren't for Peggy, my life would be ruined. She will certainly have everything; everything we planned for the two before they were born will now be hers. She is the light of my life, and her father's too. We'll do all right by Ronny, but we will *really* do things for Peg.

Dan is nine, and his prognosis is not good. He, like Jeff, is diagnosed as a quadriplegic athetoid type of cerebral palsy. Although, due to his physical condition, it is impossible to measure his mental ability, he appears to be functioning at a level of the severely mentally retarded. His speech is completely unintelligible. There also appear to be both visual

and auditory perceptual problems. He cannot sit up without being tied into a chair in a sitting position. He is not toilet trained. He has no use of his
fingers. He also has petit mal seizures at frequent intervals through the
day, and is on a regimen of both Dilantin and phenobarbital to control
the seizures. His hearing acuity appears to be defective, but accurate mea-
surements of his hearing loss cannot be made, at least in the community
treatment center which he attends. Dan is the first-born of three children,
but it was the second pregnancy. The first pregnancy resulted in a still
birth.

>   Father's comment: Dan's future is my biggest worry. His mother is
>   not here today to talk with you because she is in very poor health. She and
>   Dan constitute a real worry to me, not a burden, just a real worry. It seems
>   to me we are surrounded with doctors—and doctor bills. Wow, are they
>   heavy at times. I'm not griping, I'm only hoping that I am doing the right
>   thing for the boy. I don't know much about these things myself, you know
>   —never went to college. I'm what I guess you'd call a self-made man! Not
>   too successful at that, I guess, but enough. My biggest worry is that I might
>   have to put Dan in some institution. I guess they're all right, but that would
>   really be a defeat for me. I always wanted a son as a friend. If I could just
>   get over the notion that what happened to Dan is my fault, I'd be a happy
>   man. How the hell did this happen to me?

Anna is diagnosed as a rigidity type of cerebral palsy. Her prognosis
is the poorest of any in this group. Her mentality cannot be measured. Although she is ten, she has no speech, no bodily control, nor does she show
much movement of any type. The type of cerebral palsy which she has results in an inability to initiate movement. She appears catatonic. She thus
must be cared for by attending adults for her total life experience. Her
condition has been known since birth, and, while she has had excellent
care, treatment, and attention for ten years, she has progressed almost
imperceptibly.

>   Mother's comment: We're giving up on Anna. Our physician told us
>   to institutionalize her a long while ago, but we fought it. I've got to have re-
>   lief. She's getting so big now, and heavy, that I can't possibly lift her much
>   more. She'll never get better. We have prayed all we can. No, she'll never
>   get better. We have visited several institutions, and while there's something
>   wrong with every one of them, there are good things too. We're going to
>   place her in a private place for as long as we can afford it, and then maybe
>   we'll have to turn to a state home. One thing I have decided though, and

that's not to fight it any more. It's possible that I might even decide to do some volunteer work at the state home on the other side of town. That'll take some doing, but maybe I can make myself do it. We'll see.

These eight children comprise a typical cross section of school-aged cerebral palsied children. It is obvious that, although they are in a "group," they cannot be considered a homogeneous group so far as treatment or education are concerned. Like most physically handicapped children, several of these children through PL 94-142 could attend their regular community schools if transportation were available. More could attend, if either permanent or itinerant physical, occupational, and speech therapists were practicing daily within the school building where the children attended. Paul could certainly attend a local school, if there were transportation, receiving his therapy at the center or elsewhere. Doug, Terry, and Mary could likewise participate, probably to nearly a full degree, in an appropriate regular or special class of the community school system. Dan, Ron, and Jeff are probably not candidates for an ordinary community school. They need the more treatment-oriented programs of clinics or special schools with supporting therapeutic personnel. Anna definitely requires the latter. The residential home, perhaps the least restrictive placement for her, ultimately may be the best place for her, and, at the same time, provide her family with relief.

It can be seen that not only are there great individual differences among these children with regard to their physical and psychological characteristics, but these individual differences dictate the type of educational settings which might be optimal for the children. One wonders why they are all left in a treatment center in a state which has mandatory legislation for "the education of all handicapped children within public educational facilities." Table 9.1 illustrates the variation in this group of handicapped children, and it quickly indicates the problems confronting educators and therapists as they prepare educational and therapeutic regimens for these eight children or for others like them. What Table 9.1 does not show are the equally complicating factors of speech and communication characteristics of the children or the total familial situation with all of the inherent dynamics which are constantly present, and which surround the child regardless of his or her other problems.

In addition to the brief descriptions of the children themselves, the parents' comments, statements made to the authors, are themselves illuminating. In them one sees the spectrum of parent concerns varying from despair to hope, from ignorance to realistic understanding, from selfishness to guilt feelings. These are feelings with which all professional people

TABLE 9.1

Individual Differences Characterizing Eight Cerebral Palsied Children

| Name | Age | Subtype | Involvement | Degree | Intelligence | Perceptual Problem | | | Emotional Problems |
						Visual	Auditory	Haptic	
Paul	7	spastic	hemiplegia	mild	normal	none	none	none	none
Doug	8	spastic	hemiplegia	moderate	retardation	none	none	none	none
Terry	11	spastic	hemiplegia	severe	low	yes	yes	none	none
Jeff	9	athetoid	quadriplegia	severe	normal	none	none	none	none
Mary	8	spastic	hemiplegia	moderate	high	yes	yes	yes	none
Ron	10	ataxia	paraplegia	severe	normal	none	none	none	yes
Dan	9	athetoid	quadriplegia	severe	very low	yes	yes	none	none, but seizures
Anna	10	rigidity	quadriplegia	severe	severe low	not measurable			no affect

working with handicapped children and youth must deal and be prepared to handle adequately.

Since one cannot describe the individual differences of all physical handicaps, it is necessary to select a subgroup which is illustrative of the greatest number of individual differences found in other categories of physical disability. The eight children who have been described briefly represent a number of characteristics of individual differences found not only in cerebral palsy but in other categories of the physically handicapped as well. A discussion of this subgroup will exemplify individual differences, supply background information for the upcoming case study of a child with cerebral palsy, and exemplify the individual differences which characterize all groups of physically handicapped children including the visually and auditorily impaired discussed in other chapters.

OVERVIEW OF CEREBRAL PALSY

Although it was completed more than twenty-five years ago, the study by Hopkins, Bice, and Colton (1954) to which reference has already been made still remains the most complete demographic study of cerebral palsied children and youth reported in the literature, and it is undoubtedly the most extensive. This study has been reported in full, since the original publication is now out of print, in a more recent volume totally devoted to cerebral palsy (Cruickshank 1976).

Prevalence

The prevalence rate for cerebral palsy varies among studies from between 0.74 and 2.4 per 1,000 live births. While this is a wide range, these studies represent the thinking of some twenty separate investigators in various localities in Scotland, England, and Northern Ireland. These studies have all concerned themselves with children of school age, between 5 and 15 years. They are typical of the findings reported in other countries, including those in the United States.

Sex Ratio

The Hopkins, Bice, and Colton study, often referred to as the New Jersey study, included 1,406 children with cerebral palsy—802 boys and

604 girls. The percentages of the subtypes within this large group was practically the same for boys and for girls; i.e., spastic, 46.6 percent boys, 44.8 girls; athetoid, 23.7 boys, 23.3 girls. The other subtypes of ataxia, rigidity, tremor, mixed cases, and rare cases had similar close distributions between sexes, boys presenting the higher percentage in each category.

Subtype Incidence

The complexity of the problem of cerebral palsy is related to the subtype. For example, in the New Jersey study the highest incidence percentage related to the spastic group and was 46.1 percent when the right and left hemiplegic children were combined. In the athetoid group, the quadriplegic category accounted for the largest number of children (87.6 percent). Similarly, in the rigidity subtype the quadriplegic category was the highest (49.7 percent).

If cerebral palsy were just one thing, it might be an easy problem to handle educationally and therapeutically. But it is not. Cerebral palsy is many things, as can be seen from the above remarks. Variation in type, severity, and extent means variation in treatment programs if children's needs are to be met. Cerebral palsy is more than all of these factors, however, as shall be noted in the paragraphs which follow.

Etiology

Cerebral palsy results from many things. While there are individual variations among the subtypes, *in toto* birth injury accounts for the greatest number in the New Jersey study (430 children, 38.9 percent). Other factors of significance include such things as developmental deviations, mostly prenatal (315 children, 28.5 percent), postconvulsive (103 children, 9.3 percent), and prematurity (8.1 percent), postinfection (3.8 percent), cerebral anoxia (3.7 percent), Rh factor (2.6 percent), and postcerebral trauma (1.9 percent). It is interesting to note that some years ago the factor of Rh incompatability was assumed to be the cause of most of these problems. In reality it is seen now as a minor cause of cerebral palsy.

Morbidity Data

One of the assumptions which in the past has often been made regarding cerebral palsy as well as some other types of physical conditions is that it is essentially a problem of the first born. The New Jersey study refutes this completely. Six hundred and fifty-six sets of data contained complete birth histories. In this group 290 children were first born; 176 were second; 73 were third; and the remainder of the distribution included children born with cerebral palsy through the thirteenth birth order.

Cerebral palsied children are often born to mothers who have had other types of negative birth history characteristics. For example, in the New Jersey study a total of 143 miscarriages were reported in the 656 mothers either previous to or following the delivery of the cerebral palsied child. In the same group of mothers 35 still births were reported. These two events were reported in 134 of the mothers involved, slightly more than 20 percent of the total group.

Additional Complicating Factors—Intelligence

If this situation of multiple physical disability were not enough, the complexity of the problem is further compounded, as we have previously stated, by a much higher incidence of intellectual retardation in cerebral palsied children than in the total population. The New Jersey study reported on 1,000 children. In these children, 715 had intelligence quotients below 89, nearly three-quarters of the total group. Among the spastic, athetoid, rigidity, and ataxic subtypes, the percentage of children with intelligence quotients below 70 ranged from 42 percent (athetoids) to 71 percent (ataxics). The high incidence of mental retardation in cerebral palsy is itself significant. When one considers the controlling importance of intelligence in all aspects of learning (for occupational therapy, for physical therapy, for communication, and for social and academic learning) one can immediately understand the magnitude of the problem when it is reported in such high incidence in cerebral palsied children.

Perception

In children who are judged to be above an IQ level of 75 with a minimum mental age of 6.0 years, and chronological ages between 6.0 and 15.11 years, inclusive, the incidence of visual perceptual processing disability is extraordinarily high. For example, in studies of the figure-background relationship in cerebral palsy and normal children, a factor inherently related to visual perception processing and basic to all academic learning, the cerebral palsied children (spastic and athetoid subtypes only included in this study) were characterized by a higher percent of pathology. These characteristics, like that of intelligence, have pervading influences at all levels of intelligence, and they significantly impair all learning and school achievement when they are present in a child.

PSYCHOSOCIAL ADJUSTMENT

Visible and Nonvisible Handicaps

Another element needs mention in considering all physical disabilities, and that is the degree to which the disability per se is seen by individuals in the society in which the disabled person lives. In an age which stresses human equality, downplays the terms denoting gender, and requires affirmative action in employment and related matters, it constitutes a sad commentary that handicapped children are still excluded by law and regulation from school programs in many places. Many are yet unwillingly accepted as adults in employment and are in other ways discriminated against when the disability becomes known. Society would still prefer to forget that handicapped people exist. Old, indeed ancient, prejudices exist in the twentieth century, which have not been replaced by positive concepts of social and mental health. The bus driver's attitude regarding Terry Sloan is a case in point to which reference in greater detail will be made in the latter portions of this chapter.

There is evidence that the degree of anxiety in the handicapped person is related to the extent to which his disability is visible. In a study involving 264 physically handicapped high school youth, this fact was corroborated many times. The visibility of the handicap was reported by the students to be a pervasive factor in all aspects of the youths' adjustment, i.e., relationships with their parents, with boys, and with girls. It had an impact on their aspirations. It was a vital factor in their anxieties, fears, and guilt feelings as compared to other youth of the same ages who were not disabled. The negative function of visibility was accentuated when, from the large group of handicapped youth being studied, 71 cardiac youth were singled out for separate study. These young people, with nonvisible disabilities, responded on all measures almost exactly as had their physically normal peers and completely different than their visibly disabled friends. It was obvious from these studies that adult society defines the handicapped person in terms of the visibility of the handicap. This was not the case in terms of peer definition of the handicapped youth. So significant is the social attitude toward disabled persons that often the individual with a handicap goes to great lengths to hide the disability if he can, for fear it will serve as a factor of rejection. Obviously, the cerebral palsied and other types of physically handicapped people fall within the group of the handicapped with visible disabilities which make them constantly the subject of judgments by others.

Impact of a Physical Handicap

Just as the issue of visibility of a handicap is significant, the way in which an individual perceives his or her disability is also important. The many and unpredictable effects of a handicap interact with the individual's given potential in his or her own environment. Whether a disability is congenital or acquired later in life, it is a variable that affects an individual's physical, social, and psychological functioning to various degrees. In a major sense a handicap can and does affect an individual's total life.

Although it is possible to lose sight of the whole person in inferring and isolating the physical, social, and emotional aspects of the self, such a structured approach is helpful in describing the effects of a physical handicap on one's functioning. One often overlooked area of life, the individual's ability to function biologically, is greatly affected by physical handicap. The type of handicap helps determine both the individual's ability to provide for his or her own needs and at the same time may create special needs. For example, obstacles to eating, breathing, or mobility could drastically affect life style as well as necessitate medical and nursing care.

On the one hand, the more mobile and physically able a person is, the greater his or her chances for self-care, employment, and independent living. On the other hand, a severely disabled person may be totally immobile, with little control over excretory functions or use of limbs, and so needs assistance just to survive. Of course, there is a wide range between these two extremes.

Undoubtedly the extent of the physical limitation or dysfunction is usually but not always the primary issue for the handicapped. These limitations affect their everyday life activities, including employment, recreation, or the general capacity to manage alone or in private. It is obvious to the casual observer that many handicapped persons operate quite well on their own, but usually with great strain on their resources. Society's lack of sensitivity to their special problems in carrying on the activities of "normal" living is probably the most unbearable of all limitations.

Environment

An important aspect of physical limitation is the person's knowledge of the extent to which he or she is limited. A handicapped infant does not know that it is different. Only later, when the child begins to differentiate himself from others, do differences and deficits become important factors in adjustment. The environment, then, has an important impact as a socializing factor in the lives of the physically disabled. The point we stress here is that society does not emphasize what the individual *can* accomplish, but what he or she *cannot*. A handicapped child becomes aware of his or her "disability" through contact with others and through comparisons between his or her own skills and those of others. Due to this early social awareness the child learns to adapt positively or negatively to the handicap.

Besides actual physical limitations of many types, what does a physical handicap mean to the individual? People with amputations, deformities, or disfigurations, as in the case of burns, are faced with complicating problems when in social situations. Their physical limitations may be accompanied by psychological apprehensions, embarrassment, and oftentimes lowered self-esteem. These secondary effects, great or small, frequently become the obstructions to normal living. Attitudes such as these are not innate, but are the learned consequences of people's restrictions. A case in point is a high school sophomore.

> Bill is 15 years old, but he does not take part in most of the activities engaged in by his classmates. Bill does not participate in sports, nor go to dances; he tends to avoid social situations, particularly those involving people he does not know. At a weight of 290 pounds this short-statured young man is the object of many long glances, wisecracks, and sometimes verbal abuse. Bill has become a shy, apathetic person who is easily embarrassed. When he was twelve he began to stutter, and his school performance dropped off dramatically. He spends much of his time watching television and listening to records. He has few friends. Most distressing is the fact that Bill is an unhappy person who does not like himself.

Obesity is another type of physical disability often accompanied by a variety of psychological overtones. One can easily understand how Bill or other handicapped individuals might develop negative self-concepts when confronted with the realities of physical limitation, abnormal body image, and lack of social acceptance. The person has already been stigmatized by others as one who "cannot," and thus views himself as less than a "whole person." Where can this person meet success? Where can he find reinforcement and obtain self-respect? A handicapped individual often has fewer opportunities for positive reinforcement than physically normal persons. The implications of a negative self-concept may impinge on one's confidence, motivation, expectations, and entire mental attitude. A negative self-concept and mental attitude also can depress and deflate the individual's will to improve. To compensate for this problem the handicapped child needs constant but appropriate positive reinforcement.

Given the predisposing conditions of physical disability along with often unkind environmental situations, it is reasonable to assume that the physically handicapped boy or girl is "at risk" emotionally. The handicapped child can never seem to escape the notion that he or she is different from ordinary children or adults who knowingly or unknowingly amplify the presence of his handicap either by laughing at, alienating, or criticizing the disabled child. The child and his or her handicap are forever the object of someone's curiosity, leading to uneasy interactions characterized sometimes by pity or aversion. Similarly, even the child's parents may find it difficult to strike a balance between what the child is and what they had anticipated he or she would be or be able to be. These kinds of inconsistencies in the child's social encounters surely undermine the stability of the child's emotional growth and development.

Once a child recognizes that the physical handicap hinders ability to form and maintain human relationships, then the precursors of emotional disturbance resulting from the physical handicap have been established. If not dealt with carefully, latent emotional overlay will result in disturbed behavior manifestations. McMichael (1971) classifies the signs of difficulty in children in adjustment to their handicaps into three categories:

1. Nervous disorders: inhibited, anxious or withdrawn reactions.

2. Habit disorders: involving some disorder in speech, sleep, movement, or excretion.

3. Behavior disorders: aggressive, troublesome or delinquent reactions.

These categories, which are very encompassing, describe a large sector of the total population. Clearly, emotional disturbance is not merely an outgrowth of a physical handicap. Such disturbance refers to a lack of self organization or to a poor adjustment of the individual in relation to the environmental situation in which he lives. The presence of a disability may make the individual more liable to emotional disturbance, but this is by no means unusual within the group about which we write.

When considering emotional disturbance in this population one cannot overlook the direct impact that brain damage can have on behavior. Many disabilities, particularly developmental disabilities, are a result of brain dysfunction. It is possible that brain damage alone can account for impulsive behavior, poor judgment, inappropriate affect, and other aspects of emotionality. Seidel *et al.* (1975) report a study in which psychiatric disorder was twice as prevalent in children whose crippling condition was due to cerebral diseases or damage as with children with noncerebral (peripheral) damage. They concluded that emotional and behavioral disturbance stemmed from both an increased biological vulnerability and psychosocial hazards. It is important to keep in mind the biophysical aspects of emotional development as we continue to discuss the more important psychological aspects of these problems.

Ego Development

The authors agree with theoretical positions which state that the controlling factor in the area of emotionality is ego development. The development of ego functions—such as one's relation to reality, control of impulses, relations with others, control of thought processes, and use of defense mechanisms, among others—evolves throughout the life of the individual to determine the nature of the person. The ways in which these functions develop and are synthesized, whether favorably or unfavorably, are the independent variables which produce tendencies toward coping with or being disturbed by the environment.

In human beings, what causes ego functions to develop adaptively or maladaptively? What are the ingredients which greatly affect ego development? Besides the human needs required for survival, it has been deduced that the well-adjusted individual also needs such things as good human relationships, care and affection, guidance, a consistent and rational environment, channels for discharging tension, and the right to be seen as an equal. Each of these elements, leading to good ego development, must constantly be considered in relation to those with physical disabilities, for the disability itself may be a significant liability or barrier in achieving one or all of them. Human sexuality in all of its manifestations is one of these essential needs. Educators need to recognize this and incorporate these issues into both general and special education.

Sexuality

If the aforementioned ingredients are those by which an individual's ego functions develop adaptively or maladaptively, then human sexuality, inclusive of all of them, has a great impact on ego development and human adjustment. Freud (1935) comprehensively theorized the nature and impact of psychosexual development as the foremost principle underlying human behavior. Others have brought the same theoretical principles to bear on the psychosexual development of the physically handicapped. Most psychologists, psychiatrists, and many laymen agree to some extent that sexuality is a most important part of life. There is no reason to believe that this situation is different for the handicapped person. Most of the physically handicapped persons are capable of a range of sexual experience. Yet, because of their lack of independence, many of them have little access to privacy, to sexual partners of their choice, or guidance around compensatory devices and/or practices to minimize the limitations of the handicap.

Examined from another angle, what might the absence of healthy sexual knowledge, experience, or expression mean to a person, particularly a handicapped person? It is felt by some (Reich 1949; Abraham 1966) that interest in sexual matters is present in early stages of childhood eroticism. Sexual drive is also posited as an early natural phenomenon. Given this viewpoint, some suspect that relationships, impulses, and human motivation have strong sexual components. The way in which these components are assimilated by the child continually serves as an important dictating role in his ego development. If sexual impulses and experiences are irregular, traumatic, reacted to by defense mechanisms, or totally prevented, the ego may become vulnerable forever to these situations, and unhealthy patterns of coping with them may be established. A physically handicapped person is prone to encounter situations in which sexual impulses cannot be controlled or satisfied, or situations in which affection and tactual fondling are rare occurrences, or predicaments in which he has sexual desires which cannot be fulfilled. Though not confined to the physically handicapped, these insufficiencies are common and debilitating within this population. Therefore, it is critical that the physically handicapped receive no less than other individuals in terms of education, healthy care and affection, fondling and tactual stimulation, channels for discharge of tension and sexual drive, and opportunities to love and be loved. If anything, in the area of human sexuality, the physically handicapped need more individualized attention, encompassing an understanding by others of their unique situation. They need continual guidance, reinforcement, and assistance at all ages, in realizing the implications which their physical condition has for their social and sexual development. Finally, they need help to actualize what potential they have for integrating sexuality into their lives.

The care of the handicapped person's sexual needs has not been a high priority issue in the United States. Rehabilitation and special education services are for the most part extensive, from dental hygiene to vocational counseling. It is not for a lack of progress in these areas that sexual needs of the handicapped have been overlooked. Rather, this issue has been suppressed by an American way of thinking, a puritanical ethic and morality. The United States, as other forward-looking societies have done, must become attuned to the sexual needs of the physically handicapped and be prepared to address these needs as a part of the total rehabilitation or habilitation process. To do this, laws must be implemented that give physically handicapped individuals the rights of all persons to an unimpeded pursuit of experiences of their choice, marriage, if desired, and family development. In addition, society needs to provide opportunities which will aid the physically handicapped person in being able to find, choose, and interact with sexual partners. At the same time, the general public must be made aware that the moral and behavioral norms set by society within which most persons function socially may be inappropriate and a hindrance to the handicapped person.

Some of the prevalent attitudes and myths encountered when discussing sexuality and the handicapped may reveal the extent to which this areas of life is misconstrued:

1. Many parents and helping persons tend to see and speak of the handicapped person as neuter.

2. Early manifestations of sexuality on the part of the handicapped are frequently unrecognized by concerned adults due to ignorance, denied due to fear, or punished due to apprehension and anxiety.

3. Parents tend to view their children with handicaps as being in danger, both from the limitation per se and from sexual exploitation.

4. Many fear that pregnancy would result in the birth of a handicapped child.

5. Frequently, the abovementioned attitudes result in the parents withholding information, exposure, and experience: "What they don't know, they won't worry about and won't miss."

6. The very nature of the dependence on another for self-care, particularly at puberty and thereafter, creates an erotic situation that all persons involved in are frequently ill-prepared to handle.

7. Questions must arise for the person with the handicap: "Am I unloved, unlovable because of my handicap? Things I feel and experience —are they natural or handicap-related?"

8. The nonhandicapped find it difficult to imagine those with physical defects in a sexual situation, because sexuality as such is often linked with a certain view of the body just as the prevailing ideal of beauty is reinforced in our society.

No segment of society is privileged to ignore its role in the consideration of human sexuality of the physically handicapped or normal individual. The family, organized religion, the schools, and the community each has a proper role which is continuing and developmental in nature. Each must respond to this significant aspect of human development. The schools, particularly, must assume a positive stance in considering human sexuality as subject to teaching and discussion at all phases of a person's growth and maturity, especially the physically handicapped individual. In many countries of the world foresighted programs, providing for the fullest possible definitions of human sexuality, are a part of the assumed obligations of organized education, both for the handicapped and the nonhandicapped elements of childhood, youth, and adulthood.

In this chapter the authors have attempted to address a number of concepts which pertain to the physically handicapped without trying to individualize comments to every type of handicapping condition. Instead, the focus has been on cerebral palsy, a handicap serving as a microcosm of the totality of physical handicaps. By studying the multifaceted problems of cerebral palsy, it is possible to generalize information to most handicapping conditions. The profile of the eight children with cerebral palsy demonstrated the variations possible within this clinical category. Similar constructs could be developed for each of the other categories of physical disability. Through these summaries, the reader can become familiar with some of the factors which contribute to the handicapped children's development, family support systems, financial resources, reality identification, treatment, sociocultural environment, extent of the handicap, intelligence, and self-concept—just to name a few.

There is generic value in studying cerebral palsy as an example of not only physical disability but of "exeptionality" in general. Every chapter of this book discusses a topic which can pertain to cerebral palsy. The continuum of intelligence ranging from the gifted to the retarded is represented in this population as is the spectrum of emotional disturbance, learning disability, and sensory impairment. These concepts of exceptionality become important to consider in relation to an individual with cerebral palsy, such as Terry Sloan, who will be discussed in the next chapter.

The authors wish to express their appreciation to Martha Dickerson, M.S.W., and Martha Moersch, O.T.R., M.A., both of the Institute for the Study of Mental Retardation and Related Disabilities; and to Douglas Buyer, Graduate Student, University of Michigan, for their thoughtful critiques and suggestions regarding this chapter.

10

Cerebral Palsy

WILLIAM M. CRUICKSHANK AND LAWRENCE J. LEWANDOWSKI

Terry Sloan, who in the opening pages of the last chapter the bus driver left on the street corner, was not always a young man working in a bank as a teller. Terry Sloan once was a baby, and subsequently the young child of a young set of scared parents. The parents were in their late teens and early twenties when Terry was born. He was their first and only child. When he was born, Terry's father worked at the fire department in an industrial city of about 200,000 people. His mother, untrained for any specific type of work, maintained the home and did babysitting. Both were high school graduates; both had completed one semester at a college. Mr. Sloan had been in the armed forces for the minimum time required. They soon were to seek the help of many professional people. Fortunately the Sloans, as will be seen in the following pages, were referred to a facility where there was an interdisciplinary team of professional people prepared to assist their son.

The concept of the professional interdisciplinary team, effective with the Sloans and with many other families coping with most other types of physical disabilities, began to be accepted in the early 1940s, although there were those who were espousing this approach before that. Until the interdisciplinary team concept became a reality, diagnosis was essentially restricted to the discipline of the moment, and it pertained only to the immediate problem, i.e., education by educators, medicine by physicians.

There should be available to families and handicapped persons at least one nearby facility wherein all their diagnostic, management planning, and, if necessary, treatment needs can be obtained. Yet, O'Reilly (1975) presents statistics on 1,700 cerebral palsied individuals indicating that about 40 percent of these persons were at home despite treatment facilities being available to them. There must be a facility available to these people wherein their needs can be seen in global terms. And there must be a process of early identification and then referral to the appropriate resource. There is no reason at this writing for handicapped children and their families to run from one physician, psychologist, or educator to another, an experience which never really pieces the total study of the child together. This is a "cafeteria" approach which accomplishes little.

THE INTERDISCIPLINARY TEAM

Referral is sometimes, but not always, a logical or planned series of steps. It is often accomplished through alert professional people overhearing comments which reflect needs. In the instance of Terry, however, a nurse working in the interdisciplinary clinic learned about Terry during an evening visit to a friend's home. During a conversation with a county public health nurse who knew the Sloans, Terry was mentioned. The clinic nurse suggested that the family be referred. This chain of contacts among the nurses and the family resulted in the parents' decision to seek assistance.

Most of this chapter will pertain to material relevant to Terry's early childhood, a phase of development too frequently overlooked. Minimal emphasis will be placed on his school-age activities. At the clinic the family found an extensive number of people ready to serve them. Included in the clinical diagnostic group were pediatricians, a child neurologist, psychologist, social worker, physical therapist, audiologist, ophthalmologist, occupational therapist, speech pathologist, nutritionist, dentist, nurse, and other individuals who were able to consult with Terry's parents regarding their legal rights for Terry and Terry's needs both at that time and as he would grow older and be ready for school. We shall examine Terry's record in some detail, for all of the disciplines listed in this paragraph were related to Terry in the first few months of his contact with the clinic. Not all of the clinicians' reports will be included here, for they are voluminous. Some will be noted in greater detail than others. By the time Terry was referred, the parents had begun to notice poor to severe development of his right side, and it was this which the boy's grandmothers had reported to their friend, the public health nurse.

The reports of the diagnosticians which will be included in the following pages are those which were seen to be important to Terry's development at the time.

Critical items

Pediatrics

Birth and development history: This is the first child and second pregnancy for this young couple. The mother is 20 years old, the father is 24. The family history is largely negative for medical problems.

Miscarriage

The mother's mother also had one miscarriage. The mother's father had a brother who had a handicap of unknown type. Mrs. Sloan has an adopted sister. Mr. Sloan has one brother and three sisters, all in good health.

Bleeding

The successful pregnancy was marked by the occurrence at 2 months of an episode of bleeding. Mrs. Sloan describes this episode as being the passage of something that resembled a huge blood clot. She was told to lie in bed and rest frequently.

Premature labor and delivery

The pregnancy continued, and during the seventh month the bag of waters spontaneously ruptured. Two days later Mrs. Sloan went into labor. The labor lasted a long time, but was not really difficult.

Birth weight 2 lbs., 10 oz.

The infant, when born, weighed only 2 lbs., 10 oz., but he cried immediately on delivery, although his cry was rather weak. There was one episode of rapid respiration during the neonatal period, but the infant otherwise did well and gained steadily. Mrs. Sloan fed him once a day while he was in the nursery and he was sent home with her when he was 5 lbs., 2 oz.

Normal hospital development

At that time, he seemed to be quite normal and there were no special instructions. At this time he was about two months of age.

Normal neonatal development

The only abnormality noted at the time of discharge from the hospital was a 2-cm. raised hemangiomia (purple birth mark) on the right lower abdomen.

Developmental history: Reference is made to the detailed notes of this child's developmental history.

Problem noted in right arm and leg

His motor development has been slow but progressive with obvious and increasing difficulty in the use of the right arm and the right leg.

Clenched right fist

The right hand is held much of the time in a clenched fist attitude and the child is unable to grasp with the right hand.

DDST findings

The Denver Developmental Screening Test has also revealed a number of failures for chronological age.

By age 5½ months Terry's height was 24½ ", weight 14 lbs. He was taking a diet of Similac with iron as well as cereal, fruits, and vegetables. He was able to hold his head erect and to roll over from stomach to back. By 7 months of age, height was 25 ", weight 16½ lbs. Some increased muscle tone was noted, but no increase in deep tendon reflexes. No sitting effort even when propped in the sitting position was noted.

Suspicion of cerebral palsy at 7 months

The suspicion of cerebral palsy was raised at this time. By January, age 9 months, height was 29½ ", weight 16 lbs., 14 oz. The notation observed Terry was still unable to sit by himself. He did not crawl, but he could roll over. On physical examination there appeared to be some increased tone in the lower extremities and again the question of cerebral palsy was raised.

9–13 months. Evidence of developmental delays

Further evidence of developmental delay and increased motor tone was noted on succeeding examinations through 13 months of age, at which time he was 29½ " long and weighed 19 lbs., 4 oz.

Terry had never had any fainting spells or convulsions, and generally has had good health except for occasional episodes of respiratory infection with fevers of 103° or 104°. His tonsils have been involved during several of these occasions.

13 months, all signs negative except as noted re: right extremities

Physical examination: Reveals a 13-month-old white male infant who does not appear acutely or chronically ill. He is alert and responsive and holds himself in the standing position by pulling on a table with his left hand. He is unable to use right arm and leg in a normal manner. His head is well formed, the circumference is 18½ ". His eyes are clear and blue. His pupils are round, regular, and equal and reactive to light and accommodation. Extraocular muscles are normal; there is no eyelid paralysis. His face is symmetrical; no weakness of facial musculature is noted. His tongue protrudes in the midline, the pharynx is unremarkable. His tympanic membranes are normal, and his nose is normal. His neck is supple; no abnormalities of his neck are noted. His chest is clear; heart tones are normal; no murmurs are heard. Rate and rhythm are within normal limits. Abdomen is not tense or protuberant. Liver, spleen, and kidneys are not enlarged; no abnormal masses are palpated. There is no umbilical hernia. Genitalia are normal for male infant. Testes are in the scrotum. There are no abnormalities over the cerebrospinal axis. His skin is clear except for the hemangiomia previously noted in the birth history. His left upper and lower extremities move normally.

Right extremities
show deficiencies

His right upper and lower extremities exhibit the motor deficiencies previously described. Although there is some evidence of increased muscle tone in the right upper and lower extremity, no clonus at the ankle was noted. Hemiplegia is quite obviously present.

Developmentally
somewhat "behind
schedule"

Summary and conclusion: This infant appears to have a centrally determined motor weakness of the right upper and lower extremity. Developmentally he is somewhat behind schedule, but this must be viewed in the light of his very low birth weight and premature delivery. There is no evidence of progressive neurologic disease.

Recommendations

1. Prevention of contractures and stereotyped motor habits of the right upper and lower extremity.
2. Development of fullest possible normal motor function.
3. Parental education.
4. Periodic developmental re-evaluation.
5. General pediatric supervision.

The pediatrician had not labeled Terry, and no pediatric neurologist had yet been consulted. He noted a problem, but did not put a term on it. That may come from another discipline. The physical therapist is the first to narrow the problem to what it may actually be. It is significant to note that Terry was premature and that his mother had a history of one previous miscarriage. These factors are relatively common in the case studies of children with cerebral palsy.

Of more significance, however, is the fact that examinations of Terry at five months and at nine months raised the question of cerebral palsy. The Sloans reported that, although the term was used then, they were given absolutely no information about the problem, its implications, or treatment. One person at the hospital said, "Don't worry. It's mild. He'll outgrow it." "Whatever 'it' was," said Mrs. Sloan, "I really didn't know. But I know I cried all that night wondering what was wrong with Terry that they weren't telling us about."

Physical Therapy

The physical therapist undertook a rigorous examination of Terry and provided a detailed report to the interdisciplinary team. The parents were present during all the examinations.

1½ yrs. old, definite hemiparesis rt. side

This 18-month-old boy has a right hemiparesis (slight paralysis affecting one side) associated with cerebral palsy. He was seen in the home environment at which time a home program was constructed for him with the assistance of the visiting nurse and the clinic nurse. The home program was designed to offer the family and the visiting nurse assistance, interim management of Terry until an integrated and comprehensive program based upon the assessment of all disciplines in the clinic could take place. The home program was based on the following clinical findings:

1. Muscular imbalance leading to development of stereotype positioning of the right upper and lower extremities

    A . Right Upper Extremity

Note details of hemiparesis

    1) Scapular: resistant to motion passively, no contractures

    2) Gleno-humeral (shoulder) joint: resistant to motion passively especially in flexion, abduction and external rotation, no contractures

    3) Elbow: 30-degree elbow flexion contracture; tightness but no contracture of pronators

    4) Wrist: complete range of motion, but minimal tightness of wrist flexors

    5) Fingers: extreme tightness of long finger flexors, no joint contractures

    B. Right Lower Extremity

    1) Hip: 20-degree hip flexion contracture

    2) Knee: no tightness, no contractures; ankle: dorsiflexion (turning foot and toes upward) impossible with knee extended

2. Failure in development of support reactions in sitting to the right

3. Lack of use of the right upper extremity

4. An extreme positive supporting reaction when placed in the standing position

5. A lack of the development of reciprocal patterning

6. The maintenance of an infantile crawling pattern

When Terry was seen a month later, the neuromuscular picture was greatly clarified and possibly improved. On the basis of the findings of the physical therapist, a pediatric neurologist was added to the team of consultants. The following gains within the period of a very short training period were noted. There was also a different attitude expressed on the part of the parents.

19 months, shows   1. He crept in reciprocal pattern on his knees, left hand,
positive growth,   and right wrist.
except right side
2. He had overcome the positive supporting reaction and was standing holding on with a wide base, utilizing flexed knees and relatively dorsiflexed ankles.

3. He was cruising laterally.

4. His elbow flexion contracture had been reduced to 25 degrees and dorsiflexion of the ankle was greater. In addition, the finger flexors had been lessened so that some extension of the wrist was possible.

Based upon the findings of this subsequent evaluation, some suggestions in the home program for Terry appeared to be warranted:

Exercises   1. Standing activities should be encouraged.
recommended
2. Movements in a reciprocal fashion on the shoulders should be performed in both sitting and standing positions.

3. Internal rotation of the hip should be continued but de-emphasized.

In addition, the following were added to the exercise program conducted by the parents:

1. A ball should be suspended by a string opposite the child's right arm. The child should be encouraged to flail at the ball with his right arm. The ball should be moved so that the child gets a sensation of speed, inertia, and gravity into his perceptual motor system.

2. The child should be approached from the right in play and socialization activities.

3. The child's right hand should be placed in substances which have various kinds of consistencies such as beans, macaroni, marbles, small stones, cotton.

4. The child should have some opportunity to use his right hand when the elbow is supported on a surface. Finger extension will probably be facilitated to the degree that the arm is elevated.

Parent involvement recommended

5. The parents should be taught to stimulate the right forearm and hand.

6. Shifting the weight to the right in a standing position should be encouraged.

7. The parents are to encourage the use of the right hand in the following two motion patterns:

    A. Pattern 1: Wrist flexion and finger extension

    B. Pattern 2: Wrist extension and finger flexion

8. Parents should recite names of body parts on right side as they work with the child so as to facilitate body image.

9. In the future, it may also be necessary to consider the advisability of a right splint for the hand and ankle should progress not continue to be made.

Activity program recommended

10. It is recommended that the activity program for this child be perceived by the parents as having two components: structured activities and unstructured activities. Component one (structured activities) encompasses the exercises for Terry which were recommended earlier and are still applicable, as well as the additional exercises which are recommended as the result of this second evaluation. Component two (unstructured activities) consists of those play activities which will allow Terry to develop eye-hand coordination, bilaterality, and adaptive use of his right side by the use of imitation and play. The endpoint of this

unstructured activity would be for Terry to experience satisfaction from manipulations of his environment and to reinforce exploration of that environment so that he stumbles upon motor acts which produce new experiences. Imitation is recommended of sounds and movements which are not in his own repertoire at the present time.

Differentiated responsibilities for parents   In the beginning stages, it may be well for the mother to emphasize component one while the father emphasizes component two with the goal that their function becomes less and less complementary and more and more substitutionary with regard to Terry's home program.

Psychology and Social Work

In an interdisciplinary setting, one disciplinary representative often speaks for the total team. This reduces professional time; it also reduces the number of adults who may need to talk with the family. In the case of Terry, psychology and social work personnel met together with the family. Terry was such a young child that the traditional psychological skills were not required. However, the psychologist desired a "data base" for subsequent appraisals as Terry grew older. More important, the counseling and advisement skills, as well as the psychologist's capacities for good qualitative assessment of young children, were needed and played a vital role in work with Terry and his parents for several years. The initial interview took place in the clinic with Mr. and Mrs. Sloan.

Standing beginning speech play behavior   Description of child: Terry now at 18 months can stand alone. He can say "ma-ma-ma," "da-da-da," and "hi!" He likes to play throwing a ball and his parents have tried blowing bubbles with him as a result of a suggestion by someone from the clinic staff. According to his father, he "freaked out over them." He's a friendly child, but is leery of strangers when his parents are not around.

Mother: Mrs. Sloan is a high school graduate; she also studied for one semester at the Community College. She did not like school; she became pregnant (resulted in miscarriage) and dropped out. She is currently employed as a babysitter, going to the home where she babysits for three children, and takes Terry with her.

Social economic status: The family's earnings appear to be adequate. However, according to Mr. Sloan, he says that they are able to get by, but not get ahead. He feels that this is how the economy is set up. They are renting a two-bedroom duplex, at the average rent for this area.

Parental tensions

Family interrelationships: The parents seem to have a general feeling of despair; there's very little involvement with extended family members. However, they do have a circle of friends, but most of these are single. They appear to be mostly Mr. Sloan's friends, although they both indicated that they were mutual friends. Mr. Sloan says they go bowling together; they enjoy parties together and having friends "drop by."

Mother's concern

In questioning them about this, it seems this may be a strain upon Mrs. Sloan as this sort of puts her out and she has to furnish snacks. Although the friends may bring their own beer, Mrs. Sloan still feels this is an obligation for her.

Father's outside activities

Mr. Sloan plays football and has a large dog which he enjoys taking for walks.

Lack of goals: Parents

Summary: The general impression is that of a young couple who have very few goals in life. They married young but it seems that they may be beginning to grow apart.

Low aspiration level: Parents

They have a very limited outlook on life and much bitterness toward society. Mr. Sloan seems to have some insight and expressed that he does want to return to school or college; however, he feels that he cannot work and go to school at the same time. He says he attempted school on a part-time basis, but felt that the schedule was "too strung out"; he was wasting too much time waiting between classes. He feels that anyone going to school should go on a full-time basis. This couple needs to get some realistic goals.

Job dissatisfaction: Father

Mr. Sloan expressed a general dissatisfaction with his work at the fire department, adding that he really didn't want to work there at all. He does seem to have some sense of responsibility for his family, his wife and son, in that at least he stated that on occasion when friends call and ask them to come to parties, many times they are not able to go because they don't have a babysitter and feel it too much of a problem to take Terry.

Recommendations   1. The interpretation of the evaluation should be geared so as to help allay many of the fears and concerns that the parents have regarding their child's level of functioning and their expectations for the future. Mr. Sloan especially has expressed his concern over whether or not his child is mentally retarded.

Father involvement needed   2. There should be more involvement of Mr. Sloan in therapy or whatever management program is recommended for Terry. This would have a twofold purpose: (1) increasing the involvement with the child and (2) helping Mr. Sloan to relate to the child and have a better appreciation of his problems. This could perhaps be in the form of a physical therapy or play therapy type program.

Potential divorce of parents feared   3. Exploration counseling for Mr. and Mrs. Sloan regarding the family interrelationships (the role of Mr. Sloan as a father helping the family to set goals and planning together to help them have a better outlook on life). There is much evidence to indicate that the couple seems to be growing apart.

It is apparent that the physical disability in a child is not only a handicap to Terry who possesses it. All family members may be touched. The Sloans are typical of the majority of American people in terms of education, understanding of unusual physical problems, and economic level. These people cannot be expected to solve the problems of these children alone, whether in the home, or school, or in the larger community. The social work–psychology team has brought several very significant facts to light, and an action program must be launched.

Nutrition

Oftentimes the nutritional aspect of the child's life is overlooked. In the interdisciplinary clinic, nutrition was seen as an integral part of the professional diagnosis. The initial nutritionist's report is included here.

Terry as a nineteen-month-old boy has three large meals daily. Mrs. Sloan followed the basic four food group pattern well, but it lacked variety. Chicken and ground beef are the common meats she serves, and she only cooks the vegetables that she herself likes and is familiar with. Mr. Sloan stated that he likes all kinds of food and expressed his desire for his wife to fix a variety of vegetables as well as meats. Terry generally will try any food and seems to like everything. Mrs. Sloan states that Terry seems to eat constantly. Terry does not eat many sweet foods other than fruits and ice cream, as Mr. and Mrs. Sloan do not. Terry does not receive candy often due to his mother's fear of a "bad habit."

Negative nutri-
tional findings
Terry's meat and milk intakes are low. Mr. and Mrs. Sloan state that at times he will eat more of these two foods than others for no apparent reason. Terry's overall diet does seem adequate. He has a thin frame and is in the third percentile for both height and weight. Terry can eat finger foods with no help. When using the spoon, Mrs. Sloan has to scoop the food and hand the spoon to him. If no help is given to him, he will use his fingers.

Recommendations

1. Because of Terry's inadequate milk intake, other calcium sources were suggested to supplement this. Terry is fond of cottage cheese and ice cream. These were encouraged to be given possibly at snack time.

2. If Terry's hemoglobin level is found to be low, iron-rich foods and possibly iron supplementation are recommended.

3. Eggs were recommended to supplement Terry's inadequate protein intake, and since he favors cottage cheese, this was also recommended.

4. An added variety of foods was encouraged for a much more adequate nutrient intake.

Ophthalmology

Since the diagnosis of cerebral palsy appeared appropriate and since visual problems are known to be associated with this condition, it was felt necessary to obtain an early baseline understanding of Terry's visual development. His visual examination proved essentially normal.

Dentistry and audiology findings also were normal, but it is nevertheless considered important for these examinations to be completed for later comparative information. (Complete visual, auditory, nutritional, and dental examinations are warranted for all handicapped children.)

Audiology

Hearing normal   Terry Sloan was seen for an audiologic evaluation and was accompanied by his parents. Informal evaluation revealed an alert, friendly baby who appeared to be in good contact with his environment. He responded appropriately to auditory and visual cues and vocalized freely. The child's speech consisted mainly of jargon.

Sound field testing using warbled tones, speech, and noise as stimuli revealed a good localization and awareness levels well within normal limits for all stimuli presented. A normal startle reflex was noted for noise at 80 decibels. The child has hearing within normal range bilaterally.

Occupational Therapy

Terry Sloan was a very young child at the time of his first comprehensive evaluation. Certain of the disciplines such as occupational therapy, which may be viewed as essential in any evaluation of physically handicapped children, are often seen as playing more minor roles in working with children as young as Terry. Occupational therapy input, however, is being seen by more and more clinicians and educators as beneficial in the identification and stimulation of developmental activities of infants, as well as the more traditional roles relating to readiness programs, to perceptual-motor training programs, and to the overall development of skills which are requisite in the child's school achievement. It will be noted in the occupational therapist's comments that personnel of this discipline, as with others included here, are aware of the need for strengthening the relationship among the Sloan family members.

Terry is seen as a child who suffered sufficient injury at some time to produce the physical handicaps that he has in his right arm and leg, but who, considering his prematurity, is functioning in a low normal range in most activities. In view of the changes noted in the past six weeks, he might have suffered from a lack of stimulation during the six-week stay in the prematurity nursery. This may have continued with young inexperienced parents who were having difficulties in their own relationship. He is seen as being developmentally delayed but not necessarily retarded in the traditional sense of mental retardation.

OT recommenda-
tions focus on
family tensions
and on childhood
developmental
activities

1. The primary gain to Terry probably will come through improvement of the interpersonal relationships between his parents and between him and his parents. The process of correction of the physical problems is seen as the means as much as the end to improving his life situation.

2. Ongoing counseling to the parents on all aspects of their life together, including money management, recreation, child care, work.

3. Continued support of the public health nurse in carrying out the management plan to be worked out.

4. Increased stimulation to Terry through play, conversation, chances to explore, incentives to crawl, walk holding on to parents and furniture, and later walk alone.

5. Remove his toys from the inaccessible toy chest and put favorite ones in 4 to 6 inch cardboard boxes on living room or kitchen floor.

6. Parents need to learn how to love and enjoy each other and Terry.

At eighteen to twenty months Terry Sloan was a moderately physically handicapped child with two parents who were confused and fearful. The father dreaded that his son might be mentally retarded. Confirmation or rejection of retardation could not be determined accurately at Terry's age. This worry would have to continue. The father's interests were definitely not in Terry's direction, but in the direction of dogs, football, and things which took him away from home.

Almost total responsibility for Terry became the mother's. The feelings of the professional staff at the time was that the family was on the verge of breaking up, essentially because of Terry. Family intervention took place at the right time. Parental lack of understanding about physical disability brings confusion. Confused parents often do not know which way to turn, and as a result little happens to reduce their confusion and tension. In Terry's case, through the accidental friendship of a grandmother, a public health nurse, and the clinic nurse, Terry received what he needed. Perhaps of equal importance, Terry's parents also received what they needed.

Following the diagnosis, a total interdisciplinary staff conference was held with the parents who, for the first time in Terry's life, were given the beginning of insights, not only into Terry's problems, but into some of their own. More important, they were given avenues to follow, and through which problem solutions could be obtained. The young boy was entered into the Early Action Program of the clinic. Home teaching with weekly behavioral objectives was begun. Mr. Sloan became involved as a full-fledged partner in Terry's growth and development. An emphasis on early intervention and stimulation was undertaken with Terry and his parents were taught how to participate in these activities.

Continuous evaluation, home teaching, group socialization, and special specific examinations and therapy sessions were provided for Terry, as was counseling for his family during the next three years. When he was four years of age, as school entrance was rapidly approaching, a major re-evaluation was undertaken. The staff conference notes relating to that series of evaluations is illuminating, as are some of the disciplinary comments. Special educators had become a part of the team now as the boy has grown and developed. They began working in the Early Action Program with Terry when he was about two years of age.

Physical Therapy

1. Continue monitoring of leg length discrepancy by parents and physician.

2. Monitor girth and length discrepancy of right arm (may need to be done through growth study x-rays).

Age 4 years

3. Physician from Physical Medicine and Rehabilitation to look at right elbow joint and check on it through x-rays to determine how range can be increased or if bony changes prevent this without some other form of intervention.

4. Continue with range of motion and stretching exercises to right side, moving toward Terry's doing more of it himself.

5. Exercises and games should continue to increase weight bearing on right arm (parents now do some).

Occupational Therapy Recommendations

1. Continue exercises with emphasis on increasing shoulder flexion, abduction, and elbow supination.

2. Play games like "Simon Says," but use bilateral motions using just one joint, e.g., straighten elbows.

3. Two-handed activities: bead stringing, finger painting, play dough.

4. Use refrigerated "Silly Putty" to play with to strengthen grasp.

5. Push and pull objects to strengthen his scapular muscles.

Special Education   1. Termination of placement in the Early Action Program group session with a referral to a regular nursery school or day care center until he enters kindergarten next fall.

2. Provide experience to increase visual motor skills (especially pencil, paper) and gross motor skills in school and/or home.

Summary   A list of suggested preschools was discussed with the parents and with the school's preschool consultant. She should be asked to write a letter to whomever is following Terry in physical medicine and rehabilitation, stating our concerns and a request for follow-up. Bi-weekly home visits will be made for the next twelve-week period to assist the Sloans in anything that may arise. This will be aimed at teaching parents more skills in monitoring Terry's hemiplegia (i.e., leg length) and providing suggestions for appropriate visual motor activities. The Sloans will completely handle the contacts with the nursery schools.

The Sloans were present during this staff conference. When the last recommendation was stated, namely, referral to *regular* kindergarten, Mr. Sloan was both visibly and audibly delighted. "Best news of the century," he blurted out. The transition of a family from dependency on the clinic staff to the realities of a public school placement always must proceed with logic and care. It must be just as carefully implemented as any aspect of the management plan.

DEVELOPMENTAL PROGRESS
IN TERRY'S PRESCHOOL ACTIVITIES

Throughout Terry's preschool years efforts to bring him and his family to a high level of function were maintained. The Sloans were not completely dependent on the clinic staff, but they relied on the authority of a group of people whom they had come to like and respect for assistance they received in many decisions. The county public health nurse was a continuing contact, as she was appropriately needed. Every time a contact was made with the child or the family, a note was put into Terry's record for the information and education of others who might be involved and also as a record illustrating the boy's early development. Some of these comments are illuminating and of interest. The mother was encouraged to enter her own notes into the boy's record. Unless parents become an integral part of the team, they often are passive observers rather than active participants in the regimen developed for the child. As will be observed, Mr. Sloan was frequently involved in the activities of Terry's growth and development.

Fine motor activities	Group Session: Terry and his Mom worked on collage activities. He readily imitated the tearing and pasting that his Mom was doing. He was also cooperative during the rest of the group activities.
Stair climbing	Ms. D. took him out of the room to work on stairs. He must hold on to another person, as the railing is quite high for him. He is being encouraged to alternate feet going upstairs, and to lead down with his right foot.
Gross motor activities	Group Session: Terry threw bean bags with fair eye-hand coordination into a box and through a hula hoop. He worked with Mrs. Jones making valentines for Mom and for Mrs. Jones and for his Dad. Later helped paste small hearts on card. Fairly quiet throughout session.
Language development	Terry's expressive language seems advanced for his age. The cerebral palsy doesn't seem to interfere with his articulation. He is very resistant to using his right arm and hand, but playful activities seem to encourage such use.
Gross motor arm and leg activities	Terry worked well in all activities presented. He again threw bean bags into a container with fair accuracy. He interacted with the other children, mainly Suzy, and at times would imitate their behavior, sometimes nearly getting out of control. During the session, he worked well making a play dough man and after several tries, caught on to the idea of "the magic bag" (he kept wanting to look at the objects first). He was very resistant to using his right arm to put the objects into the bag. In the sack race, he

was able to keep his balance while walking in the pillow case and did well keeping his balance for a short distance while hopping in it. (Occupational Therapist)

Matching and classification activities

Group Session: Terry did well with matching concrete objects and picking out same and different. His mother was introduced to the concept of classification with him by color, use and make-up, i.e., wood, plastic. Terry appeared also to be catching on to this idea. He did use it to stabilize when using the rhythm band instruments. (Physical Therapist)

Socialization and group participation

Group Session: Terry was in late, 2:00 P.M. Terry worked with building blocks. He was encouraged to carry blocks with both hands and to rationally count. He and his Mom worked on copying a model that had been built with different shapes. Tom and Ann kept knocking his model down, and Terry became quite upset. He was told it

Dealing with anger

was all right to feel angry that the other children were wrong. He was praised for his restraint. (Special Education Teacher)

Group Session: A physical therapy student did some gross motor activities with Terry to observe and evaluate his skills in this area. He was very cooperative; especially liked playing with the ball.

Body image

Terry and his Mom then went on to body image activity. Mrs. Sloan outlines his body, then Terry worked on coloring it in. He was encouraged to grasp the crayons correctly. We modeled using the flat crayon to roll it and cover more paper. He did this somewhat. It was noted he had some difficulty with spatial concepts of placing belt, facial features, etc. After snack Terry sat and listened to the stories and initiated ring-around-a-rosy. His face showed apparent concern and several times he showed definite approach behavior to Suzy. He tried to give her a ball, etc. (Physical Therapist)

Upper extremity problems and recommendations

Group Session: It has been noted that Terry's right arm appears tighter. He is keeping his hand fisted and his elbow flexed to 90° during most activities. During the water play he was encouraged to do more bilateral activities. However, when specifically asked to use his right hand, it seemed to tense more. In pouring, he used his right hand to stabilize and poured with good age-adequate eye-hand coordination. He helped to mix the juice and participated in our story time. Mrs. Sloan remote-viewed until story time. (Physical Therapist)

He played cooperatively in pin the tail on the donkey and allowed us to blindfold him.

Upper extremity use encouraged

He was encouraged to use his right hand to hold the tail, but he switched at the last minute. He also used a board as a slide, but preferred to go down it on his stomach, head first, rather than to sit up. John and Terry played tiger and chased each other through the obstacle course. (Physical Therapist)

Language development

Terry's language participation reached a height not previously seen. He sang entire songs and remembered "modifiers" discussed during circle time (plant: "smooth," "spider"). (Speech Therapist)

Gross motor activities and social awareness

Terry was able to jump off a low step while keeping both feet together. Tried to push big ball with both hands (i.e., using his right hand also) when requested. Has trouble doing somersaults (lack of support on right side). Able to roll horizontally on mat, both going down mat and coming back up again. Participated in clean-up (washed his cup). Unable to grasp cup in his right hand. Very alert; heard Ann asking clinician where her doll was. Since clinician gave evasive answer, Terry called to Ann and told her where the doll was placed. Terry speaks in complete sentences. Correctly matches subject of sentence and inflections on verbs. (Speech Therapy Student)

Father involvement

Home Visit: Mrs. Sloan was leaving for work; spent time with Mr. Sloan. We worked on dressing skills using Dressy Bessy and special book. Terry better able to handle some tasks like buttoning today. He is becoming more skilled at buttoning using one hand, his left. His father reports increasing independence in toileting. Note: Too often fathers are completely omitted from the therapy program. As with Terry, this is essential with all handicapped children.

Acting out behavior

Group Session: Terry arrived late during circle time. He participated in toothbrushing, but stayed back with his Mom when the other children got into dress-up activities. He was given a comb which he used. He was then brought over to the group to initiate bead stringing. During free play we saw more acting out behavior than we have ever observed before. His mother took him aside to handle it. Terry did enjoy the story and seemed pleased that his birthday was remembered. He did report he would be "almost" five when asked how old he would be. (Social Worker)

Stair climbing improves

Group Session: Terry arrived late and was met by Ann, who brought him to the circle. During play time Terry and I went up and down five steps, four times. He often alternates the leading foot going down the steps and when reminded, will go down using only one hand to hold the rail.

Going up stairs appears easier for Terry. He is now leading with right foot when reminded. Hemiplegia is still very evident. (Speech Therapist)

Motor progress reported

Opened *R* hand to move table, hold paper, etc. Did fairly well managing scissors on short, three-inch straight lines. Did staircase, one foot at a time, holding on with left hand. Much improved balance. (Occupational Therapist)

Number concepts; counting

Home Visit: OT evaluated right arm. Spent some time looking at Count and See Book. Terry seems to know well by sight numbers 1–6; 7–10, some confusion. Needed some prompting for rational counting above 7. Introduced counting 10s to 100. (Physical Therapist)

PT evaluation in social settings

Home Visit: Went for walk to check walking tolerance. Also worked on heel-toe gait; still tends to strike with full foot on right side; brace probably interferes. While walking, his right side does not fall behind as much as previously noted. This becomes more apparent as he runs, but this also is improving. Also worked on reciprocal arm swing. Left arm swings; right arm tends to go into flexion pattern. Practices rolling down hill, catch. Throwing pattern now much more advanced: evidence of diagonal patterns with weight shift. Terry stood on right leg to "kick off" his football. (Physical Therapist)

Mother's chart entries

Enjoyed obstacle course, but got so involved and overexcited that he refused to stay for storytime. Buttoned his coat! (Mrs. Sloan)

Dressing

Home Visit: Worked with lacing boot with moderate amount of direction, i.e., showing him how laces crisscrossed. He moved on to doing entire boot with minimum amount of verbal directions. Terry can tie simple knot, and we started to work on making a loop to tie shoe lace. Terry still needed to be reminded to correctly hold pencil. Last time he did automatically hold it correctly. (Mrs. Sloan)

On group project, Terry did a super job of following straight lines and cutting if assisted to hold paper up with his right hand. Needed reminder to hold marker pen the right way. Walked balance beam holding one hand.

Last time in; Terry seemed sad when we sang goodbye song. (Physical Therapist)

New behavioral objectives discussed   Home Visit: Terry played while Mom and I went over Vineland and discussed parents' objectives. Mom will let me know when to schedule next visit. Also, she may try to contact nursery schools. Terry was told next time we would work on some dressing activities and then the play dough. (Physical Therapist)

Just prior to Terry's beginning kindergarten, two home visit notations are of interest. A new responsibility is being placed on the parents for the first time, as can be noted in the comments below; namely, the Sloans will be asked to think about becoming resources for a new set of parents who live in the vicinity. A "buddy" system is in the making through which a set of experienced parents will begin to share their learning with those who are facing what the Sloans faced four years earlier. This type of personal support often can be even more effective than that which professional people can provide. The Sloans, defeated a few years earlier, will now become counselor-teacher-friends! They will be assisted in their new roles as they need it.

Positive parent attitude   Home Visit: Mr. and Mrs. Sloan seem to enjoy hearing how much we count on Terry to cooperate and lead some of our activities. They feel that he is really receptive to trying new things.

They are very pleased that he is gaining more independence in toileting. Dressing skills are still a big concern. Would like to consult with special educator about moving to a chart to monitor progress of independence in dressing as long as toileting is going well.

Parental guidance still needed   Mr. Sloan tends to sit back and observe, and yet offers encouraging comments on Terry's work on dressing.

Both parents need some guidance on how much to help and how much to let Terry struggle with things like snaps and buttons.

Home Visit objectives

1. Discuss with the parents the aggressive behavior we have seen in Terry over the past few weeks. We wish to assess their concern.

Parents are asked to help others

2. Tell them about new family (Polly) and ask for their help in working with this family, since both children appear to have similar problems.

3. Have Terry work on body parts puzzle, assess level of understanding for body parts that are more uncommon (shoulders, hips, etc.) on himself and puzzle.

4. Introduce scissors, crayons, paper folding to introduce skilled use of left hand, right hand to stabilize.

5. Fit a circle puzzle-beginning seriation and a two-handed activity.

Counseling session between father and PT

Mrs. Sloan was leaving for work and Terry was asleep. I spent first half-hour discussing with Mr. Sloan his feelings concerning first two objectives. Mrs. Sloan also had noted the increase in Terry's more aggressive type behavior. Mr. Sloan reports that although they hate to see it, they both realize many children exhibit it both in their neighborhood and in the Early Action Program. Mr. Sloan goes along with idea that it is a part of growing up. He feels Terry must learn to hold his own. They would like to work on changing these feelings into what would be more appropriate activities.

Father reports growth in independence

Mr. Sloan reports Terry is growing increasingly independent. He does insist that Terry tell him where he is going when he leaves the yard. The neighborhood children tend to take care of Terry to assure that he can keep up with them. Mr. Sloan says this may sometimes be too much help. He feels Terry is now doing a good job of keeping up in general play as long as terrain is not too rough.

Father accepts challenge of helping others

Mr. Sloan was quite willing to meet and talk with Polly's family. He stated that he and his wife do not feel they have too much in common with families of the children who are definitely retarded. They are looking forward to a parent group with those parents who have similar concerns and interests.

Mr. Sloan also said he is starting to talk to Terry about his arm and leg so that Terry will understand. Mr. Sloan really wishes that Terry would use it more. They bought Terry a pinball machine for his birthday that Mr. Sloan insists Terry use his right hand to play with.

Mr. Sloan was encouraged to stress using Terry's right hand as a helping hand and the left as the one for skilled dextrous activities.

TERRY'S SCHOOL ENTRANCE ASSESSMENT

One final home visit before Terry's enrollment in kindergarten was made. The purpose of this was to assess Terry's self-help skills so as to be able to advise the new kindergarten teacher, a person anticipating Terry's arrival, regarding the positive areas of his development as well as to be able to point out those aspects of self-help which would require the teacher's attention. Present during the assessment were the physical therapist, the occupational therapist, and Mr. Sloan. It is important to comment on the frequency of encounters which the Early Action Program team members had over the years with Mr. Sloan. It was terribly important for Terry's development that Mr. Sloan was available. It cannot be assumed, however, that fathers can always be present as frequently as has Mr. Sloan. The nature of his job at the fire department has made it possible for him to be in the home when Mrs. Sloan was babysitting or doing other work or home-related things.

Age 5 years, 3 months When we entered the home, Mr. Sloan and Terry were present. Terry had just gotten up from his nap and was partially dressed, i.e., underpants and pullover shirt. He is able to ambulate around the house without his short leg brace.

Behavior He appears to be an active, alert child with no difficulty communicating verbally. Terry's initial behavior was uncooperative when asked to get his clothes to complete dressing. He was uncertain and threatened by my presence and demonstrated this by acting out throughout the entire home visit. Finally, he got his shoes, socks, and pants from the bedroom and threw them on the floor.

Putting on Sock   Type—all cotton with elastic band. With assistance, he is able to place fingers into sock opening, but he cannot maintain right hand position. Once the sock was over his toes, he used his left hand in pulling the sock up. Verbal encouragement and assistance was given to complete the activity.

Suggestions   Selection of socks without the elastic top band. Purchase socks the next size larger to make it easier to get the sock over his heel.

Continue bilateral hand activities which encourage finger extension and strengthening.

Comment: The information regarding dressing is important to the kindergarten teacher. While it is rare that complete dressing or undressing would ever be required, many of the activities of a normal kindergarten routine involve boots, overshoes, mittens, and warm hats. It appears from what has been said regarding the evaluation of Terry's dressing skills that the school administration may need to assign an aide or volunteers to assist Terry's teacher in making successful the attempt at integration of him into the ordinary classroom.

It will be recalled that Terry has been wearing a short leg brace (normally defined as a brace from above the knee to foot). His ability to put this on or take it off is also a skill which must be evaluated and about which the teacher must have information.

Putting on Brace   Type—short leg brace.

Manipulate and handle brace: He needed assistance in lining the brace up and putting his foot into the shoe. He appears to know the sequence of placement in order to put the brace on his leg. He is able to manipulate the straps, but he lacked the strength to tighten securely. He was able to buckle partially, and was shown how to use his right hand to help assist in fastening the buckle through the hole. He demonstrated difficulty in getting his foot into the shoe by curling his toes.

Suggestions   He needs verbal support and assistance in managing this activity. Try different body positions when pulling on the brace: for instance, sitting on a bench instead of the floor or putting his foot in dorsiflexion to encourage toe extension when placing his foot into the shoe. Have him stand and use a long-handled shoehorn to get his heel into the shoe. Check his shoes periodically to make sure he has the proper fit.

Comment: It is obvious that this boy still needs help with his steel brace. This is not uncommon, and it need not be a reason for avoiding an integrated educational experience. It means, however, that when the brace is removed for one reason or another, some adult must be around to assist the child to get it back on. Shoes are another factor. His right shoe is a part of the short leg brace; hence only his skills in manipulating the left foot into the shoe need to be evaluated.

Putting on *Left Shoe*	Type—high back, lace, scuff toe. He is able to grasp the shoe with one hand. He is not able to loosen shoestring and maintain tongue placement in order to put his foot into the shoe. He is able to tighten the shoe string once the therapist starts and he can make the cross tie to the first part of the bow.
Suggestions	Tying a complete bow is not a five-year-old skill; however, continue to encourage through such activities as a lacing board, Dapper Dan, lacing shoe. At a later date, you might try one-handed tying techniques. Also, there are several types of adaptive shoe laces, as a last resort.
Putting on *trousers*	Needs minimal assistance in pulling up. Type—straight-legged corduroy with elastic waist band.
Suggestion	If the clothing seems to be fitting snugly, check his clothing size. Measure his waist, height, hips, and inseam length with his brace on. Height is the deciding factor when a child's height and weight fall into different sizes. Suggest styles which lend more room or fuller cuts, such as bellbottom slacks, front opening with hooks instead of buttons for waist closure. Always consider shrinkage. The use of Velcro on right seam pant leg will facilitate getting his leg into the pant with the brace. It also saves on wear and tear on the material.
Putting on and *taking off shirt*	Type—pullover, short sleeve. Taking off—needs assistance in getting it off his head. Difficult activity for a five-year-old.

Putting on—has difficulty putting neckband over head. He is able to get his arms through without assistance.

Suggestion   Until he becomes more proficient at this skill, suggest button-down type shirts or shirts with a zipper-front opening. Buttonholes should have vertical opening.

Coat and jacket   He is independent in putting on and taking off his coat. He needs some assistance in adjusting his clothing and buttoning. He was able to unbutton with the horizontal buttonhole. He had more difficulty with his short jacket with elastic wristband. The therapist demonstrated an alternate technique in putting the jacket on which he accomplished with a fair amount of success.

Comment: It is obvious that Terry still needs assistance in many self-help activities. However, one must also consider how many physically normal children enter kindergarten who cannot put on shoes, tie shoelaces, button or zipper clothing, and who need assistance with winter clothing. Terry is not entirely unique. While some of his underdeveloped skills are related to his disability, in many areas he will be equal in performance to the other children in his classroom. The teacher and other adults in the kindergarten must be assisted to see the "normalcy" of Terry's development as well as the specific areas which are interwoven with the fact of the handicap per se.

Because of the significance of the early years of the child's development, and because these years are often ignored in total planning, more emphasis has been placed in this chapter on early intervention than on the school years. The importance of the multidisciplinary team has also been indicated.

THE RESULTS OF EARLY INTERVENTION

Much progress has been achieved by the Sloan family during Terry's first five years. At five Terry began his long educational experience which culminated fourteen years later in his completing a community college program in "banking services." His community college training program was financed through the cooperative efforts of the State Division of Vocational Rehabilitation, a service to which all physically handicapped persons over sixteen years of age are entitled by federal law. His progress was not always academically smooth, but he performed quite well in school. He is obviously of normal or above normal intelligence. At five he was immediately integrated into an ordinary kindergarten, and he remained in an integrated situation throughout his school experience. This both produced problems and solved others, depending on the degree of sophistication of the teachers he encountered. Not all handicapped children could tolerate a regular grade placement.

Terry's father and mother have grown close. There has never been a question of their separating since Terry was six years old. They have profited from parent counseling, and they both have become equal partners in Terry's growth, therapy, and development. Terry has had his share of unhappy experiences, and these do not stop. There have been other bus drivers, and the bus driver of the previous chapter is representative of many unsympathetic peers and adults with whom Terry has had contact throughout his life. His father, however, has seen to it that Terry excels in something physical. Bowling has become a family activity. Terry went through the activities of the YMCA, and he swims, rides a bicycle, was the "bat boy" of a Little League baseball team when he was in junior high school, and he has friends.

The parents were much worried as Terry reached puberty. They, interestingly enough, returned to the personnel of the Early Action Program at that time, personnel who had visited with them regarding their earlier marital problems. This time it was to get an orientation regarding Terry's physical and emotional growth. Numerous conversations with people who could assist them served to assure them of the normalcy of the boy's development, helped them to appropriately understand and deal with sexual exploration in which Terry found himself with two neighborhood boys, to accept without being threatened Terry's masturbatory activities, to discuss nocturnal emissions, and otherwise to assist Terry through adolescence in this often difficult area of growth. Thus he was able to discuss freely sexual topics with his father, not in the sense of guilt or dependency, but in the sense of a good male relationship. Terry has had girlfriends, although not a great number. He started going with a girl at the time he got his first job in the bank, and this apparently is continuing.

What are the significant factors in this set of excerpts regarding Terry Sloan? There are several.

1. Communities do not yet have fail-safe methods for the early identification of all children with physical disabilities. It is too often an accidental happening. Although there were positive findings at 5½ months of age leading to a diagnosis of cerebral palsy, nothing relating to a treatment program was initiated until after Terry was thirteen months old. This is a very significant delay.

2. Early intervention, to insure the fullest possible total development of the child and his family, is important and is required. If Terry had not had the experiences he did, beginning at the age of approximately one year, he would probably not have been able to be assimilated into the ordinary community school at kindergarten age. A special school would have been his lot, a school which serves many children admirably and is a needed service in most communities, but not a school needed by Terry. Terry continued to receive necessary therapy during his elementary and secondary school life, and as a young adult still received speech therapy and some physical therapy. These are requisites to keep him in condition to participate in the normal community life.

3. The physical problem of a young child may be the real reason or it may be the excuse for parental tensions. It may be the reason for the male partner separating and leaving, when, as in Terry's case, the father has difficulty in accepting a handicapped son. Consultation for parents is an important service need in every community.

4. Complex problems require complex and interdisciplinary diagnostic efforts. Insight into the problems of a physically handicapped child will not come from a single discipline, regardless of which one it might be.

5. As Terry reached young adulthood, he still presented physical problems which were visible to himself and his friends. There may have been potentials which as a child were not exploited for this young man; perhaps there were services which could have been made available sooner or in greater depth. Under no circumstances can it be assumed that a perfect solution was available to Terry or his family. Certainly they received good, very complete, and long-term assistance, but there is yet as much to be learned about cerebral palsy as there is now understood about this severe and difficult problem.

6. Insofar as Terry's biological functioning is concerned, he is able to operate quite satisfactorily. Not all cerebral palsied persons or others with other types of physical disabilities are so fortunate. Terry is able to walk, talk, hold a job, and to engage in social activities. As a child, he was slow to toilet train; ultimately he could bathe, dress, and groom himself without the assistance of others. He has made a good adjustment to the opposite sex. He is capable of having sexual relations, of maintaining his own family, if that be his choice. Other handicapped adults are not so fortunate, and, as has been stated, they may need assistance in obtaining full, complete, and satisfying social and sexual experiences.

7. Earlier in this chapter it was indicated that many physically handicapped children with poliomyelitis, congenital deformities, or other types of disabilities demonstrate a variety of emotional problems. Not

too much has been reported in the case material regarding Terry's emotional development. Early aggressiveness, however, was noted, but this is not uncommon. When handicapped children, seriously restricted because of disabilities or prosthetic devices, begin to learn independence and try to move into the center of social activities, short-term personality problems are frequently observed. While Terry, with the support of clinic personnel, made a smooth entry into adolescence, he was also always a relatively easy child to handle in his home and his school.

8. It is obvious from the description of Terry Sloan that a child with a moderate physical disability has been under consideration. His entrance into kindergarten and his maintenance in the regular grades of his community schools was not a serious problem to the teachers or other children. All children deserve this opportunity, yet there are those whose disability is so severe that they cannot easily be integrated. The term "mainstreaming" has been used in educational circles to express the concept of integration. This is not a new concept. Physical disability alone is apparently not the basis on which acceptance or rejection of a crippled child is made by classmates in an integrated situation. Personality factors, similar in nature to those characterizing physically normal children, are the issues which cause a handicapped child to be rejected or to be seen as a "star" in sociometric studies. Thus as with Terry, children with problems of club foot, incipient muscular dystrophy, moderate forms of paraplegia or hemiplegia, and those with other moderate forms of physical disability or disease may find good educational experiences in regular grades. Children with severe forms of physical disability may require resource rooms or special classes, and some may require home teaching. An evaluation of the bases on which integration of exceptional children can be accomplished in the regular grades as well as the limitations to this concept has appeared in the literature (Paul 1977). Undoubtedly, more physically handicapped children could be integrated than are at present if general elementary and secondary educators and administrators were attitudinally more ready to accept them into programs other than the special schools or classes.

CONCLUSION

The education of physically disabled children, those with orthopedic, neurologic, cardiac disabilities, or long-term diseases or illness, is a problem of both parental and professional interdisciplinary concern and action. Although certain disciplines have legal responsibilities for specific portions of a disabled child's life program, the medical and the educational professions are not alone responsible for the total management plan. The concept of interdisciplinary diagnosis, treatment, and life planning is one in which disciplines are seen as equal among equals and in which the parents play a role as significant as any professional discipline. The historical dominance of programs for physically handicapped children by one or two single professions must give way, as in Terry's case, to that of total team function in which each discipline plays its legal and ethical role, brings to the handicapped child its skills and expertise, and jointly, with the parents, creates a regimen which assists the child to adulthood functioning. Problems of physical disability, whether diagnostic, habilitative, rehabilitative, educational, or vocational, are too complex to be trusted to the understanding and skills of a single discipline, whether that discipline be medicine, education, psychology, or another.

Society itself creates problems for the successful education, rehabilitation, and adult adjustment of the handicapped. Through a lack of fundamental information, social attitudes continue to be molded and directed by historical stereotypes, myths, outmoded attitudes, and discriminatory laws and regulations. One has only to witness the attempts to place adult handicapped in community living homes to see the outworn attitudes of non-handicapped adults come to the fore as forceful deterrents. Housing codes, discriminatory personnel and employment policies, lack of adequate transportation facilities, inaccessibility of public and private buildings, in spite of state and national legislation, all militate against the physically handicapped. Society is slow to change these barriers to full community living and participation. Large segments of society do not want to change but would rather ignore.

The poor attitudes of adult society are quickly accepted by children and youth and are perpetuated. The bus driver in the first page of the previous chapter characterizes a national problem. There is hardly a segment of our society, from adherents of some religious groups to the manufacturers of toilet seats, which does not discriminate against some or all of the physically disabled. There are problems with which special educators must cope and which are in no way fully solved. These issues are reflected in other chapters of this book as other types of children with problems have been considered.

Unfortunately the class action suits of the 1960s, concerned essentially with the mentally retarded but having implications for the physically disabled as well, have been allowed to spiral down significantly into a community attitude of disinterest and often outright avoidance. Concerned community leaders, concerned special educators and lawyers must renew the actions of the earlier decade, and undertake to stop the perpetuation of unfortunate attitudes toward the physically disabled. They must release that which is now a stopgap to change and improvement in the education and lives of the disabled, and bring to fruition an educational and social concept in which the physically disabled are not only legally equal to all others but, in actuality, are.

11

The Problems and Promise
of Special Education

WILLIAM C. MORSE

W̲ₑ ʜᴀᴠᴇ ᴀᴘᴘʀᴏᴀᴄʜᴇᴅ sᴘᴇᴄɪᴀʟ ᴇᴅᴜᴄᴀᴛɪᴏɴ through the individual lives of children with handicaps. This is a little like looking at trees but not seeing the forest, and there is a forest. From time to time controversies, alternatives, and problems were mentioned as the histories of the pupils evolved. It remains for us to pull together these general issues and consider what the future may bring. Any teacher working with even one special education pupil will of necessity be responding to these issues. An awareness of the ferment in special education is necessary to make reasonable professional judgment.

Special education is a significant portion of the educational enterprise with unique characteristics. And like any major institution, it develops a momentum of its own with strain and stress as changes are introduced. Though special education has come a long, long way, it has yet to fulfill its destiny. Gallagher (1970) estimated that less than half of the legitimate exceptional children and youth were being served. There are other estimates even less encouraging, indicating that only about one-third of the eligible children are being served. Still current special education represents a massive service enterprise, costing an estimated *$2.6 billion,* directly employing about 125,000 professionals in addition to many lay persons and ancillary support specialists to serve 2.26 million children and youth (Annual Report 1969). There is a vigorous national organization, the Council for Exceptional Children. National and state legislation is monitored, and lobbying is part of the game. Most categories of exceptionality have their own professional and lay groups. There are state and local associations. The national special associations as well as local ones want changes for their children which are deemed in keeping with best understanding.

301

As in the case of any social operation, special education has become institutionalized, with stated and unstated provisos and customs. Change is often resisted and aborted. When there is this much momentum in a time of vast social re-evaluation, such as we have had, the result is predictable. There will be factions, controversies, panaceas, experiments, and proposals for radical instant solutions. Above all there will be new terms even if for old substance. Is mainstreaming a new idea or a return to pre-special education practice? In the area of methodology Mann (1975) has shown that long-buried "faculty" psychology has been resurrected under new names in special education. It is the teachers who carry the actual burdens for programs. If we want to know what is actually going on in special education, we must study the experiences they provide children more than the pronouncements of the remote individuals. Frequently those describing the big new world forget the actual school day of the pupil. On the other hand, change in a democratic society rests on the convictions held by the participants. The function of leadership is to provide new options, insights, and values for the teacher's consideration. Even when they are absurd, such as the zero reject concept that every child must be educated in the public school setting, we must evaluate the degree to which this is reasonable. What each professional thinks and does about the controversies of special education is of crucial concern. After all, this is a field where decisions will make or break the lives of our fellows, and the responsibility is as great as in the medical profession. We should keep in mind that special education does not stand alone but is part of the total educational establishment. Being a part of a larger operation restricts the freedom to move independently. Money here means less money there. Mainstreaming changes the function of both the regular teacher and the special teacher. It takes a lot of doing and a lot of counter balancing, for there are huge financial and administrative conditions involved. Sometimes those who influence legislation and those who direct training act as if the special education world which *should* be already is. One can even be trained for non-existent roles. Conversely, if one does not appreciate the nature of the current scene and the changes which are taking place, it is difficult to be prepared.

While it would be impossible to summarize all of the current special education issues brought up in the chapters, some are of overriding importance. The following sections deal with mandatory legislation, labeling, mainstreaming, and other modes of service delivery, accountability, and multidiscipline problems. How these concerns are handled will define the character of special education in the next decade.

MANDATORY LEGISLATION—WHERE ARE WE HEADING?

Without legal sanction for universal special education, there is nothing. With it comes the right to demand and sue for service. You do not remake professionals or create programs by law alone, but the legal shock waves continue to violently shake up special education. Even with mandatory provisions, court action is often required to obtain services. State laws differ greatly. Some start at age zero and run to 25 or more; others cover the usual school age. The use of law to obtain services is not only with regard to special education. Rehabilitation in mental health and penal institutions has been forced by judicial process. In special care for children, the balance of the rights and protective needs of the child, the rights of the parent, and the obligation of special education are as yet undefined but are being clarified by case decisions. The Council for Exceptional Children has been active in monitoring the development.

We should recognize that the law embodies our social aspirations, and we can take pride in the fact that federal and state laws are aimed at making quality education the right of each and every child. Other countries have preceded us, and it is about time this degree of humanness became the law of our land.

Since mandatory special education is an expression of our democratic ideology, most professionals are using the opportunity in good faith. However, it is also evident that some administrators are fearful, and since even teachers can be sued, protective action can become the central goal. Meetings, forms, and rituals are designed to follow the law regardless of the program which eventuates. A lawyer's call to the state office of special education can cause a local school superintendent to issue a decree: an instant program is to be produced by the local special education officer regardless of the appropriateness of what is done. Parents' groups have been known to think in terms of opportunities to sue rather than cooperate, an impulse born of long experience with and mistrust of professionals.

Legislation has created the expectation of an immediate solution to all special education problems, but most of the legal mandates are not adequately financed for the programs defined. Decrees without cash bring another series of pressures. Until we have the money, we generate a contest over the limited resources. Keogh (in Wedell 1975) has worked out the index of the per pupil cost for special programs over regular programs: the highest is physically handicapped, 3.64; visual and auditory handicaps come next at about 2.98; emotionally disturbed at 2.83; learning disabilities 2.16; retarded 1.92; speech 1.18. Costs for the multiply handicapped are put at 2.73, which seems low. While these figures do not tell us what the range and cost of the best program might be, they do emphasize the cost factor. Regular education and the unions have only just begun to realize what has happened and have begun to question responsibilities and the use of resources. Federal resources are being expanded but not in any sense sufficiently to fill the gap.

Several consequences are already evident: parent groups are competing with each other for programs; the multiply and seriously handicapped provisions are very expensive and are being resisted; there is expansion without qualified personnel; other agencies—notably mental health—are divesting themselves of responsibility since schools must provide; paper programs, inadequate programs, and superficial programs are being developed. One proposal is to count mainstreamed children double or triple in regular classroom enrollment. There is even a move to count special children as special only that percent of time they are *not* in regular situations and thus save the money. Reimbursement would be for only the 10 percent or whatever time the pupil was actually in a resource room or special service. Yet the same children are still required to be certified even to get the 10 percent help! The sooner we face the fact there is no cheap or cut-rate special education, the better. It would be informative to see the budget for the special services for each of the cases in this book.

The converse is also true: much real progress has ensued. Many systems have reorganized their services, expanded their concerns, and sought added funds as well. Regular education is beginning to deal with its part of the responsibility. It is important to note that the new federal legislation carries with it a funding plan. It is intended that, by 1982, this shall be 40 percent of the national average cost per school child. The figure is estimated to be more than three billion dollars. When this day arrives, the other 60 percent of the financing will be competing on the state and local level with all other services, especially other educational services. As one teacher's union official put it, "The state now mandates the service but pays a decreasing portion. The standards and expectations are far higher and more expensive than provided for regular pupils."

The expansion to preschool children has received a boost, and this may bring the needed emphasis on early intervention and prevention. Such expansion will also require new expertise. Schools dealing with the young adult will also need a new approach.

"Mandatory" means force was necessary. It is evidence of mistrust which must be melted away. Only by honest facing of issues will suspicions be reduced. It is particulary important to realize the deep and immediate concern of parents. They have the present child's welfare at heart and will not be put off by five-year plans or the "long haul" expectations. The most important need is to work together for more adequate appropriations and quality programs.

Perhaps the most myopic aspect of the present mandatory phase is its limited perception of programs for the handicapped. The school is a creature of the state and an easy and visible target. Further, it has a most critical part to play in rehabilitation. But schools cannot go it alone. The mandatory legislation should cover all society, all agencies, and all services. While there are sometimes regulations for provision for special children in services like Head Start or vocational rehabilitation, even then enforcement is difficult. What is to be done about health and welfare? Handicapped care is everybody's business.

WHAT SHALL WE DO ABOUT LABELING?

The controversies around labeling are both real and spurious. Without some sort of a category system, there is no access to differentiated special service. The negative effects of being named are not in the names themselves but in the implications which reflect social attitudes. Not all labels are negative. Parents have their children tested to get them entitled exceptionally bright. To be categorized as learning handicapped is more acceptable than to be emotionally disturbed, though the prognosis may be less favorable. There is a natural reluctance to have one's child categorized as anything which could be assumed one's fault as a parent. Research on attitudes indicates that mere diagnostic labels increase the teacher's perception of the child's incapacity compared to the same description of the child's behavior without the label. Even special teacher trainers hold negative stereotypes of the emotionally disturbed. Our own research has indicated that student teachers of the disturbed see these children as both "bad" and "powerful" on the semantic differential. It is interesting how many teachers who give help to the disturbed are reluctant about getting personal help for themselves, when they need it, though they feel good about giving help to the "unfortunates."

Those who decry categories have often ignored the fact that most children are given some such name or category by parents or peers long before they come to professional attention. Sibling comparison may label the slow or bad one in the family, and there is the literature on family scapegoating. Comparative sibling evaluations often become internalized by normal children, regardless of the accuracy. To this is added peer names such as "nutty," "stupid," "wild," "weirdo," "crutches," "goo-goo eyes," "fatso," "skinny," "runt"—any of which can leave a deep imprint on the child thus singled out. The normal child may spend his lifetime to rid himself of feeling dumb. Unfortunately the mass media frequently uses atypicality as a source of humor which adds to the negative stereotyping. With the handicapped, there is a reality reinforcer to add to what is said: the child really doesn't "get it," does lose control, can't talk or run as well as his or her compatriots. Even without the name, the performance differences are there and evident. While small children seem to accept differences as a natural thing, at the elementary age and certainly adolescence, competitive pressure often makes "the difference" a source of ridicule. Be that as it may, to have an official legal label after being diagnosed by the man in the white coat or the man with those funny "games" has implications of another order. The lack of knowledge of or bizarre interpretations pupils make of their condition on their own has been brought out in the chapters. Children will walk to different pick-up places so as not to be seen by their neighborhood friends boarding the special bus. Even the opportunity which diagnosis heralds may be bad, for help makes you more different than others, and "different" is what is generally perceived negatively. This may more than counterbalance the help. And people expect you to react as that special pupil regardless of what you do. You begin to fulfill their prophecy. Any one of us who has tried to change our reputation for a given set of behaviors knows how difficult it is. Our friends still see the clown, the shy one, or whatever, even when we have ceased to send out the cues. The label has become the self.

The problem of getting help without having a label is most perplexing. One of the truths which has become only too evident is that we should not discard categories as an isolated act. The whole system has to be overhauled along with getting rid of categories.

Now it should be clear that we are dealing with social attitudes and not the condition itself. A name does not change the nature of the actual condition, but it most often changes the way the person and others perceive or misperceive that condition. Other societies do not have our set of difficulties with names. For example, in *Village in the Vaucluse* (Wylie 1964), the parents, teachers, and peers openly acknowledge individual differences in ability and expect performance related to ability. There is no secret about it. While it made the American visitor cringe, the local people considered the efforts toward pretense of equality in ability as distorting reality. Because of our attitudes, to label is to affix a set of behaviors to the individual which are usually detrimental.

Current federal legislation requires that there be a state procedure for identification of the handicapped. Frankly, in one way or another there will be labels. The magnum opus on this problem are three volumes by Hobbs (1975), where every aspect is dealt with in detail. Some sort of nomenclature is necessary and will persist; what will be most useful to the child should be the determining factor. In addition to the social and personal difficulties, there are other significant questions about labels as now used—and this is as true for educator's labels as the medical ones which special education has tried to replace with their own set.

There is growing attention to a competing system which is based on severity rather than category. This represents a horizontal vs. the usual vertical categorical system as mentioned in Chapter 1. In the old vertical demarcation, emotional problems from minor to most severe, or retardation from minimal to severe would each be considered in a single category. The horizontal division would put together minor LD, MR, ED, and so on as one level to be handled as one category while severe problems in all areas would be grouped together. The combination is comprised not of a deviation type but on level of intensity. There are those who hold that autistic and severely retarded have similar treatment needs. Such a system goes on to equate the intensity of service with the intensity of problem. For the professional it means a different style of training. Some teachers would be trained to work with the combination of mildly retarded, disturbed, language disabled, and speech problems while another would work with combinations of severely handicapped. Most would agree that specialization by category for the blind and deaf would still be separate. Administratively the horizontal makes a neat package, but there are problems which will be discussed subsequently.

If we look at the basic issue, the purpose of a label is to indicate what the intervention style and substance should be. As presently used, this is seldom true. A label of "retarded" or "disturbed" is not definitive: it gives a teacher no specific help. Labels are often based upon erroneous data. Labels often lie. Research is available which throws doubt on many of the particular educational tests and scales used to categorize. Since many of these tests are the life blood of special education they are still used as if they are definitive, even when the factors claimed do not appear to be real. Both reliability and validity of many scales are questionable. Whole programs are built upon unwarranted assumptions about certain tests. To one clinician a child may be disturbed and to another a healthy ego in conflict with a punitive environment. While this misidentification may be less a condition in certain medical diagnoses as we have seen in the chapters on certain anomalies, misdiagnosis can happen there too.

There are really two functions to whatever we do in labeling. One is entitlement: is this child a legitimate candidate for special education service? This is the in or out function. We should note that again this is an artifact of having special education rather than meeting all of the special needs of any school pupil. If a teacher, parent, and, one would hope, the child, too, indicates a problem but does not pass the magic line to become special—what then? In many schools as special education upgrades its services, it reduces its intake with no or very inadequate services left for the inbetween. One point in IQ has to be lost to get help! As long as we do not have complete services for all children, we are faced with the problem of what to do with pupils who need help but do not fit the legal categories. Parents of special children often guard the entry gates to protect limited resources.

With the limited money dedicated for "special education" pupils, unless a student "has something," there is a great reluctance to provide service. Early intervention and prevention are being stymied. Some professionals have developed ways to bootleg service to children who are not yet "bad enough" to fit the state categories. The advice to a special education child is to have it "bad" but only in one category or you will not get proper service.

With some progress being made during the current cry for declassification, we have witnessed the reverse happening at the same time! The case of the learning disabled is a point. Parents demanded help for such children. But neither special education nor regular education was eager to assume responsibility for a category variously estimated from 3 to 30 percent of the school population. Some said it would take all the special education funds for this category alone. Thus while declassification was being proposed elsewhere, a new classification was created as the only way to secure assistance for the children who needed special help. With this come new diagnostic procedures, new certification requirements, and new training programs. William Rhodes once commented that we will end up with more categories than children. But a category is often the key to special education resources.

In addition to the decision function, the second major purpose of any categorical schema is to assist in drawing up specific intervention plans. After all, each pupil is to have a unique educational sequence according to law. The current labeling systems do not provide the data for this. The argument still remains if the child is autistic does one use a particular style of nonpersonal behavior modification or relationship therapy for each and every one? The fact is, the range within labels is so great as to make an educational program impossible from the title. A schizophrenic, primary behavior disorder, or neurotic pupil could be a "delinquent." We are too complicated to have our needs satisfied by a simple rubric. At best labels can only tell us to what general issues we must attend. One functional escape is individualization, where categories are submerged in the particular prescription for each child. There is a way to make diagnosis the key and labeling of minor consequence and a way to make the diagnostic workup serve individualized planning. First off, we examine dimensions of behavior in the major realms—cognitive, affective, and motor. By compiling a succinct but comprehensive set of dimensions under each, we can formulate a grid. The dimensions are then used to assess the conditions by column. Column 1 summarizes what we are confronted with in day to day living, with relevant diagnostic data on cognitive, affective, and motor functioning coming from etiological data. Column 2 becomes an analysis of the assets and limitations in the person and in the surroundings. Column 3 lists interventions already tried, with results. Column 4 includes the new plans, short- and long-term goals related to column 1. This is the source of the IEP. Column 5 is evaluation and recycle planning in the future. In fact, as special education moves toward more services for the very seriously and multiply handicapped, there is a vital need for this grid to summarize the multidiscipline contributions from education, psychology, social work, and medicine. Some educators do not distinguish between the so-called medical model which uses terms and a concept of intervention related to that discipline from the use of medical data. Medical information may be of the most sophisticated nature though it contributes to educational plans rather than dictating them.

The danger of stereotyping is as true of the new educational modes in special education as of the old. When there is no attention to anything about a pupil but graphed behavior and mechanical plans are made on this basis alone, one has again violated the individual's nature by artificial abstraction to the tune of the "educational model." How many are the reasons a pupil may not sit in his seat enough of the time to please the overseers? Is it disinterest in the seat work? Anxiety? Defiance? A migratory propensity? Distractability?

Making all children fit a set intervention is labeling by practice. To label all "behaviors" which look alike to the casual observer as identical in meaning and thus requiring a common intervention is actually unfair categorization of children whether named or not. There are no short cuts to psychologically valid planning based upon a broad spectrum of knowledge and practice. The recognition of the multidisciplinary nature of the field is evident especially when it comes to research: a great deal of the progress is made from non-special educators. Gallagher has edited a volume of this genre, *The Application of Child Development Research to Exceptional Children* (1975). Teachers need to know what prognosis to expect for they are faced with gauging task relevance and difficulty as well as rate of progress at every interchange. There is only one model in a teacher's system, and that is the human model, complex and varied as the subject is.

As was pointed out, the mandate of special education is to do the best things possible for all special children. Frequently it may be "how" or "who" does something rather than the specific "what" that is done. In our own studies of disturbed children, some had changes in their life space out of school which produced new hope or motivation on one hand or despair on the other. The impact of these forces may override the specifics in the educational program. But programs and methods earn the credit or debit regardless of their external factors. There is also a tendency to overapply any technique which has a reasonable modicum of success in a given situation. Yet we know there is hardly anything which is not appropriate and which does not work in some instance, and conversely nothing which will solve all the problems. In the course of this book we have seen that there are deep differences of opinion regarding methodology in some fields. For the teacher there is likely to be blood, sweat, and tears even when one has discovered the methods which are more adaptable for the particular children. There is nothing cheap or easy about special education.

If we recognize the interactive multiple causation in many of the children's problems, even new professionals can understand why progress is so slow. Adding to the basic question of what is best to do is the cost in money and energy of giving a child what he would need if we are to maximize his potentials. Since there is rarely any instant cure, we are faced with endless hours of work—far in excess of that invested in the typical child. Tommy required an intensive and extensive interaction to get things moving: weeks of intensive one on one work were required. Perhaps the most flagrant violation of proper investment is related delinquency where it is more probable to find counterproductive than preventive programs. Program failure can be a consequence of lack of energy or knowledge, but there are also failures due to lack of application of available knowledge because of cost. This is not to imply that with proper special education all children could eventually perform within one standard deviation of the average on all counts; what we are implying is that we already know enough to help many live more full lives than they now enjoy.

MODES OF PROVIDING SPECIAL EDUCATION SERVICES

The mystique of special education was around special classes. In fact, being in a special class (since the program might not differ from the regular class) may have been the only real element of difference. Then came institutionalization. If a special class was not enough for the serious cases, institutional warehousing was the final answer. When special educators found salvation during the recent cultural revolution, all of this was rejected both on humanitarian grounds and studies which, while far from definitive, gave reason to doubt. Many of the same leaders who were rabid for special classes now decreed there was no place for them and ushered in the new era. As you consider the children in the various chapters, it will be clear that no single mode of giving help was sufficient even for so small a sample as we have studied. In fact, several procedures might be adopted at even one and the same time.

Any teacher can verify that "mainstreaming" special children is nothing new. Historically the child had to make it in the regular class or get out. Unfortunately much of this has persisted even with special education. When the first efforts to break down the segregation into special classes took place, regular teachers offered to take a pupil if the special class would in return take another they already had in the normal classroom.

It is popular today for special educators to advocate the zero reject model. By this is meant that there should be no escape from administrative responsibility once a child is enrolled in the mainstream. There should be no removal for any reason. This concept of zero reject from the mainstream is quite other than the concept of zero reject from an adequate and relevant educational experience.

Effective mainstreaming of a large number of exceptional children requires massive changes in the present structure. We have a long way to go. Can our present educational system accommodate to the wide range of differences in the typical school population? It has been pointed out by many that getting the mass of public school teachers to change their methods is most difficult. Legal "demands" produce as much subterfuge as real change.

Mainstreaming is a process, not a place. As one reviews the examples, it is clear that whenever possible, special youngsters should be with others of their own age with the added help infused. It goes without saying, if the unmodified regular classroom could provide all that is needed, the pupil may not be special in the first place. Regular classrooms differ widely in their capacity to provide for individual differences because of teacher skills and philosophy, peer cultures, and subject matter. The less adaptable the regular stream, the more candidates for special education. But let us begin with the recognition that, for the special child something must be added. There are significant differences between special and general education: special education is deficit oriented, does not mirror regular education, and is based on clinical diagnosis and assessment. Sometimes what must be added will not be educational: medical and psychological therapies may not involve the educational complex specifically.

What can be added to make the regular classroom the effective mode for providing special education? The first and universal criterion is peer acceptance and a social climate of mutual care and support. When this does not exist, it must be cultivated. More is learned from peers than from teachers, and self-esteem is impossible without peer acceptance. When integration of the special child is anticipated and the proper conditions do not exist, the available consultants will have to work it through. It has been said that integration provides a learning experience for the normal child: the question is—what kind will it be? At growth periods of high social tension, such as adolescence, rejection and scapegoating are common with regard to normal peers; much work will be required to give the help the special pupil needs at this time.

The mainstream teacher may be prepared to provide for the exceptional child. Most will need information, skill training, and consultation before and during. It should never be forgotten that mainstreaming increases the obligations of the regular teachers, many of whom have very difficult classes to teach already. Materials and methods will have to be practical. As one such teacher put it, "Theory is OK, but you can't teach a deaf child with theory." Consultation for the classroom teacher has a role to play. Unfortunately much consultation is spread too thin, deals in advice and not demonstration, and is not there when the teacher most needs it. But a good consultant, even of the migrant kind, has been helpful to many mainstream teachers.

The next step is the adding of direct service and not just advice. In many of the chapters the pupils could be mainstreamed and helped on a crisis or time-allotted basis by a special education teacher. Resource rooms in schools or itinerant specialists who actually work with the youngster are examples of added support to the classroom. The issue is whether episodic intervention of such a nature, no matter how well executed, is adequate to meet the youngster's needs. A severe LD case will not respond to a half-hour-a-day tutorial. But even the severely handicapped may be able to function (not just exist) in the mainstream for part of their school day. There are junior high cases who can only function in a classroom two periods and spend the rest with their special teacher. Many of these children need more input of the type which a lay tutor can provide. If the older retarded can teach some of the younger ones, we should realize that peers, older pupils, college students where available, parents, and other volunteers can be the added ingredient which makes the mainstream appropriate.

One of the least appreciated elements related to mainstreaming is the relationship to diagnosis. It is naive to assume that the less severe can always be mainstreamed while the seriously handicapped are candidates for more segregation. The analysis should be made on the basis of what interventions have to be marshaled to meet the assistance plan. Would it be better to separate temporarily and intensify interventions or go a more gradual route? What is the necessary set of resources? Some very handicapped individuals can be helped in a regular setting: there are physically restricted who do well, even certain schizophrenic children have been able to use the regular classroom. On the other hand, a minor ego intact social deviant may require more supervision and structure than a teacher of twenty-four children can devote.

Schworm (1976) believes that the hierarchy of services concept indicates where a student should be placed for instruction, not the instruction the student is to receive. He argues for using evaluations of the affective, cognitive, and motor performance. This is by way of caution relating placement to severity.

The next step beyond the resource teacher supplementation is the separate classroom. Again, flexibility is the rule, maximizing the time spent out of the classroom in the mainstream when it can be productive. But when we think of it, there is in the small class two and a half times the regular teacher per youngster, and the person has particular skills. When the special class is nothing but a replica of the regular class with intensified social problems, we cannot expect anything good to come of it. The pupil's attitude toward the "opportunity" will be most important. Riding on the "special bus" for considerable distances may be a more potent experience than the classroom. Some children find in the adjusted demands of the special class their first peace and copable environment. If this is a chance to recover and grow, so much the better: if it is only a place to retreat, it makes prognosis more limited. The relevance and quality of each pupil's experience, not philosophical prejudices, constitute the criterion of judgment about the class.

There are cases where the total environment must be controlled to maximize the pupil's future. Some families are ineffective or detrimental and unable to carry out a supportive effort. The family may need a restorative rest. The multidiscipline input around the clock is another condition available only in a totally planned life setting. For the few, such a setting is not only a treatment institution but a protected halfway house or living center for life. Sheltered workshops or "living communities" provide work and social roles. Here there is the continual role of adult special education to stimulate lives in whatever ways possible. It is unlikely that we shall provide treatment towns for caring for the handicapped as is done in some European countries. The next best is a protected total environment in an institutional setting.

Many leaders have discussed the need for a series of programs. But that is only half the problem. If we have the gamut from regular classrooms to long-term institutions, there is still the perplexing concern about placement. Which child needs what style to help to maximize his or her growth? As one moves toward the very serious problems, there are fewer and fewer children who require the ultimate in intensive care. However, without a fully articulated sequence of services, children will be put where there is an opening whether it is adequate or not. If the only available service is the special class, that will be used. What is present will be used and misused simply because it is available, regardless of fit. There is a great tendency to overload services with cases too complex for the given resources since there is so little for those who require extreme programming. Any total special education program will include access to a spectrum of delivery modes—mainstream to living in institutions. When stages are missing, there is overloading of other services and misuse of what is open.

Age considerations are becoming increasingly important in the design of services. By and large, the elementary age has been best covered in the past. Often this has been too late, and the present concern for preschool children is an effort to redress the balance. If we review the cases, the critical need for early intervention has been evident. Yet, for chronic handicaps and because there may be new difficulties with the age, adolescence cannot be neglected as it has in the past. The worry of many an elementary teacher is the lack of follow through in junior and senior high. The transition from high school to adult life status may be delayed for the handicapped. All of this means there is no age for which services can be ignored.

There is pressure to design delivery systems based upon logic or cost. A special teacher for ten children is costly and more pupils could be served if the teacher gave up the class and became an itinerant teacher. Thus that teacher could serve more children but serve them much less, which could still be a quality program or could be a façade. From a psychological viewpoint the design of the delivery system is secondary. What is important is the match between the pupil's needs and what is actually being done for him or her. If the match is as close as possible, how it is rationed out is incidental. What is needed in planning delivery systems is precise study of the remedial input required. Whatever the mode, the consumer (and his or her parents) must see the help-giving arrangement as positive; beyond this attitude is the actual substance of the special program.

THE HUMANIZATION OF TREATMENT

It is a sad commentary that it took law suits to curb the bureaucratic institution of special education. As noted in several of the chapters, parents were often regarded with suspicion and handled in a cursory fashion by professionals. After all, if one is doing the holy work of helping the handicapped, who should be asking questions? Once parents finally had legal sanctions behind them, nothing was about to stop them. They have united to form very strong pressure groups. Certain special education prophets promise solutions to everything through such cures as vitamins, rigid conditioning, or crawling to maturity, to mention a few of the many. Parents, in their hopes for their children, are of course anxious to try what experts suggest. Sometimes they attempt to dictate program design and content. It is interesting how many parents become lay-professionals: reading, taking courses, and attending conferences they acquire a knowledge bank in advance of the regular professionals. Some serve as teacher assistants while a few go on to professional careers in special education. There are books written by parents. One group has spent tens of thousands in court cases to protect their rights to get help for their handicapped, and they have confronted the governor, powerful agencies, and local boards of education. They do the research and get the consultation to speak with authority. This democratization of special education is bound to increase the humanization of service. When the parents serve on boards and face the realities of budgets, they are less inclined to demand the impossible. Parents and professionals can be adversaries or allies: it is one of the choices to make in the next decade.

Because of the history of suspicion over the years, the new laws have also produced definitive regulations to assure parent participation at all levels. The parent must be notified at all stages, must agree to the program, and must be presented information on progress. The decision-making conferences may include as many as eight to a dozen professionals. In one instance, the meeting was even larger and went on for 6 hours! Some parents do find participation in such sessions painful and prefer to work through a trusted professional. Part of the problem is that psychological reports, histories, test results, and the like are not easy for most experts to discuss before parents. We have been too prone to discuss children as "cases," and we lack skill in describing conditions sympathetically. In some places there are little meetings before "the meeting" with the purpose of getting the things worked out ahead of time, so real is the difficulty of talking together. A parent may wish to bring an ombudsman to help him participate.

Whatever the difficulties, the mandated involvement of parents is a huge step forward for special education. As we learn to work together, let us hope that the ritualistic elements recede to be replaced by teaming.

One of the most prominent conditions in the accounts of the children in this book was the role of the parents. Except for the period of institutionalization, no professional care can equal the time and significance of the parent relationship. We saw again and again the decisive role they played, and there is no way to replace their function even if we so wished. In essence, the humanization of special education means that all parts of the operation must deal with people and their rights. Gone are the days of covert decision making or informing parents after the fact. In its place is a partnership which adds more than could be paid for were it a cash transaction.

There is yet another task in the humanization process which has a long way to go. It is traumatic at times to hear pupils spoken about by teachers and others as if they were not present or could not hear. In common with the nonhandicapped, the most vital core of the special child is that child's self-concept and self-esteem. Because of the hazards we have noted, self-esteem is even more tenuous for them than for the normal youngster. We are at the threshold of counting them in as well as parents. He who is most involved often knows least about what is going on. Things are done to and for the pupil that are not understood. Learning disabled pupils often have no real comprehension of their plight. Adolescents are both hurt and resistive when they are not given information about themselves. Obviously some special children cannot handle much or any of this while others can become highly involved. Decisions are made without benefit of consumer advice. It is not easy to deal with the issues the youngsters are considering: Why am I different than other children? Whose fault is it? What do other people think of me? What will happen to me if my parents die? Their questions are life questions not to be taken lightly. A teacher's superficial comment, "That's good work for you," is not enough. Any alternatives in special education programs should be discussed with those who can understand. Their rights are to be respected in any placement.

Humanization is also apparent in the de-ritualization of special education services. Time was when only the fully initiated were considered able to do anything helpful for the special child. Appreciation of the many ways of helping has changed matters a great deal. Peers and peer groups are an influence we seek to convert to positive input. Older youth are often the critical figures in younger children's identification images. College students, lay adults, paid aides, and volunteers often have acquired understanding and patience because they have lived through many problems. These persons constitute a reservoir of support in special education. Many programs now depend on parents for major intervention strategies, especially for the young child.

No special education teacher can go it alone and offer the degree of help needed. As mainstreaming increases, the delegation of tasks to other than the formal teacher will necessarily be accentuated. As we more than double special education to serve all who are entitled to it, we can never invest the time necessary without volunteers.

As the chapters are reviewed from this light, one thing stands out. The family constitutes the most significant expansion area for helping the special child. Time after time we saw how family acceptance of the true nature of the condition had to be achieved before any significant program could be worked out. Then came family cooperation, and finally the families conduct certain special education functions on their own. In the past parents were often seen as the enemy. Democratization means making parents the allies, a process which includes the teacher's ability to work with and through parents. Along with this is the new concern to provide "respite" care for families, some relief and freedom for families who may be virtually collapsing under the stress of trying to deal with the problem. One of the functions of school is to give this help to the home.

The definition of children's rights has become a matter of supreme court decision, so important are the issues. The age and conditions relative to rights of treatment and protection as well as the right to refuse has become critical. Parent rights and the rights of the state are also involved. As is usual with our process of change we go from no rights to ultimate freedom in attempting to redress former conditions. At what age have children and youth the right to decide to leave school or home or refuse help if what is happening is not compatible with the youngster's perception of self-interest? Lawyers have sought out test cases regardless of the child or parent interests. One state law requires that every schizophrenic child be informed of his or her right to leave the treatment institution. One such youngster, unable to comprehend the nature of his new option to freedom, thought he was being ejected. With tears he begged not to be put out, saying, "Why do you do this when you know I have no place to go?"

Only recently has the scope of rights expanded from the legalistic to conceptual human rights. We have fixated more on freedom than the opportunity and right to have help. Handicapped people have equivalent rights to their normal counterparts: this means the right to move freely in society, to be employed, to marry, to vote, even to spend money as foolishly as normal people can. The function of special education is to prepare them for all of life. Even sexual knowledge has been neglected until recently. With a teenager the right to a driver's license is the most obvious sign of maturity: for the learning disabled a written test may be impossible. There are added rights for special people such as the right to be protected from exploitation, the right to specialized training and placement, the right to sheltered workshops and sheltered living—the overall right to be cared for. We can start this process by always involving the handicapped pupil in his or her own welfare to the extent of the student's ability and by helping the student to assume more responsibility for his or her life.

There are particular ways to talk with handicapped children. The sad thing is, most handicapped children are not given the opportunity to participate. With the severely handicapped, of course, parents and special educator advocates provide balance. In the final position stands the law. The delicate balance between forcing, manipulating, and counseling is most difficult to maintain. Adults tend to either err on the side of having all the wisdom and patronize the youngster or underestimate the child's investment in his or her future and ability to grapple with real problems. Those who work with teenagers have the adolescent developmental struggle to add to the problems brought on by special conditions. Counseling with this age becomes more complicated. Special education children are not "patients" or "clients" but young human beings. This constitutes the ultimate test for the level of humanization of services.

ACCOUNTABILITY

It used to be that the value of a program was attested by its existence: it is, therefore it is useful. Accountability has entered into all education but is particularly evident in special education. After all, the revolution in special education came as a result of studies of special classes which were found to offer no more promise than the mainstream.

In the discussion of diagnosis it was pointed out that from this analysis we set goals and these in turn are subject to evaluation. The difficulty is the "'round robin" nature of this operation, with the teacher being the culprit if the plan is not realistic. The goals set vary greatly. In one place they may be narrow and specific—to make the letters A, B, and C on command. In another instance, they may be global—to return the child to the mainstream in three months. Systems have even used Bloom's taxonomy and demanded goals for all aspects of the three domains—cognitive, affective, and motor. What teacher could expect to accomplish such a list?

Without goals individual programs tend to become amorphous and general. Limited goals can be restrictive. Unrealistic goals can produce frustration on the part of those responsible and punitive action on the part of others. Whose goals should be accepted—psychologist? teacher? supervisor? parent? child? Obviously this is a complex issue, and several people will be involved, especially the child whenever he or she is able. After all, it is the child's life and energy involved.

Once both short- and long-term goals with some indication of priority have been set, the interventions must match. Hoping to "cure" a delinquent by once a week contact with a "big brother" is unrealistic. Episodic tutoring sessions may assist a retarded child, but are they enough? If the goals are set in good faith and with an eye to their reasonableness, they form the basis for accountability.

Periodic re-evaluation and re-setting of goals should be based upon the progress. Accountability requires realistic expectations: for some children prognosis will be more limited with only minor alteration possible. With others the long-term goal may be normal behavior, through a series of specific changes, step by step. Putting expectation too low is irresponsible, and setting them beyond possible fulfillment is cruel to the child, parent, and teacher alike.

Basic psychological considerations can be tested in examining progress. Just what needs to be changed in the individual and/or the environment to make for a more promising future must be pinpointed for accountability. What are the preferred strategies of intervention? Should particular methods be utilized? How much time must be invested? Does the family need to change, and if so how? Is there a factor of peer rejection or teacher incompetency? This analysis of needed input is crucial. Parents and the children are involved as well as professionals. To avoid the damage of too little or too great anticipation, the plan must have a degree of openendedness. There are so many examples of under- and overestimation that honesty requires tentativeness.

Psychological accountability, then, is making the most perceptive plan we can, executing the most appropriate actions, and conducting careful evaluations. It is a painstaking process where superficiality is ruled out by expertise and experience. Just doing things to or for a youngster is not accountability: what is done must be important. There is no better way for training in accountability than to participate in the analysis, planning, responsibility, and evaluation for the life course of a special child. Each chapter provided the opportunity to watch the process unfold and judge the accountability level in each instance. The authors provided information on what might have been done as well as what was done.

But it is not enough to hold a teacher accountable as an individual. The total program should be subject to accountability. Was the proper intervention indicated? Adequate time provided? Did the teacher get the other help implied? Are the parents meeting their obligations? Does the pupil have a morale problem and no real investment in the activity? The goal of accountability is to maximize the handicapped pupil's performance. It cannot be used to nullify those who are doing the best they can with impossible odds.

CONCLUSION

Both special teachers and mainstream teachers stand to be overwhelmed when the complications of even the cases in this book are considered. There is so much to do and so much expected. It should be noted that this is an introduction only: for each chapter's handicapped, volumes have been written.

One thing expected of all of us is to be advocates for all the handicapped. There are three ways one can function in the advocate role. The first advocate role is the new professional advocate recommended by the *Crisis in Child Mental Health* (1971). This is more than an ombudsman function of helping those who request assistance: it is riding forth to contest wrongdoing as a profession (Paul 1977).

The second concept of advocacy is not new but renewed. There have always been advocates for child welfare, a host of advocates ranging from classroom teachers to national leaders. These advocates have gone beyond the comfort and protection of traditional professionalism to seek a better life for all children as well as those with whom they are working at the time. It has meant endless confrontations with authority, use of personal persuasion, and being counted on critical issues. In fact there are teachers who have gone the last mile and put their jobs on the block. This is personal advocacy as against role advocacy.

The essential thing to remember is that the true advocate does not have the luxury of dividing people into "good guys" and "bad guys." There may well be a few psychopaths in the field, but most people are doing the best they can, given their capacity and the situational forces under which they operate. These conditions need to be analyzed. The individuals we see as the "bad guys" blocking righteousness are frequently caught in a bind even as are we all.

True advocacy is attempting to help resolve unfortunate conditions and to work through more adequate solutions. To do this, the professionals need not only skill in working with people but an understanding of the dynamics of systems and modes of change, as well as self-understanding. Assigning blame is the most prevalent and useless form of advocacy. This advocacy is not a new role in special education but a function or stance for all in the field regareless of role. As one might expect, parents, sometimes singly but more often in parent associations, are the most vigorous and productive advocates. It is one thing to argue for causes as a part of one's professional job; it is quite another to fight for the rights of one's own child, as parents do. Fearless and driven, they go where many professionals fear to tread. Professionals have an opportunity to become co-partners with parents at every possible turn.

The third style of advocacy is through one's own direct efforts with the handicapped. One must affiliate with kindred spirits who are also concerned—parent groups and professionals. Political and social decisions must be made, and this is the cutting edge of real advocacy. One must embark on some relevant, specific, and definable task in keeping with larger goals. Practice of highest quality in one's own professional responsibilities to the children in one's care is vital. There is always more to learn and new ideas to try. Movements come and movements go, but we remember the test of accountability is the quality of service the special children receive, and this just happens to be in the hands of those who directly teach and otherwise serve them. It is an interpersonal transaction. Nothing takes the place of the professional morale each one of us must establish and maintain.

It has been said that we are on the threshold of a second generation of special education. If it meets expectations, it will be because of laws, appropriations, and new concepts. Most of all the promise lies in the hands of the teachers who will be spending thousands of hours in educating these children in the next decade.

Bibliography

Allan, K. H., and Cinskes, M. E. "General Characteristics of the Disabled Population." *The Social Security Bulletin* (August 1972).

Barsh, R. H. *Achieving Perceptual-Motor Efficiency, Vol. 1.* Seattle, Wash.: Special Child, 1967.

Bellefleur, P. A. "TTY Communication—Its History and Future." *The Volta Review, A Bicentennial Monograph on Hearing Impairment* 78(4)(1976):107–12.

Brown, R. *A First Language: The Early Stages.* Cambridge, Mass.: Harvard University Press, 1973.

Bruce, R. V. *Alexander Graham Bell: The Conquest of Solitude.* Boston: Little Brown, 1973.

Cornett, R. O., and Henegar, M. E. *Cued Speech. Handbook for Parents.* Washington, D.C.: Health, Education and Welfare, Office of Education, Media Services, and Captioned Films, 1971.

Council for Exceptional Children. "What is Mainstreaming?" *Exceptional Children* 42(3)(1975):1974.

Critchley, McD. *Developmental Dyslexia.* London: Whitefriars, 1964.

Cruickshank, W. M., ed. *Cerebral Palsy: A Developmental Disability.* 3rd ed. Syracuse: Syracuse University Press, 1976.

Dale, P. *Language Development: Structure and Function.* 2nd ed. New York: Holt, Rinehart & Winston, 1976.

Delacato, C. H. *The Diagnosis and Treatment of Speech and Reading Problems.* Springfield, Ill.: Thomas, 1963.

Denhoff, E., and Robinault, I. *Cerebral Palsy and Related Disorders.* New York: McGraw-Hill, 1960.

Douglas, J. D., ed. *Deviance and Respectability.* New York: Basic Books, 1970.

Dunn, L. M. "Special Education for the Mildly Retarded—Is Much of It Justifiable?" *Exceptional Children* 35(1968):5–22.

Dunn, L. M., ed. *Exceptional Children in the School: Special Education in Transition.* 2nd ed. New York: Holt, Rinehart & Winston, 1973.

Feldhusen, J., and Kolloff, B. "A Three-Stage Model for Gifted Education." *G/C/T Magazine* 1 (4)(1978):3–5 + .

Fillmore, C. J. "The Case for Case." In *Universals in Linguistic Theory,* edited by E. Bach and R. T. Harms. New York: Holt, Rinehart & Winston, 1968.

Gallagher, J. "Unfinished Educational Tasks." *Exceptional Children* 36(1970): 709–16.

————. *Teaching the Gifted Child.* 2nd ed. Boston: Allyn and Bacon, 1975.

Getman, G. N. "The Visumotor Complex in the Acquisition of Learning Skills." In *Learning Disorders, Vol. 1,* edited by J. Hellmuth. Seattle, Wash.: Special Child, 1965.

Grossman, H. J., ed. *Manual on Terminology and Classification in Mental Retardation.* American Association in Mental Deficiency Special Publication, 1973, Series No. 2.

Guilford, J. P. *The Nature of Human Intelligence.* New York: McGraw-Hill, 1967.

————. *Way Beyond the IQ.* Buffalo, N.Y.: Creative Education Foundation, 1977.

Heber, R. F. "A Manual on Terminology and Classification in Mental Retardation." *Monograph Supplement American Journal of Mental Deficiency* 64 (1961).

————. *Epidemiology of Mental Retardation.* Springfield, Ill.: Thomas, 1970.

Hirsch, K. de. "Two Categories of Learning Difficulties in Adolescents." *American Journal of Orthopsychiatry* 33(1963):87–91.

Hobbs, N. *Issues in Classification of Children.* San Francisco: Jossey-Bass, 1974.

————. *The Future of Children.* San Francisco: Jossey-Bass, 1975.

Hopkins, T.; Bice, H. V.; and Colton, K. *Evaluation and Education of The Cerebral Palsied Child.* Arlington, Va.: CEC, 1954.

Ingram, D. "The Acquisition of the English Verbal Auxiliary and Copula in Normal and Linguistically Deviant Children." *Developing Systematic Procedures for Training Children's Language.* ASHA Monograph no. 18. Washington, D.C.: American Speech and Hearing Association, 1974.

Johnson, G. O. "The Mentally Handicapped—A Paradox." *Exceptional Children* 29(1962):62–67.

Johnson, Vicki M., and Werner, Roberta A. *A Step-by-Step Learning Guide for Retarded Infants and Children.* Syracuse: Syracuse University Press, 1975.

————. *A Step-by-Step Learning Guide for Older Retarded Children.* Syracuse: Syracuse University Press, 1977.

Kakalik, J. S., et al. *Services for Handicapped Youth: An Overview.* Santa Monica, Cal.: Rand, 1973.

Kaplan, S. N. *Providing Programs for the Gifted and Talented: A Handbook.* Ventura, Cal.: Ventura County Schools, 1974.

Kaplan, S.; Madsen, S.; and Gould, B. *The Big Book of Independent Study.* Santa Monica, Cal.: Goodyear, 1976.

Kaufman, M. J.; Gotlieb, J.; Agard, J.; and Kubic, M. B. *Mainstreaming: Toward an Explication of the Construct (Project PRIME).*

Kephart, N. C. "Perceptual-Motor Aspects of Learning Disabilities." In *Educating Children with Learning Disabilities,* edited by Frierson and Barbe. New York: Appleton-Century-Crofts, 1967.

Kirk, S. A. *Educating Exceptional Children.* Boston: Houghton Mifflin, 1962, 1972.

Lee, L. L. *Developmental Sentence Analysis.* Evanston, Ill.: Northwestern University Press, 1974.

Lerner, J. W. *Children with Learning Disabilities.* Boston: Houghton Mifflin, 1971.

Lloyd, B. C.; Seghini, J. B.; and Stevenson, G. *Igniting Creative Potential II.* Sandy, Utah: Jordan School District, 1974.

Lowder, F. "The Status Quo Must Change." *Programs for the Handicapped.* Washington, D.C.: Office for Handicapped Individuals, August 11, 1975.

McMichael, J. K. *Handicap.* London: Staples Press, 1971.

Mann, L. "Cognitive Training: A Look at the Past and Some Concerns About the Present." In *State of the Art: Diagnosis and Treatment,* edited by K. F. Kramer and R. Rosonke. Des Moines, Iowa: Midwestern Educational Resources Center, 1975.

Marland, S. P. "Our Gifted and Talented Children—A Priceless National Resource." *Intellect* (1972):16–19.

Martinson, R. A. *The Identification of the Gifted and Talented.* Ventura, Cal.: Ventura County Schools, 1974.

Murphy, J. T. *Listening, Language and Learning Disabilities, A Guide for Parents and Teachers.* Cambridge, Mass.: Educators Publishing Service, 1970.

O'Reilly, D. E. "Care of the Cerebral Palsied: Outcome of the Past and Needs for the Future." *Developmental Medicine and Child Neurology* 17(1975): 141–49.

Paul, J. L.; Turnbull, A. P.; and Cruickshank, W. M. *Mainstreaming: A Practical Guide.* Syracuse: Syracuse University Press, 1977.

Payne, J. S., and Mercer, C. D. "Definition and Prevalence." In *Mental Retardation,* edited by J. M. Kauffman and J. S. Payne. Columbus: Merrill, 1975.

Rawlings, B., *et al.,* eds. A Guide to College/Career Programs for Deaf Students, rev. ed. Gallaudet College and National Technical Institute for the Deaf, September 1975.

Renzulli, J. S. "Talent Potential in Minority Group Students." *Exceptional Children* 39(1973):437–44.

_____. *The Enrichment Triad Model.* Mansfield Center, Ct.: Creative Learning Press, 1977.

Robinson, H. B., and Robinson, N. M. *The Mentally Retarded Child: A Psychological Approach.* New York: McGraw-Hill, 1965.

Sarri, R., and Hasenfeld, Y., eds. *Brought to Justice? Juveniles, the Courts, and the Law.* Ann Arbor, Mich.: National Assessment of Juvenile Corrections, The University of Michigan Institute of Continuing Legal Education and School of Social Work, August 1976.

Sato, I. S. "The Culturally Different Gifted Child—The Dawning of His Day." *Exceptional Children* 40(1974):572–76.

Schein, J. D., and Delk, M. T. *The Deaf Population of the United States.* Silver Spring, Md.: National Association of the Deaf, 1974.

Scholl, G. *The Principal Works with the Visually Impaired.* Washington, D.C.: CEC, 1968.

Schworm, R. W. "Models in Special Education: Considerations and Cautions." *Journal of Special Education* 10(2)(1976):179–86.

Seidel, V. P.; Chadwick, O. F. D.; and Futter, M. "Psychological Disorders in Crippled Children: A Comparative Study of Children With and Without Brain Damage." *Developmental Medicine and Child Neurology* 17(1975): 563–73.

Sontag, E., ed. *Educational Programming for the Severely and Profoundly Handicapped.* Reston, Va.: CEC, 1977.

Taylor, C. W. "Be Talent Developers as Well as Knowledge Dispensers." *Today's Education* 57(1968):67–69.

Terman, L. M., and Oden, M. "The Stanford Studies of the Gifted." In *The Gifted Child,* edited by P. Witty. Boston: Heath, 1951.

Treffinger, D. J., and Barton, B. "Fostering Independent Learning." *G/C/T Magazine* 1979.

Vinter, R. D., with Newcomb, T. M., and Kish, R., eds. *Time Out. A National Study of Juvenile Correctional Programs.* Ann Arbor, Mich.: National Assessment of Juvenile Corrections, University of Michigan Institute of Continuing Legal Education and School of Social Work, June 1976.

Wolff, S. "Overview of Educational Opportunities for the Profoundly Deaf Child in the United States." In *Deafness and Learning: A Psychological Approach,* edited by H. G. Furth. Belmont, Cal.: Wadsworth, 1973.

INDEX

327